HOSTAGE
TO
HEAVEN

HOSTAGE TO HEAVEN

*by Barbara Underwood
and Betty Underwood*

 Clarkson N. Potter, Inc./Publishers   New York
Distributed by Crown Publishers, Inc.

The authors are grateful for permission to quote from James Agee, *A Death in the Family*, © 1938, 1956, 1957 by James Agee Trust; © 1957 New Yorker Magazine (Chapters 8, 13) and by Grosset & Dunlap, Inc., New York; Laile E. Bartlett, specified excerpt from *New Work/New Life*, copyright © 1976 by Laile E. Bartlett, reprinted by permission of Harper & Row Publishers, Inc.; T. S. Eliot, "Little Gidding" in *Four Quartets*, copyright 1943 by T. S. Eliot, renewed, 1971 by Esmie Valerie Eliot. Reprinted by permission of Harcourt Brace Jovanovich, Inc.; D. H. Lawrence, *Women in Love*, © 1920, 1922 by D. H. Lawrence, © 1948, 1950 by Frieda Lawrence, and reprinted by permission of Viking Penguin, Inc.; Jack London, as quoted by Joan London, *Jack London and His Times: An Unconventional Biography*, © 1939 by Joan London, Americana Library edition © 1968 University of Washington Press, Seattle, Washington; Thomas Merton, *Disputed Questions*, copyright © 1953, 1959, 1960 by The Abbey of Our Lady of Gethsemane. Reprinted with the permission of Farrar, Straus & Giroux, Inc.; Adrienne Rich, *Of Woman Born: Motherhood as Experience and Institution*, copyright © 1976 by W. W. Norton and Co., Inc.; an adaptation of a statement by Allen Tate Woods, in "My Four and a Half Years with The Lord of the Flies," December, 1975; William Butler Yeats, *Collected Poems*, "He Wishes for the Cloths of Heaven," copyright 1906 by Macmillan Publishing Co., Inc., renewed 1934 by William Butler Yeats, and "The Shadowy Waters," copyright 1907 by Macmillan Publishing Co., Inc., renewed 1935 by William Butler Yeats.

Inquiries should be addressed to Clarkson N. Potter, Inc.,
One Park Avenue, New York, N.Y. 10016
Printed in the United States of America
Published simultaneously in Canada by
General Publishing Company Limited
Design by Robert Bull
Library of Congress Cataloging in Publication Data
Underwood, Barbara.
 Hostage to Heaven.
 1. Segye Kidokkyo T'ongil Sillyŏng Hyŏphoe. 2. Moon, Sun
Myung. 3. Underwood, Barbara. 4. Underwood, Betty. I.
Underwood, Betty, joint author. II. Title.
BX9750.S4U52 1979   289.9 [B]   79-13689
ISBN 0-517-53875-X

To a Daughter

There is
An ache
In me
For houses
Which
Do not
Have
A daughter.
The air
They hold
Must sometimes
Be thin
And sharp
And hard
To breathe;
Their space
A cell,
Their light
A filament—
No luminosity.
Their color?
Bleak,
Not felt
As spun,
As motion.
Their degree?
Colder,
Yes.
Their tone?
More harsh
Than clear.
Their emptiness?
Not Tuesday,
Not a month,
A year,
But forever.

—BETTY UNDERWOOD, 1975

Acknowledgments

Ray Underwood's insights, steadiness and fortitude helped build this book.

Gary Scharff added a very special dimension of care and understanding.

Clarence, Scott, and Lauriel Anderson gave of themselves in time of need, as did Russell, Douglas, and Jeffrey Underwood.

Carl Katz generously let us share some of his notes on certain days of the court hearing.

Eve Eden and Jeff Scales were initiators and counselors.

Jean Naggar and Beth Rashbaum believed in the book.

Authors' Note

To respect the privacy of those who probably would prefer it under the circumstances, real names are not used except in the case of people who have had intensive media exposure.

Contents

Foreword by Barbara Underwood

The genesis of my voice in this two-person account goes back to April 1973, before I entered the Unification Church. As a student of sociology at the University of California at Santa Cruz, I had intended to keep an objective account of my experiences while "studying" the Unified Family. But I never predicted an account of four years duration. Nor did I predict such a totally involving and personal record. In short, I failed to anticipate the overwhelmingly seductive power of an experience to which I eventually surrendered without reservation.

I waged an inner battle about keeping my journal while I was in the Church. At first writing seemed like a personal, selfish attachment. So I stopped. Then I conceived of my writing as a testament by a living disciple of the Messiah; I thought my journals might one day be a chapter in the "Completed Testament." I also began to cherish my Church brothers and sisters whose personalities and character traits I felt compelled to preserve, with the intention of writing a series of biographical sketches some day when there was time—presumably when the Kingdom of Heaven arrived.

After leaving the Church in April 1977, I worked with my mother on an account of the events of the preceding four years, years that had transformed our lives. Our decision to write together, as mother and daughter, reflected a need to bridge the chasm those years had created. As I read her story of the pain of rejected parenthood, my love for her took deeper root. As she read my story of sacrifice and visionary hope, she recognized a reflection of her own youthful idealism.

The Unification experience is complex. Within the Church or without, there are no ultimate victors and no easily defined enemies. And within the Unification membership there are decent but fallible human beings demonstrating a desire to love, to weave myth, to claim for themselves the glory of God. Unfortunately, the passion for God and goodness can lead to severe violations of the freedom of the individual. And worse.

Was I "brainwashed"? My mind was certainly manipulated through my intense desire to believe and love, my freedom was lost, my values distorted. But even now it is difficult to say for sure which cult experiences are dangerous, how to evaluate them, how to strike a balance between spiritual commitments and secular freedoms. Having seen both sides of the issues involved, I have no easy answers.

Foreword by Betty Underwood

"How the Moonie Magic Is Turned On"; "The Battle for Mind Control"; "Out of the Shadow of Moon Madness"; "What that Spaced-Out Look Means"; "Judge Gives Moonies to Parents"...

On and on they went, the lurid yellow journalism headlines about cults and cultists.

When I came from my daughter's court hearing, the last thing I wanted to do was write a book. I wanted instead to forget.

But after I'd regained my strength, I did put together the notes on the hearing in order to give them to a trusted young journalist friend.

Meanwhile, those sensational headlines kept proliferating and added to my sense that the cult phenomenon was being treated by the media as though it happened only to weird people.

I can't remember the exact moment when Barb and I came to an agreement to try a book, probably sometime in June 1977, after she had left the cult.

By the fall it had already taken rough-draft shape as Barb clattered upstairs at the typewriter while downstairs in the den I did the same. Every now and then we shouted up the stairway to confirm a point or ask a question.

We were trying to write a book which would say, among other things, that our experiences could happen to any American family.

Look up and down the street (and inside your hearts) and, yes, it could happen.

More by unspoken understanding than by grand design, we began this two-person account, some of it based on journals and tapes that both of us had kept at various times during the four years Barb was in the cult.

A book which we hoped would tell what we knew to be our truth as we understood it.

HOSTAGE
TO
HEAVEN

Barb:
Who Is the Captive?

"And I know not to this day
Whether guest or captive I."
—SIR WILLIAM WATSON

AUGUST 1976.
"Come immediately to Hearst Street. Pack for a week. You've got to look mature, up-to-date. This is a very special mission so I can't tell you over the phone. They're probably listening in. All right?" The voice was not waiting for an answer. It had delivered its command.

"Teresa, there's one thing. My mother's flown all the way to San Francisco to spend the weekend with me. I haven't seen her in two years. She's coming to Washington Street tomorrow morning."

/ 1

"Don't worry about your mother. You can pray for her," the voice advised, determined and dispassionate.

"Shall I call her tonight?" I asked hesitantly. "What shall I do?"

"No, absolutely don't call. You'll have to explain too much. Leave a note at the front desk and someone'll treat her gently when she arrives tomorrow. Say you've been called out of town on an unexpected emergency," Teresa ordered. "Now come quick. Amos and Irene are waiting."

I hung the phone up, nervous with the excitement of imminent intrigue. Racing upstairs two at a time, I thought of my sparse wardrobe packed in brown grocery sacks in various closets. I had nothing fashionable to wear, only corduroy pants and turtlenecks, my daily uniform for flower selling or Boonville ranch life. As I rooted around the sisters' wardrobes, I suddenly felt inadequate, wrongly chosen for the mission. Trying on dress after dress, I appeared to myself too young, too baby-faced, too tomboyish.

All the dresses were too short.

"Oh, no, my poor mom," I thought abruptly. "She'll never understand." But I knew such thoughts were looked on as total faithlessness; I had to extinguish them.

Finished packing, wearing a tailored blue dress a staff sister had lent me, I scribbled a note which read: "Dear mom, I'm sorry I can't see you. I've been called out of town on an emergency because a Family friend of mine needs me. I'll write you later. Love, Lael (Barb)."

As I was driven across town, guilt was replaced by a secret sense of power which flooded me—after all, *I'd* been chosen to represent God and the Lord of the Second Advent. *I* was being given this chance to help establish the Kingdom of Heaven on Earth.

Irene, an elegant, angular-faced Jewish woman from New York with a gutsy, omniscient manner, greeted me at the door of the palatial Hearst Street center. I'd never felt comfortable around her. I'd been in the movement two years longer than she, but she had swiftly ascended to a higher position of responsibility and power. I knew too well about myself what Teresa had once told me, "Your problem is, you came as a wild rose and you've never been properly pruned." Irene was already pruning others.

Amos, tall and restrained, disguising his urchin spirit, waved me a good night as he crawled into his sleeping bag next to the front door to guard the entrance to Hearst Street center. "Heavenly dreams," he called out in a paternal voice. "Get some sleep. In the morning we'll tell you what's about to happen."

Irene and I marched up the three flights of newly carpeted stairs. We opened our sleeping bags, removed our first layer of clothes, and, in order to execute a quick wake-up in the morning, hopped in, slips, hose, and all. "Let's pray, then I'll tell you the plan," Irene said.

"O.K. You and either Jonah or Amos will be flying to Columbus, Ohio, to try to free Michele Tunis from deprogrammers and bring her back to the Family. We know where they took her after her parents kidnapped her because she left a note with her wallet in the San Francisco airport indicating Phoenix, Arizona. Then two days later she left a message and address in the stall of a john in Illinois; someone mailed it to us. She's at the Alexanders' house in Munroe Falls, Ohio, being deprogrammed. Of course, she's there against her will, and we don't have much time before they could break her. They could even be torturing her right now. You're to go along to help influence anybody in the state government or courts, or police departments, to help release her. This is criminal. We'll talk more in the morning. We only have three hours till we get up. Good night."

"Amazing," was all I could answer; my shivering I kept to myself.

"Hurry, Amos," Irene yelled. "Onni and Abba are expecting us for breakfast by eight!" Onni (meaning "elder sister" in Korean) was the handsome, forbidding spiritual commander of Sun Myung Moon's Unification Church in California. Her will was undisputed, her decisions about policy matters autocratic and final. With her mystically manipulative aura, she was Moon's most faithful and accomplishment-oriented disciple, was called his "daughter-in-spirit," and was often bodyguard and caretaker of Hak Ja-Han, Moon's wife, when she attended special public events in New York and San Francisco. Although everyone worshipped Onni's passionate and indefatigable ambitions for God, privately she was regarded as impersonal and scary by certain staff members and novitiates alike. Abba (meaning "father" in Korean) was the name Onni had given to Dr. Mose Durst, a kindly, philosophical, tender Jewish college professor whom she'd handpicked as her husband and been married to in a "blessed" service performed by Moon himself. Dr. Durst, a credible public performer, had developed a benign front organization called New Education Development Systems, Inc., whose generalities about love and sharing appealed to and brought in many innocents, who later discovered they had somehow become members of the Unification Church. Together, Onni and Abba formed the leadership of the Moon mission on the West Coast.

We piled into the car. Within minutes, Amos, Irene, and I entered Onni's magnificent western-style Berkeley Hills mansion, named The Gardens, through a controlled intercom system of electronic gates and doors.

We took off our shoes, stopped for pious and grateful prayers, and looked to each other for further directions. Soon someone beckoned us into the kitchen, where breakfast was being served: pancakes, bagels, yogurt, cheeses, eggs, juice, coffee. Preparations were always dignified and bountiful around the local "true parents."

Onni came in with a flourish and indicated we should sit. Abba trailed in behind, fatherly, affectionate, with his arm around Jonah, one of the business-brain-children of the church.

I rose to shake hands with Dr. Durst. We all waited to see what kind of mood Onni was in. Our spiritual lives—which is to say everything that mattered to us—depended on pleasing her.

She wore curlers in her striking black, usually stylish hair; she was the least adorned I'd ever seen her. She radiated impatience, anxiety. Dr. Durst, too, looked more than usually upset.

"So, Jonah, you know how to get Michele back?" Onni barked in her idiomatic Korean-American blend.

"Well, we know where she is, but we don't know who to go to when we get there. Play it by ear, I guess," Jonah answered.

"You mean you don't know what to do?" Onni accused. An oppressive silence followed.

"Amos, you go instead. Jonah, you don't have head for this." Jonah, shocked and speechless, turned to Dr. Durst for support. But there was no help there, either.

"Amos, you know all legal part? You and Lael make plane reservation right now. Lael, do exactly what Amos says. You must get Michele back. She so stupid to go with her dad. Good luck." Onni got up and went out of the room.

Dr. Durst seemed near to tears. We knew he, too, saw deprogramming as the violent death that stripping away one's spiritual life meant to the Church. The end of all hope for Michele ... He showed us out the door, offering unspoken encouragement.

Amos and I stood for a moment on the doorstep. We had our orders, but no strategy. We'd have to devise a battle plan, using only God's intervention and guidance.

At the airport Amos immediately assumed the parental role. From now on, I was to be his "object" and support, his obedient assistant ... his attractive child. He purchased the tickets and we boarded the United airliner.

Picking out window seats, Amos motioned me to sit down. He took my hands in his and, as older brother-in-charge, urged, "Let's pray: Heavenly Father, we're so sorry for your misery. We know you'll never have a moment of happiness until our Father has subjugated Satan in the spirit world and started the Kingdom on Earth. We'll do everything we can to claim our sister, Michele, back from Satan's grasp." His beseeching voice concluded, "We pray that you can work through Lael to follow Amos exactly, and that together we can bring victory to our True Parents. Amen."

It was a long ride. Amos opened his attaché case and handed me piles of news articles and leaflets on the recent barrage of kidnappings and deprogrammings by parents of various cult young people, from Unification Church to Hare Krishna to Children of God. To the Church, the real devils appeared to be Ted Patrick, a black man known for his forceful snatches; Joe Alexander, senior and junior, noted for their legally sanctioned deprogrammings; and the Alexanders' "mercenary" attorney, young Michael Trauscht from Tucson, Arizona. Michele was being held captive by the legal device of a conservatorship her father had just been granted by a California court. Her father had claimed she was in need of temporary parental guardianship because she was susceptible to "artful and designing" people in the ranks of the Unification Church. This was the first I'd ever heard of such a legal tangle; it sounded threatening, and I agreed with Amos that conservatorships must be fraudulent. We made a solemn vow to use any means necessary to spring Michele from her captors.

The plane let down in Columbus after two hearty meals, a catnap, and lots of earnest prayer and discussion. It was midnight.

Determined to save every penny for God, suitcases in hand, we walked arm in arm two miles down a straight highway to the Holiday Inn. Stiff and formal, I felt like I was enacting *American Gothic* amidst the hayfields and cricket sounds of the Ohio summer.

I hid outside while Amos rented a single room. Dr. Durst had advised Amos to "be careful," which, in the puritanical Church doctrine of total chastity before marriage, meant "no compromise" or, practically speaking, two separate bedrooms. But, eager to be frugal, Amos simply prepared a separate bed for me—the tub in the bathroom! We both laughed uncontrollably at the primly propped pillow, delighted we'd "obeyed" Abba without spending the extra cash.

At 5:00 A.M. Sunday we woke for Pledge Service. Together we carried out the Familial Unification Church ritual, chanting our lifelong devotion to God and Moon and our burning antipathy to Satan—who was everyone opposed to Moon.

Honoring the sacrifice Moon had made for us during his imprisonment in North Korean prison camps years ago, we drank orange juice and coffee but couldn't eat till noon. Amos, in an elaborate and sanctimonious gesture, put sugar and cream in my coffee. To serve another in the Church is the highest honor; inverting usual habits, the server becomes the victor. A cup of coffee or tea offered and taken has cosmic significance.

Amos rented a silver Dodge and we drove to Ohio State University and made ourselves comfortable in the faculty club. Chanting under my breath for a good lead into our puzzle, I sparked up a conversation with what turned out to be the head of the dental school. After hearing my careful story, it developed that he'd graduated from Berkeley and knew the dean of a law school in northern Ohio very well. What a gold mine!

Amos was pleased with God's effort so far.

After several phone calls, Amos made arrangements to meet with the dean of the law school that night. We knew Munroe Falls, where Michele was being held, was a suburb of Akron. Only two hours' drive away, we were getting warmer. . . .

The dean of the law school invited us into his orderly office. Calling himself a follower of New Education Development Systems, Amos pleaded Michele's case. After Amos finished, our dean promised us that his assistant, Dean Reece, who'd handled the Vietnam Calley case, would help us the next day. The dean showed us briefly around his law school, bought us hot chocolates, and offered to let us sleep in sleeping bags in the student lounge. Surprised but grateful, we declined the hearty invitation because we needed to be where we could plan more privately.

Monday morning we charged into the Akron Public Library, fighting crowds of people swarming to see the famed Soap Box Derby, and combed through thousands of feet of microfilm of newspaper and magazine articles about the Alexanders, Michael Trauscht, and deprogramming.

The microfilms led us deeper into espionage and masquerade. We discovered there was an Akron person who conducted deprogramming from a subterranean office in an alley beneath the haunted-looking Brown Derby Hotel. The label on his door read Mind Freedom.

Inside worked a young, slapstick psychologist who claimed he knew everything about the recruitment methods of Hare Krishna, T.M., Scientology, and, worst of all, in his opinion, Unification Church.

We introduced ourselves as Amos and Lael; soon he'd handed me a *New Age Magazine* article by a journalist named Bob Banner about our own Boonville ranch. I recognized the magazine writer instantly; the article was all about Bob Banner's experience in *my* group (and he named me) up on the recruitment farm! I excused myself hastily to go to the bathroom while Amos—unaware—kept presenting himself as a deprogrammer with special expertise in the neurophysiology of brainwashing. Amos, however, was soon handed the article, came across my name, and shortly excused himself, too, to fulfill "other obligations."

Close call! we breathed, out on the street.

Dean Reece met us that afternoon. A gentle southern hulk of a man, he took in every word of our story and scoured it in his mind. I trusted him at once, but Amos made it clear by several sharp looks that I was not to reveal so much information. Reece himself, a loyal Baptist, said he didn't care for the deceptions and dubious goals of some of the cults, especially Moon's army (whom he suspected, despite our circumspection, we had some connection with), but he was concerned for the civil rights of "a woman being held against her will." He promised that if we could verify Michele's presence in Joe Alexander's Munroe Falls house, he would go there accompanied by the local chief of police and talk to her. He recommended we do some sleuthing that night and find out exactly where she was.

Equipped with new Penney's tennis shoes, a can of chemical eyespray, and a deafening noisemaker, I stole through the molasses-black woods behind Prentiss Street, while Amos patrolled the pleasant rural neighborhood from the car, its headlights switched off. I'd never spied on a suspected house before, but I was well versed in stealth; flower sellers for the church dare illegal entrances to restaurants, bars, and office buildings, all of which forbid solicitations, from San Diego to Toronto. I prayed to be invisible and for the chorus of neighborhood dogs to stop yelping so suspiciously.

I crept up to the back of what I was sure was the right house and clung to one side of a tree. Finally I dared to look in.

Sure enough, Michele herself sat in the kitchen with a group of people. She looked tired and high-strung, but that was to be expected. After all, she was surrounded by the worst people on earth, the ones God raged against.

Yet, as I watched in fascination, eight ordinary-looking people around the dinner table bowed their heads and prayed. Then everyone laughed and talked companionably as they ate.

I grew more and more outraged. How could they pray, even presuming to address God? How could they pretend to be happy? I remembered Dr. Durst's lecture: "God and Satan, good and evil, look exactly alike. But one is for world benefit, one is for self-benefit." Who, the thought flashed in me, dictates or defines world or self-benefit? I let the troublesome wonder escape, seized as I was with the abrupt desire to let Michele know that her saviors had come, that her true Family was nearby, that her captivity was about to end. . . .

Then, through the gold-lit window of the homey kitchen, I watched Michele get up, yawn, stretch, and leave the room with three young people. Eventually I edged across the moonlit lawn on hands and knees, hiding myself in the shadows alongside the back porch in order to eavesdrop on the people who had just entered it. A pair whom I guessed to be the Alexanders were talking with another couple whom I recognized from photographs as Michele's parents. I studied their faces, earnest and worried; they looked malevolent, plotting. . . .

Then a phone rang. When it did, I recognized my only chance to dart away unnoticed in the flurry of interruption.

Panting, and fearful of discovery, I caught up with Amos's car and climbed in the window to avoid the noise of the door banging. Amos yelled when I stepped on his hand. I shushed his cry, only to sit down on the noisemaker in my back pocket! The pair of us, unintentional clowns that we were, eased the car through back streets to the main highway.

"Amos, she's there! I saw her! We've got her!" I exulted.

"Is she tied up? Does she look bruised or beaten?" he demanded.

"Mostly just nervous. Out of place," I replied, more slowly.

"Great, we'll have her out by tomorrow. The dean's reliable.

Thank you, Heavenly Father. Let's pray." Then, "You hungry, partner?" Amos coaxed.

"Anytime you are, chief," I joked.

"We haven't eaten all day. Let's stop at the Red Barn. You order
and I'll call and give the good news to Onni."

"Give her my love," I offered awkwardly.

"I expect she gets all she needs from God," Amos rebuked me. I felt
like Cain, whose offering had been rejected.

After we ate it was midnight, but Amos's and my night watch
wasn't over. Shortly after Michele had disappeared with her father in
San Francisco, Mitch, a responsible Church member, had been seized in a
hotel by his uncle and father on a conservatorship order and flown to
Ohio to stay with one of the Alexander sons. Amos was intent on
recovering Mitch, too, though his loss to the church was considered less
disastrous than Michele's, as she was a top staff member. We roved from
one end of Akron to the other blindly searching for every Alexander
listed in the phone book. We turned in unsuccessfully at 4:00 A.M. after
singing boisterously to keep ourselves awake.

We·met Dean Reece at ten sharp in his office the next morning.
Amos told him the results of our reconnaissance the night before, filling
in more details about my part than I'd supplied him. Reece listened
closely, then put in a call to the Monroe Falls chief of police. An
appointment was set up an hour from then in the sedate bedroom town.

As we crowded the dean into our rented car, he talked about an
episode a month earlier when a boy had come bursting into his office,
insisting that he buy some peanuts. Reece, from Georgia, couldn't refuse,
but he fumed to us now about the brazen intrusion. "That was Unification, wasn't it?" he pressed. "I tell you, that kid acted like a little demi-
god, as though his work was more earthshaking than any I'd ever heard
of." Amos and I, in silent fraternity, winked at each other. Someday it
would all be clear. . . .

The sterile beige police station didn't offer us much relief from our
anxiety. We chanted incessantly in a lifeless cubicle while Reece conferred with the cop. When both insisted on going to the Alexanders'
home without us, Amos rebelled.

"No representation without us. Satan could get into the dean, especially with that policeman beside him. He's not sympathetic," Amos muttered to me confidentially.

More conferring.

Amos lost.

But as soon as the two men left, Amos instructed me to stay behind in the jail and pray hard. He was going to take the rented car and park outside the house on Prentiss Street anyway. After all, God had made *him* Michele's guardian.

Amos later told me that at the very moment of his arrival, Michele and her mother had driven up from an errand. The dean and chief were with Esther Alexander on the front lawn awaiting their arrival.

Amos had hurled himself out of the car and run toward Michele.

"Michele, Michele, Lael and I are here. Onni and Teresa love you," Amos shouted.

Instantly Michele turned to Esther, wild-eyed. "Get me away," she begged. Esther Alexander grabbed Michele's hand and ran with her into the house.

"Hey, you go back to the police station," the chief came out on the porch and angrily shouted at Amos. "We told you to stay away."

In dismay, in anguish, Amos drove back to join me. He didn't interrupt my chanting nor did he offer any insight. Instead he held his head in his hands and cried for the pain of Michele's betrayal.

The minutes we waited were merciless; more like light-years.

Dean Reece and the chief finally entered our room, sober-faced. The chief said, "The girl doesn't want to see you. She says she cares for you both but she plans to stay with the Alexanders. She believes the conservatorship is justified. So do we," added the chief.

I shot a hard, blazing glance to Amos. "But I thought conservatorships were a fraud, a setup," I backed him up.

"What did Michele say about Onni or Teresa?" Amos begged.

"I heard someone say—I can't remember who—that Teresa has a devil's mesmerizing ability," commented the chief; he seemed open to that possibility.

"That's a lie! *They're* the devils!" Amos pounced.

"Now listen here, you're a nice-looking pair of kids. The woman you claim is being held against her will wants to be there. Something's fishy," the chief remarked.

Dean Reece stood, judgelike hands behind his back. "It seems

Michele's undergone an experience called deprogramming. You've heard of it, of course. . . ."

"Yes, and that's exactly why we're here. They've just finished intimidating, maybe even torturing her, ripping God out of her life in hateful cold blood," Amos exploded in fury. "If Michele doesn't come back with us, it's because they've planted false, evil fears in her about a life she loved just two weeks ago. They're the ones doing the brainwashing, can't you see?"

"Look," calmed Reece, "she appears to have control of her senses, and although she appreciates what you're trying to do for her, she's happy where she is and wants to stay there."

"What makes you so afraid of deprogramming?" suddenly asked the chief.

Shocked, vulnerable, I waited for Amos to speak up. "Well," he said, "my faith must be deeper than Michele's ever was, but all the same, I wouldn't relish having it threatened in inhuman ways."

"How do you know it's inhuman? Michele speaks highly of both the Alexanders and her parents."

"She *must* be brainwashed," I concluded.

"They've taken the Messiah out of her life and Satan's possessed her spirit. She's no longer responsible," Amos added.

"Nonetheless, you two had better think pretty hard before you go traipsing all over America trying to uproot people from a situation they prefer to be in," warned the cop.

"She no longer knows *what* she wants. She's captive. Michele can't be herself," I spoke up.

"That, my girl, is a very serious accusation. Who are you to go around legislating or determining one preferred reality for another?" Reece moralized.

The policeman jumped on me. "Who told you to do this anyway? Maybe *you're* the captive?"

I didn't care what he said; I knew I was absolutely right. He simply didn't understand God. How could he know that the final Truth of God had been proclaimed by the Lord of the Second Advent, who was living in New York at this very hour?

"I hope we're still friends. I expect you'll hear from this Michele again. She seems like a sweet person, and sincere. Let me take you both to lunch back at the Holiday Inn," offered Reece. Since we'd been trained never to refuse a gift to a heavenly child, Amos and I accepted. But the meal was pervaded by our stunned silences.

On the phone to Onni before our return to San Francisco, Amos tried to explain Michele's action. He told me it seemed beyond Onni's mental capacity to accept. Michele, Onni said, was lost in Satan's hands. Then Amos surprised me by a more practical note: Onni feared that Michele knew many secrets about the inner operation of the Church and would tell.

We were ordered home immediately. We owed God a thousand repentances; Onni left us with customary guilt.

"Amos," I summarized on the plane, "one thing I've realized through this disappointment is how vicious and deceiving Satan is. Satan turns everything upside down. And God is helpless without our faith. I could never be deprogrammed. God needs me and I love Him too much."

Two weeks later I finally talked by phone to my parents. Teresa told me my father had called our centers repeatedly trying to find me. I explained to my mother the mission I'd been on; she made little comment about being abandoned on the Washington Street porch when she came to visit.

What I couldn't tell either my father or mother was that in June, when I'd begged them to come down just once more to a weekend seminar and they refused, I'd gone out and spent two hours in the dark crying under a tree in Lafayette Park.

That evening I'd finally given my mother and father up. I'd prepared never to see them again in my life, if God demanded.

When I'd come in from that heartbreaking darkness, my real parents had irrevocably and eternally become Moon, Hak Ja-Han, Onni, Dr. Durst. As I had been repeatedly taught in the cult, it was they who were my True Parents.

Betty: Growing Up–Barb, Her Family, Their World

"Out in this world
(Which is not
Gentle)
He breaks
Who has no
Sense of place;
Who has not belonged
When young
To special earth,
To sky,
To shapes,
To winds,
To smell;
Who can't—
In mind
Or fact—
Within himself,
Go home
Again."

—BETTY UNDERWOOD

"Every morning I partake of the ritual watering. I shower first, then with a coffee cup I shower my plants, not every day the cactus. I resist watering the straw flowers. My movements teach me appreciation of my people, myself, my habitat. They teach me I'm the only one who can change my life. They teach me I love to live rejoicing, I can't bear to live lukewarm."

—BARBARA UNDERWOOD, *aged 18*

NOVEMBER 1943, Wartime—MARCH, 1973.
Barb's father, Ray, and I married at a silent Quaker service in a little college town in the Pennsylvania Alleghenies. Ray was a conscientious objector. A Chinese ambulance project for which he'd volunteered failed to materialize, so we spent the first four months of married life in jerry-built shacks in the teeth of the winter gales in a C.O. forest camp in upper New York. Ray then volunteered as a medical guinea pig for malaria experiments at Massachusetts General Hospital, Boston. I got a job as a young editor in an old publishing house, and we spent the next four years in a cat-smelling slum apartment on the unwashed-windows side of Beacon Hill.

The great war ended. Having come through the medical experiments all right, Ray finished Harvard Law School.

Our first son, Doug, was born in 1948 and brought home to an attic apartment in a small Pennsylvania city where Ray was teaching government in a men's college. Our second son, Jeff, was born in Eugene, Oregon, in 1950 where we had migrated so that Ray could work in public law.

We were poor, stubbornly idealistic, insecure, ambitious, hardworking, goal-minded, and much united in spirit when, on February 17, 1952, our third child, and only daughter, Barbara Lael, was born. Three weeks after her birth we moved to Portland, Ray to join a large private law firm and begin life as a pressured professional, I to care for our three children, all under age four.

Barb grew up as a tomboy, fleet, hard-swimming, straight-ball-throwing, a favorite with Jeff's friends. From babyhood she had been very much her own person, with dark blue eyes, heavy brows, silken dark hair. She was small and wiry. Spunky, self-disciplined, perfectionist, sunny, stormy, bright, and tenderly sensitive, she was also an accomplished tease and daredevil. Honesty was a marked quality. So were independence and determination. At school, she was apt to get perfect report cards and be named school citizen of the month.

Each child, including her, had a satisfactory herd of friends. In that more optimistic age, we were typical; Ray's and my involvement in many community projects silently said to our children that we believed the individual counted and a relatively just and humane society was possible. Rightly or wrongly, they picked up from us that fine things were possible for their futures.

The kids' grandparents on Ray's side were old-fashioned, bluff, affectionate people from a barn-shadowed New England homestead.

Fascinating, globe-girdling parents on my side led agricultural teams in the Philippines and Israel and wrote books for young people that won English Speaking Union awards.

For ten years we lived in a fine old Portland colonial house with a tree loft in front and a kid-built shack in the back. It was here our children learned how to work every Friday afternoon in a sweeping house and yard clean-up that was the envy of all the mothers on the block. It was here we held Quaker meeting in our living room.

But play occupied large chunks of time: Cub Scouts, Indian Guides, Campfire, 4-H, lessons in everything short of breathing and shouting; vacations by tent in Vancouver, ocean science camp and Shakespeare festival in Ashland, horseback riding on Mt. Jefferson, train trips back east to view history.

Just before we moved out of Portland to the suburb of Lake Oswego, when Barb was about thirteen, the huge brown house next door was sold to a bizarre and mysterious group, apparently followers of some little-known Korean prophet. At night the strange songs of his disciples carried across our driveway and into Barb's bedroom as she drifted to sleep. Years later we were to learn this was one of the first Moon centers in the United States. At the time, we didn't take seriously a plaintive young man's voice calling from an attic window one morning, "I'd like to get out of here but they've taken my pants away."

Through it all, there could not have been a more loved young girl.

Weary of shuffling money from one person's pocket to someone else's, after thirteen years Ray left his law firm to return to the public law he loved, as legal counsel to Oregon's Governor Mark Hatfield. Though he was a political liberal of another party, Mark's early brave stand against the Vietnam war—tragically beginning to scar the nation and do permanent damage to many young people and their families— cemented Mark's and Ray's relationship.

In the fall of '66 Mark Hatfield ran for U.S. Senator and won. We would leave our new cedar-beamed home in Lake Oswego and follow him to Washington. Ray went on ahead; Jeff, Barb, and I stayed behind another six months to finish the high school year, sell the house, and pack endless boxes. Doug had entered Pomona College in southern California; in June, at the end of his freshman year, he flew to Washington to be with Ray and take a summer job with the city park system.

Barb, Jeff, and I drove out of Portland one July afternoon in 1967. Our new house in Virginia backed up to a rustling oak woods. After we got settled—with Ray off to his exciting job in the Senate Office Building and Doug sitting between two old inner city blacks collecting trash from city parks—Jeff, Barb, and I sniffed out our new world, the impact of our transplanting beginning to really hit us. "I wonder who lives out there?" Jeff asked at the window. "The most exciting thing I have to do today is knit my sweater," wistfully from Barb, waiting for school to start.

Waving hopefully, Barb and Jeff set out for Jeb Stuart High School on Peace Valley Lane. Jeff was an instant frenetic success, but for Barb it was to prove the fighting Quaker siege of a Cavalier outpost. In frequent confrontation with peers and teachers about the legality and morality of the war in Vietnam, Barb soon began to slog back and forth to school in a heavy mood. She longed to go back to Lake Oswego.

Slow to develop physically, in early high school she was a little over five feet tall, weighed just over a hundred pounds, was lean, long-limbed, flyaway, with a round, lively face, soft blue eyes, and the curious manner of a thoughtful child. Very bright and creative, she seemed typically, healthily adolescent in her ambivalences, her conflicting needs and desires. She had a passion for independence and an almost helpless hunger for care; a tendency toward aloofness and a desperate need for intimacy; a mind more mature than most and a child's capacity for capriciousness; an awakening sensuality and a distrust of sex; a sweet, soft manner, and a waspish moodiness; a marked inner strength, a waifish vulnerability. Perhaps we should have, but we noticed nothing in the way of significant rebellions or hostility from her. As with the boys, over whom we were sometimes impatient or troubled, our central feeling for Barb remained love, and she seemed to respond to us in a positive way. She idolized Doug, though they quarreled, too. Jeff, the catalyst for the three, became one of her best friends. Jealousies, competition, anger, alienation seemed not to assume crisis proportions in our family.

By spring of her sophomore year in high school, things took a turn for the better when she found friends with whom she could go off for weekends in West Virginia to spelunk, or cave. When narrow, uncharted cave tubes needed to be wriggled through, the cavers called for her, our gritty adventurer, our young self-tester. In school, an understanding teacher assigned her to teach eight black students black literature for six weeks. One of them told her she was the "realest" person he'd ever met. She seemed to be coming into her own.

In a terrible April week in 1968, smoke swirled almost up to the

Capitol dome as Washington burned after Martin Luther King's assassination. Carrying a homemade identification card on his windshield, Ray drove into the evacuated city through cordoned-off streets littered with used tear gas cannisters, to help bail out blacks who'd been herded to jail in the panicked roundups.

Ray and I took our first trip to Europe that fall, after the bloody Democratic convention in Chicago and the Republican convention that nominated Nixon. *Fled* would be a better word than *took*. And, fleeing, we knew our Senate time was up; Ray didn't want to be part of a Nixon Washington. By late spring 1969, our course was set—we'd return in the summer to Oregon, where Ray would be Chief Counsel for the Board of Higher Education, the management agency for Oregon's public colleges and universities. We would be headquartered not in Portland but in Eugene, where we'd begun our Oregon life and where Jeff and Barb had been born.

Barb began keeping journals her last two years of high school. In Spring, 1969, her journal recorded her thoughts on politics, places, and people: "Would the Vietnam War end not because we ran out of willingness to kill but they ran out of willingness to die?"

She described letting herself down a rope into Elkhorn Mountain Cave, a one-hundred-and-sixty-foot dark drop. "We played tunes on the drapery formations." Characteristically, she and her special friend, Steve Lau, climbed up first. Later they explored Nut Cave, which she said was "beauty embalmed in a stone tomb."

By contrast, the next night she was visiting her friend Bev in inner-city Washington. "Her musty apartment was in a neighborhood with a plaid network of taxi-alleys."

One morning she woke up to note that the "woods were a leaf green Seurat painting below a sky of hesitant dots."

She thought about Steve a lot. "He loves me. He's one of the wonderful people I've known but it's too early."

Steve invited her to Lynchburg to stay for a weekend in the college dorm; unable to find space, they camped in a nearby forest. We gave her the dickens and she wrote: "We didn't do anything wrong. It hurts for a parent to tell you they're disappointed in you—it hurts a lot. I think I deserve to be trusted."

She described how her students were acting out *Raisin in the Sun* in the black literature class she was teaching. "Blacks seem to marvel over the accomplishments of a black person; they don't seem competitive like us."

She submitted two poems to the literary magazine: "They chose the one that meant more but ached less."

With Doug, a friend of mine, and me, Barb walked in the Poor People's March at Washington Monument. "On every side people walked along singing," she wrote. Having camped a number of weeks in lean-tos on the Mall, thousands surged, streamed and gathered to hear leaders of the disadvantaged like Coretta King. Coming home weary, moved, concerned, we feared that during the next few Nixon years poor people wouldn't be listened to.

Of a June caving trip Barb wrote:

It seems natural to thank something for the thud of cave drops, the bubble gum smell of mimosa tree buds, the two-weeks-after-Christmas taste of sassafras leaves, for one lost cloud separated from its clan, for soft native grass which lets itself be thumped on but never falls down in convulsions, for damp seat pants from early slopes, for shadow, for riverbed pebbles, for little boys even if they do point popguns, for Canada geese, for people who call you up to go caving.

Just before we left Falls Church for the west she wrote in her journal:

I feel guilty about going back to Lake Oswego to finish high school with our friends the Marmaduke family rather than following mom and dad to Eugene and finishing my last year there. I know I'll miss them and I know it hurts mom particularly (at least she externalizes the feeling more than dad) because I'm the last child. But I can see this guilt brings no alleviation to the feelings; it only intensifies upset.

Good-bye to Steve. Shock's in the staying, the being left behind.

Since Doug had a summer job in the torrid heat of a southern California cement plant and Jeff, after high school graduation, had flown to Portland for a summer government job, it was left to Barb, Ray, and me to chase our moving van across the country.

From her journal: "We camped out at Hungry Mother State Park on the way to the Smokies; I swam under a waterfall after a three-mile hike."

In New Mexico she was amazed by "skies supporting miraculous wall hangings—dangling elephants, gnomes, rattlesnakes' vertebrae."

And she was discovering that "the hurt comes not in being away from where you love, but on arrival at a new place, discovering you're the same person."

Near Jackson Hole she took an early morning horseback ride. Up on the mesa the wrangler tried to catch a sage hen with rocks—"more silent than with guns out of season." He didn't catch the bird, and Barb breathed a sigh of relief, galloped through lupine and sage, reined in at an abrupt rimrock cliff. She looked out and asked herself, "Who can graph the blind joy of a bird singing in flight?"

In the Tetons she wrote about "floating down fourteen miles of the Snake River in a rubber raft. Saw moose, heron, bald eagles, magpie, night hawk, beavers."

On this raft trip Ray suffered acute eye symptoms. By Boise he was blind in one eye from a detached retina. He was flown right out of Boise to Portland. Barb and I drove in from Idaho not even knowing what hospital they'd taken him to. He was operated on successfully; with quiet valor, convalesced.

We bought a house facing a tawny butte on the outskirts of Eugene. Jeff got ready to go to Pomona, Barb to live with the Marmadukes in Portland and be spared three different high schools in four years. Ray and I spoke little of it to her; we knew she wanted it and felt it was best for her.

She confided in her journal that she had been afraid her memories of Oregon would be bigger than life. "But they aren't. I feel so good. I hear the throbbing of Heceta lighthouse, I smell bits of autumn. . . ."

Steve came west for a visit, and Barb, Jeff, and Steve took a twenty-mile pack trip on the Pacific Crest Trail in Crater Lake, slogging 3,000 feet up over loose pumice. "I love my brother Jeff so because he's not afraid to enjoy himself. It's his instincts, which are so right."

She reacted to a phone call from Doug. "He'll be in Eugene soon. He's a major event—his voice, his exciting mind, the unsureness of an underneath shy personality like the giving of a homemade gift at Christmastime."

Then we drove her up to the Marmadukes and she wrote: "Lake

Oswego. Home with the Marmadukes. I was afraid I'd get to the Marmadukes and then wonder "what next?" But for the first time, my immediate experience seemed as comfortable as my expectations. I'm living in now."

On October 15, 1969, Barb participated in her first Vietnam peace march. It began at 6:30 in the morning when she was squeezed in the crowd at the doors of the Portland induction center, with three hundred young people blocking the entrance against police and inductees.

Afterward, there was a five-thousand-person march from Portland State University to Front Street. At noon the marchers sat in the financial district and observed ten minutes of quiet, followed by church chimes. Barb watched the nonparticipants on the sidewalks "tiptoe past in confusion" and wondered, "Will what we do here, matter at all over there?"

That year she had some physical problems and her pituitary gland was x-rayed for a possible tumor. In her journal she wrote:

I was scared about dying. I'd just finished reading John Gunther's *Death Be Not Proud* about a boy dying of a brain tumor. For the first time I sensed my own mortality. Before I died I wanted to have the assurance of God and romantic love; I wanted to build a close community; I wanted to go to Europe and to college; and I wanted to have a hallucinogenic or "other-reality" experience. About this time, too, I sensed that my parents wouldn't live forever. They seemed older, although there was something about their spirits I felt must never end, must be more than an influence on memory. They were the primary source of love in my life. If they ever die, I wonder where love will come from? Perhaps eternal love as a resource is true. That leads me straight to the possibility of God.

The journal of her senior year ends abruptly there.

As my daughter matured, I became increasingly aware of the powerful and little-understood symbiosis between mother and daughter. I grew more and more convinced that one of the most important things a mother could do for her daughter was to illuminate and expand the daughter's sense of life's possibilities by expanding the limits of her own. The last year in Falls Church, after illness that put a halt to my writing on a series of historical novels for young adults on the women's rights movement, I went to work in medical public information. In Eugene I helped manage the work life of a minister who counseled alcoholics.

Ray was also involved, very intensely, in public policy work. Single-handed, he gave legal advice to the seven colleges and universities of the Oregon system during two riotous, war-torn years. Seldom a week passed without a campus crisis involving problems of civil liberties versus private war protest rights. One night Ray's office building was bombed. Angry students later staged a week-long sit-in in it, rushing the Chancellor's office where Ray was headquartered.

Reflecting the anguished upset of the period, in early March 1970 Jeff dropped out of Pomona, came home to Eugene, talked of homesteading in Alaska, seemed oblivious he would soon be drafted. Doug was struggling his way through a C.O. application from a draft board which had never granted one. There were times when I felt my family was being broken by social forces I could never in my wildest thoughts have anticipated.

In June Doug was elected to make the senior speech at Pomona's graduation. His speech made newspaper headlines because it was the first conciliatory one the parental generation had heard in some time. Hair flying, mortarboard on his chair, Doug gave a moving address. We got back in time for Barb's high school graduation at Lake Oswego. Newspaper editor and first in her class, Barb walked across the stage to get her diploma from Don Marmaduke, school board president, who stooped to kiss her while my heart burst.

After she'd worked that summer as a motel maid, Barb and Jeff, with their mountain-climbing eastern friends, took a camper safari back to Washington, D.C. In a hilarious transaction in Indianapolis, Jeff and Barb exchanged Jeff's respectable but mechanically disabled VW camper for one with a usable engine but no reverse gear. Grinding day and night, the pair returned west, the only direction they could go, and we woke one morning to look out at the most disreputable vehicle ever to offend suburban America—a worn, dented, leaning pastiche of enormous peace symbols. All that next winter Jeff drove the ark to his University of Oregon classes but, being of an absentminded stripe, spent a lot of time pushing it out of the cul-de-sac he'd unwittingly headed into.

In fall 1970, we drove Barb south to Santa Cruz, that controversial new addition to the chain of campuses comprising the University of

California. Built into the uplands, UC Santa Cruz was two thousand matchless acres of gold meadow edged by sun-filtered redwoods above the Monterrey Bay. Only five years old, it consisted of Oxford-like individual colleges in a cluster; Barb entered Adlai Stevenson, the social sciences college. She had very much wanted to go there and was one of only a few out-of-state students to be admitted that year.

The university was intended to be an oasis for bright but goal-driven students who needed breathing time to figure out who they were and what they wanted to do about it. As one administrator said, "Perhaps we shouldn't have to baby-sit the identity crises of our students, but they come to us so scarred by education, in a state of suppressed rage, so crammed with facts and pushed to compete for grades, they've no idea why they should think."

We left Barb with a combination of longing, trepidation, and high hopes, and headed back to Eugene where Doug, after graduating, couldn't find the teaching job he'd trained for. He settled into his attic room, went to journalism classes and started his first novel. He and Jeff shared a job at a gas station, scene of many brotherly conferences. All winter Ray tried to keep the lid on campuses that continued to erupt around the state like so many roman candles. We sympathized with protesters' aims but often deplored their methods and targets.

Soon Barb was writing us from Santa Cruz that it was "fantastic." Lots of classes were held in teachers' homes and "no one has to worry about grades or courses." Socially, there were beach parties and hikes; she'd met some freshmen boys but "I like the juniors and seniors better." "I'll be taking 'University and Society,' 'Folk Dance,' 'Introduction to Religious Studies,' 'Marine Biology.'"

In late winter Barb, the tender lover of wild creatures, went to Pacific City to help on the beach with bird life dying in the slick from a leaking oil tanker. ". . . Grebes flounder in the surf," she wrote, "struggling grotesquely like wizened women falling downstairs; crude oil cakes the sand and penetrates the world of siphon dwellers. My work's simple—gather tar and residue, spread straw, wait for birds to restore. I scrape my way through the muck and pray for those wings to spread. . . ."

Drug use on campuses was at its worst about that time. We knew Barb had smoked marijuana occasionally but hadn't seen much in it. We were to survive her taking of a hallucinogen, which she wrote about in a disturbing but fascinating paper called "Sunday Rite, Santa Cruz." Excerpts:

I study both eyes in the mirror. Then my will directs the clear capsule containing dusty-colored particles into my mouth. It's done; no more agonizing about the effects of psilocybin. Peering from one eye to the other, I speculate about the coming drama.

Marty, Sue, Janet, and I are in it together, Marty and I being the only two uninitiated.

A stoniness prevails the first half hour, or is it merely the intensity of anticipation? Soon I'm aware of a body buzz like the twitch and expansion before a sneeze, but sustained and transmitted all through my being. Then my entire body seems to turn suddenly into a skeleton; I can't decide if my bones are hot soup or crushed ice. Shall I laugh or cry? Regurgitate or urinate?

I lope with a hum and a sizzle to the pitch of Dylan's "Day of the Locusts." Where's Marty wandered? I mustn't lose him; we mustn't separate. Ah, out on the rope swing in the quad. Marty and I compare conditions, then go to the courtyard lawn where Janet and Sue wait us.

She described in vivid imagery staring at a bare foot from which "globes of sparks fly out and veins flow with a sludgy sheen. . . ." She watched multilevels of clouds "form maneuvers" and wondered why she couldn't always see them that way, then realized the mind had a capacity to order, organize, synthesize perception, but it was "only a thin membrane combating all the chaotic, disintegrative life forces." She said she didn't suffer from loss of being, "but my being loses its separateness."

Then she gave up describing:

Words aren't any good. I marvel at their inadequacy to record with their linear logic a curved, four-dimensional experience.

Myself, I feel relatively secure, whole.

But I frightened myself, looking in the mirror.

At 12:30 that night we're pretty well down. Zingy, but exhausted. I still hallucinate in sundown blues after closing my eyes in bed.

We never had reason to doubt her promise to us that she wouldn't do it again.

She wrote papers called "A Reaction to *Education and Ecstasy* by George Leonard" and "The Comparative Role of Suffering in Religions." Then she let herself go in a very girl-paper called "A Comparison of Veblen's Women With Current Attitudes Toward Feminine Beauty and Personality," which she transcribed from secret tapes of friends' rap sessions. She found men still liked women to be playthings.

She seemed to make good friends, both men and women.

And then in February 1971 we got the first of what were to prove typical spring phone calls. This one told us that Barb wanted to go to Vancouver, British Columbia, for spring term. Her sociology class—all twelve of its students, plus teacher Bobby Minden and assistant Richie—planned to live in a basement and research the lives of American draft decliners in Canada. They intended to get to know the decliners and the network of people helping them, then write a group paper. The college would presumably give them credit.

Barb wrote in her Santa Cruz journal before they headed north: "Why do I want to involve myself in a study of American draft exiles in Canada? . . . I'm curious about the morale, motivations, and life-styles of these disinherited people. As a Quaker opposed to the draft and a continuing war," she said, she empathized with the circumstances of the draft decliners, wanted to know what it was like to live "sundered, with no or little chance of reconciliation, in a society antipathetic to one's beliefs." Her readings of R. D. Laing, Peter Berger, and James Agee, made her ask "how much balance can *I* maintain in the face of so much cultural falsification in my own society? Perhaps the discovery of the draft exileship may reinforce my own ability to live as an outsider, a volunteer fugitive from the war engines of American society."

She said of their group of thirteen, one was a dream analyzer and one a fine baker. Kent was a fine musician and Sam "an up-and-coming fiddler." Lynne and Dean "wear coveralls and keep their garden growing." "Bobby is our teacher and keeps us young and alive. He plays dulcimer. Richie, graduate student in social psychology, reads poetry and plays baseball."

The group camped out at our place on their way north. Upon arrival in Vancouver, she woke up "in a tomb." There were no main windows in their main basement room, a "dank, shoulder-tight hobbit's den." One main sleeping room, a single bathroom, two side rooms, a space which served the multiple purposes of kitchen, laundryroom, study, dining room, "brewery and sports equipment storage room."

One of her first mornings in Vancouver she trotted by Pigeon Park, the drunks' corner, got caught in a Salvation Army band, and found herself standing next to a "lean, piratical guy with black hair and turtle neck" who, when she said she was hunting Americans, tried to sell her dope. She escaped in relief to eat dinner with the group, "Richie and Bobby getting more lively as the bottles were emptied."

But soon troubles set in. The group, she wrote, had held a disturbing meeting. The problem: how to resolve a group commitment to share experiences and write a report with a laissez-faire concept of individual self-interest? Besides an inability to come to a basic agreement about goals, the group also faced the loss of their leader and teacher, Bobby Minden, who had to return to Santa Cruz in April to teach another class.

Continuing with her research for the project, Barb visited two young Canadians whose address she'd been given. Their life-style, Barb wrote, "and their lack of options in life depressed us. Everyone in the house is on welfare, gets about $100 a month." There was no work and, unlike in America, Barb found most kids "can't go on to university." Barb asked one if she got bored during the day. "I mostly diddle around, listen to the radio. . . ."

One of the draft evaders asked Barb a belligerent question: would *she* move to Canada as a draft evader? She was ambivalent. "Once out of America, I couldn't be part of its struggles. From somewhere else I couldn't work for minority rights, creative politics, health care, environmental concerns. . . ."

One day on Hastings Street, Barb wandered into a craft shop, soon realizing that it was filled with Jesus freaks. At a loss for words, she asked about their craft items. No reply. So she asked about their religious newspapers on the wall. "More comment, but reserved. Then the inevitable 'Jesus-loves-you' rap followed my statement that a friend of mine was doing her thesis on religious conversion." Of the three men in the shop, all were between eighteen and twenty, Barb reported. One was running from the Montreal police, one was a native Vancouverite, another—who quickly slid into the back room—was a draft exile from Michigan. "Unable to accept the 'Jesus is right, you'd better join up' attitude, I left and sighed with relief to be outside. I can't endure the Jesus freaks' intolerance of me while I pity them. They think they're righteous and can judge others. Man is morally obscene."

Fragmentation, Bobby Minden had warned before he left, was the natural tendency of a group. After Bobby's departure, Barb began to believe group cohesiveness was nearly impossible without a natural leader.

Barb and another pair took off for Vancouver islands, Quadra and Cortez, to adventure. They caught the ferry to Cortez to visit Hans Froese, who lived there with his family; Hans would be able to tell them about any exiles living in the Georgia Straits, they'd been told.

In the evening, Barb was invited in to talk to Hans and his wife, Shirley. Hans theorized: "Yes, there's a major difference between American and Canadian societies. America clings tenaciously to the concept of freedom; but in Canada, justice seems more important, justice as a fair principle, an equal treatment."

Barb went away thinking of the difference between:

"one ideal which encourages individualism and self-will and another ideal which generates commonality, group commitment, community. I let the thought burrow in my brain for an hour." Does our group-living experience hint at the truth of Hans Froese's conjecture? The majority of the people in our group adopted a laissez-faire policy of individual freedom; any policy suggesting self-sacrifice for the benefit of all was attacked as coercive and then rejected. So here we are, a group of Americans fighting the concessions necessary even to write a study of exiles, a group of Americans raised on freedom, electing independence, subjectivity, and, ultimately, fragmentation over community.

I wonder if freedom as practiced in America leads to the imperialist mentality, if freedom finally brings isolation, then alienation. Yet I also know that freedom allows creativity, enterprise, excitement, turmoil, change, too.

When they got back to the basement apartment in Vancouver, "divisiveness was rampant." Dean and Lynne met them without welcome. An argument brewed between those who wanted a final communal dinner and those who didn't feel obligated to participate. They had the dinner. "Magically," Barb wrote, "music and Chilean wine brought us together for a while. Later Kent and I talked about our melancholia at month's end, about the lack of consensus for the written project. Marginal communal living—eating out of grocery sacks and cooking on one hot plate—has been frustrating for everybody. Hunting draft decliners has made me uncertain about sociology; my future at Santa Cruz is at stake. Right now I simply want to spend a few days with my family in Eugene to restore confidence in myself, to be with people I know care for me without conditions. I've grown critical of myself in Canada and though it's a weakness to admit, I long for a time of unqualified love."

Kent, Sam and Barb were the last to leave Vancouver. They cleaned a month's accumulation of dirt from the floors, then quietly closed the backyard gate. "I knew I couldn't look back for fear of catching a flight of angels chased by ghosts."

A week later, back in Santa Cruz where she discussed with Bobby the events of the month she'd just been through, she wrote:

There must be a way to moderate the extremes of individualism and communalism. But how is it possible to breed a new sensitivity encompassing the best qualities of each without imposing an oppressive censored utopia? Bobby and I are baffled.

Bobby Minden, Barb's trusted teacher, left Santa Cruz that June. Barb's farewell gift to him was a record of her Vancouver experience called "Spirits in Exile." Her preface said: "Because our group never could agree to put out a report together, this is the impression of only one person out of thirteen. But remembered days will disappear in the wake of time, and before they do, this is written for Bobby."

Of his last written evaluation of Barb, Bobby Minden told her he had simply advised, "Don't make her stop long in college. Send her straight on to graduate school. . . ."

Later Barb concluded:

Vancouver made me aware of the oppressiveness, the acute limitations in absolutes and universals. I realize now I'm not in college to hunt down a philosophy which defines human nature or which outlines a fixed utopia. I've discarded my early freshman search for something I could neatly fold and mount.

The summer of 1971 we moved from Eugene back to Portland when Ray became chief counsel for the attorney general's Portland office, his public law focus shifting to Oregon's Department of Environmental Quality. I went to work at the state American Civil Liberties Union office; Doug was waiting to go into an Appalachian poor white neighborhood in a Cincinnati VISTA project; Jeff had joined up with a companionable living group at the University of Washington in Seattle. When Barb finished her motel maid's summer job, she, Jeff, and eastern friends spent two weeks climbing in the wilderness meadows of the Wallowas Mountains. As Barb sat on craggy rocks and around campfires, she was trying to reconcile herself to the breakup of the Marmadukes' marriage. She experienced it as the loss of a second family.

In September, I drove her down to Santa Cruz for her sophomore year. It didn't take long to unpack her clothes—by now a brief assortment of boots, jeans, tie-dyed shirts, and a couple of long India-print dresses. She poked her head in the car window, said softly, "You're my friend," then ran up the dorm slope.

Soon she hated it. When Ray and I visited her in October and went to some of her predictably stimulating classes, we were struck by the enervation and aloofness of the students on that campus. Leaving Barb depressed, we were worried.

In a month, sounding more cheerful, she wrote us that she was beginning to co-counsel, a confidence-building, do-it-yourself group therapy which had grown from Gestalt. But conflicts and disappointments were in the poetry she wrote:

#1

Look to the tyger
For tales of our ancestry.
All deeds lie in the paw—
In the dual design of fur and claw—
The primeval tool of passage
Between birth and death and back;
Fur-cradle of nurture,
Instrument of rude plunder,
Mother and slayer are one.

#2

So I got freedom
Which is laissez faire,
Noninterference.
The Constitution
Protects my right to:
Make love randomly,
Travel without itinerary,
Cruise L.A. freeways,
Be silent,

Look to the night
For tenderness and woe,
For the moon
Both soothes and incites.
The hands that cradle
Are the hands that prey.
The palm of birth
Becomes the grip of death
In the errand from womb to womb.

Smoke dope
Get smashed,
Dig on Playboy,
Boycott mama—
All because no one is there,
No one cares.
Man, I got so much
Constitutional freedom
I got the world's indifference.

I tell you in tears,
I tell you bravely,
We must learn to live knowing
There is a dark side of the moon.

That winter Barb was becoming involved in the feminist movement, then spreading on campuses. Out of this interest, she wrote a paper examining Shakespeare's views on women.

Right after Christmas, with her friend Joanna and several others, she rented a house not far from the ocean, in Santa Cruz. She had met a special friend, Evan, and seemed to be happier. We were just breathing a sigh of relief about her when Jeff's newest hobbies hit us: fast motorcycling and skydiving.

And then Barb called one early spring night, laughing into the telephone: "Guess what! Molly Martin and I are going to Europe spring term. I've got the money saved. We're headed over in April."

"Barb!" Ray yelled, visions in his head of being *forever* beholden for the education of this one.

"Don't worry, Dad," she soothed. "I'm going to get art credit this time."

"Some sociology major," he retorted.

But we were the last people to dismiss the value of travel, and we loved like a daughter Barb's childhood friend, Molly Martin. We knew that for years the two girls had cherished the dream of going to Europe together.

March 20, we put them on a London-bound plane to join the regiments of barefoot young Americans in blue jeans looking for somewhere they liked better than home. The girls appeared two such innocents I had to be dragged out from behind an airport rubber plant where in anxiety I'd gone to cry.

Their trip lasted three and a half months, beginning with Orthodox Easter spent with a Greek family on Corfu, and ending in Killarney, Ireland. They bicycled in Belgium; fished and worshipped (and quarreled) on Corfu; toured Athens and Delphi; museum and cathedral watched, awestruck, in Italy: "Firenze was like turning around and around under a blazing night sky and then at the end expecting to stand up straight." Barb particularly remarked on, and later seemed haunted by, the overpowering Michelangelo sculptures of captives struggling to come out of their unfinished stone.

In Winchester, England, Molly and Barb parted with tears and whispers, Molly to go on with her family and Barb with a newly met friend, Jackie, to Ireland.

Back in London, having picked up her mail at American Express, she wrote:

I read my letters: Evan, Joanna, Molly. Love is a silent explosion and I feel it all through me. Evan wrote me he'd dreamed June 22 that I was frightened: "It's all right, Barb, it'll be all right. . . ." He wrote that to me from a continent and an ocean away the very night of my most nightmare of nightmares.

Magic is real; it doesn't speak distantly.

I've passed something. I've gathered something in.

Tomorrow I go home.

That summer, after she'd come back from Europe, we realized Barb had fallen in love with Evan, a talented artist. Thirty-two, and married.

"Barb," I pleaded, "if you just go on loving him and ignoring everybody else, the years will pass and you'll have missed your chance for someone who's free."

"I don't think I'll let that happen," she answered soberly.

But she wrote:

Evan:
Poised in the eye
Of your own typhoon,
Your mind gnaws and swirls
At my heart.
You smile,

You reflect,
You conjure
Gale warnings.

In September Ray and I went to San Francisco where I was given a national award for my first book, *The Tamarack Tree*, for "excellence in writing on the theme of brotherhood." Barb joined us at the award giving. I resigned my job at the ACLU to begin work on my second book, *The Forge and the Forest.*

Returning in 1972 to Santa Cruz for her junior year, Barb was advised into the so-called Radical House by one of her professors. Its communal living arrangements (a dozen men and women living and working together) attracted her more than its violent, revolutionary politics, which did not sit well with Barb's libertarian, pacifist, Quaker soul. But she was intrigued that the house was centered around a student-run news service she could write for.

That winter she spent hours researching and writing a long article for the news service on nursing homes in the Santa Cruz area. Careful, bleak, and poignant (and buckling with outrage), it was published early in spring. She also wrote a short, mischievous account of her tangles with the city of Santa Cruz trying to harvest unused oranges from the front yard of City Hall.

That Barb had a deep and continuing interest in the formation of communities was apparent in the sociology paper she wrote that year called "Oneida Community: Failure in Socialization." She concluded:

> Oneida demonstrated that the first generation of perfectionist societies with a self-selected ideology can survive even while suffering social opposition. But seldom is socialization so complete that the second generation will adhere to, and believe in, inherited imposed values enough to continue to struggle against outside forces. Or, to phrase it romantically, perhaps every young person likes to dream his or her own dreams.

Apparently she was searching for a contemporary community to test out her ideals. She told us that she had twice visited a farm in Boonville, California, in October 1972 and early February 1973.

It was a family group, with both the Boonville farm and a house in Oakland. Barb wrote that she had visited her college friend Joanna, who had moved into the house. "These people are incredibly loving and live like a universal family. Everyone works hard together in harmony. It reminds me of Oneida Colony. But it scares me a little because it's so structured and organized and virtuous."

She called us, late in February 1973, from Santa Cruz. "I've got college permission to go into this religious community in Oakland and write my senior thesis on it," she announced.

Ray groaned. "Freshman spring term you went to Vancouver to study draft decliners; sophomore spring term you took off and went to Europe. When are you going to graduate from college?"

"I'll get credit for this."

"Barb, I don't think you should." Apprehension beyond credits and graduation stirred in me.

"I'm going to, I've decided," she said stubbornly. Three or four phone calls later, we still couldn't dissuade her.

"You'll have to pay for it yourself," Ray warned, grim by now.

"I know. I can handle it," she answered confidently.

She came home for spring vacation. My journal noted: "Backpack strapped to her, our dear girl arrived at the airport. She looks and seems good."

We'd just bought a Portland house that faced out on a sweeping view of the Coast range and the ever-boiling Oregon sky. Barb spent hours photographing still life objects by the light of our wide-angle windows.

Unease in me had caused me to suggest that while she was home she make tapes of her life in the Radical House. I wasn't prying, but her last year in Santa Cruz had deeply concerned me. Listening much later to the tapes she had left behind, we were struck by her soft, reflective voice, that alive voice that seemed to be the first thing to change when she went into the cult.

She started off by recalling a big rally Santa Cruz students held to protest the killing of black students at Jackson State in Mississippi. In the planning of the rally, someone had suggested that a woman should make a speech. "No one was willing," Barb said. "We're not experienced, we're never given a chance. I didn't volunteer; I was tired of picking up the energy pieces. I went to my room. All of a sudden I felt impelled— one of us had to make that speech. I opened James Agee's Let Us Now Praise Famous Men and picked out a quote."

At the rally the women were overlooked, Barb said. "I got so pissed. By God, I *am* going to do it. I jumped up and asked them to wait a minute, and I gave my speech. Afterward, I felt good. You just have to act."

Of the Radical House itself she said:

We started with meetings, films, discussions of issues, organizing antiwar and civil rights demonstrations. I was involved with a committee on the news service. Yet our efforts all along were pretty individual. I worked on my nursing home article, some wrote for socialist newspapers, some for feminist magazines. Others worked for a local radio station.

When I think about leadership, there's almost none in the house. What there is is haphazard, and bounces from one to another. Things don't get done.

On division of labor, everybody is supposed to take their part; each, for instance, should take a turn once a week getting dinner. At first some dodged work, especially in the first semester. I did more than my share and the tension was high in me because I was trying to impress people with my communal zeal. That's when I went home at Christmas and evaluated my life. Was *I* wanted in the house at all? Did I want them? Thank goodness, I went back and really confronted them. After that, I did my share of work and didn't worry about what didn't get done.

I want to talk about drugs, rip-offs. It's a self-centered rationalization that you have the right to get at the establishment that way. Everyone in our house rips off books and food. It's hard for me to take.

As far as drugs, four of us don't smoke dope. Basically, I'd rather get high just on people. But we did have a heroin addict here for a while and that was frightening. Finally, after we tried our best, we told her she had to give up heroin or move out.

The House has three women lesbians. Homosexuality was theoretical to me before I moved in; I felt threatened. I thought I'd have to relate to lesbians only in sexual terms. So I kept my distance. But soon I realized they didn't see me in terms of gay or straight, they just wanted to know me. I got involved in watching them change pairings, suffer loss of love. Still, I found out I'm not impelled physically toward women in the way I am toward a very select few men. I set limits, though maybe part of that's still a fear factor. I couldn't say I was a political lesbian, either, though I was pushed hard to take that stand. But I resisted Radical House pressure to have feminism adopt a lesbian emphasis. When I talked to mom at Christmas, her point was that it was a civil rights issue but the women's movement shouldn't be overwhelmed by it. . . .

I'm trying to think of the commitment in our house. There's something lacking. What would we do with children? We all admitted it was far beyond our sense of responsibility. We don't know that kind of personal bond. We're too fragmented, too concerned with our personal lives.

Though a feminist, Barb didn't share the separatism of some of the other feminists in the House; her feelings are apparent in this poem:

A close circle of women
gathered on the eve
of winter solstice
to stir a brew of soup
and pass the pipe—
not phantoms of history
but friends
of each other.
their love lingers logical
more resolute
than true.
they celebrated
cozy cabinward,
a shared secondary status
praising experience,
ridiculing performance.
addicted to memory
together
they silently mourned
their missing men.

She talked several times on the tapes about Evan, still the most important part of her emotional life. Yet there continued to be no resolution of the problem that he was married.

She also mentioned that in January 1973, she'd gone to a co-counseling retreat which hadn't worked out well for her. Coming back crushed and desolate, she said:

I just wanted to be a person who could love and receive love. The weekend hadn't fit that need. Groping, for the first time in my life I really prayed. I didn't know exactly to what. I woke up the next morning and the sun was golden. It poured through my stained glass windows. I felt literally enveloped by an unconditional love that didn't ask anything in return. I simply *named* this "God." I felt changed. I cried for two hours, with a towel wrapped around my head, because here I was in a Radical House, where religion was "the opiate of the people," and I didn't know how I'd tell anyone who might hear me cry that I'd just found God!

The tapes finished with this comment:

One thing I have to face is why I'm going to Oakland into the Family. I suppose the main thing is the height of the personal standard in the living situation. In Oakland community it's very high, very deep. When I try to espouse that high a personal standard in Santa Cruz, nobody believes it.

Joanna has led me into the Family, largely through the changes in herself, changes I desire for myself. There's a lioness quality about Joanna, a courage quality as well as a lamb quality, a tenderness. Innocence, openness, humility . . ."

Parenthood is tough in the twilight zone between childhood and adulthood, as one struggles to allow a child independence without surrendering all authority. Perhaps we should have insisted Barb leave the Radical House, if not ruggedly individualistic Santa Cruz itself. If we had, would we have won a less severe reaction than the cult?

But there are two things God doesn't grant twice: life and parenthood.

Betty and Barb: Going Into the Cult— a Combined Account

"A good parson once said, that where mystery begins, religion ends."
—BURKE

"Huge and mighty forms that do not live
Like living men, moved slowly through the mind
By day, and were a trouble to my dreams."
—WORDSWORTH

APRIL 3, 1973.
On the way home from a visit to the Japanese gardens in Portland, Barb talked to me about her decision to move in with the religious community called the International Reeducation Foundation.

Suspecting that more was involved than writing a senior thesis, I kept questioning her.

"I want to test the ability of the individual person to change, then change society," she told me.

On the more emotional level under the intellectual, I sensed she was excited but also frightened. Was she?

Yes, she said, she was both.

But why frightened?

She couldn't seem to be clear, ended by saying she was afraid the Family would stall her.

"For good?"

"Yes, maybe..."

"But that's a capture like your Michelangelo stones. If that's a possibility, why in the world do it?"

"Oh, I don't believe I'll get stuck there for good," she reassured me. (Was she reassuring herself?)

"What makes you want to do this?" I insisted, juggling traffic lights and anxiety. (Why *hadn't* I heard about cults?)

"They're such good people," she answered, "and they live such a good life."

"Well, what do they do?"

"They work hard," she answered me. "They work from five in the morning till eleven at night."

"But what do they *do?*"

She couldn't seem to say.

I did find out there would be six people to a room, sleeping in sleeping bags on the floor, and their possessions would have to be stripped down to fit in one dresser drawer.

We went back to the excitement side and Barb told me that people in the Family were growing to be people of character; young persons who went there in conflict and pain and confusion were finding a new way, were happier, stronger, less self- and more other-concerned.

As she talked, I squelched my intuition that something was wrong, because I knew how important this kind of self-testing was to her.

But in that intuition was only the faintest intimation of what was ahead. If I'd known what was *really* ahead, nothing on God's green earth would have let me say good-bye to her the way I did.

Which was on Wednesday, April 4, when, as my journal said, "On a summerlike morning I drove Barb to the airport to go down to the

Family. I put her on the plane at 10:20. Seeing her walk down that runway, fear suddenly gripped me. Things happened the rest of the day but I don't remember them."

Innocent of all the information about Moon and Unification which has since become available, Ray and I waited, stoic, naïve, and hopeful, for this, too, to pass. . . .

Barb called at Easter, three weeks after she'd gone into the Family. It was a strange call and left us disturbed. She was into the Family with both feet, loved it and them, and hinted it would be a *long* stay. She still couldn't be exact about its theological principles except to say that love was preeminent and if there was wrongdoing it should be countered by reconciliation. For the first time, however, she spoke of a leader of "the movement"—a Reverend Sun Myung Moon, "a great person." We had never heard of someone with such an unlikely name; her brief characterization didn't reassure us. She wanted to take all her money out of her savings to give to the Family. Ray resisted. "I'll send you fifty dollars a month . . ."

"This has to wait for a visit, either you to us or we to you." We hung up, Ray and I, and talked in consternation. We questioned the soundness of her responses. It was as we'd feared—the religious "rush," the comaraderie, had cancelled out her ability to be objective.

It seemed to us a cruel turn of events. In co-counseling she'd been working through a lot of problems, had seemed more confident, more serene in herself.

We called my brother and his wife in Berkeley. They'd seen a lot of her, said she was on a real religious "high." She'd invited them around to the Family, had been equally vague about philosophy but very clear that the movement needed money. Scott had good-humoredly said to expect no support from him. Lauriel was astonished but intrigued at the speed and intensity of the commitment.

To us the group's aims seemed so vague, the meager philosophy, as Barb expressed it, so banal, and the implications of some unknown guru taking advantage of all that young labor so obvious, that we were horrified at her naïve transformation. Her voice had sounded strange—flat and hoarse. She said it was because "we sing so much."

For the first time another apprehension hit me. The Family's gain might be our family's loss. We could lose her. Overpowering fear washed over me. A small beginning anger followed that fear. A guilty anger directed at myself for somehow failing her; at the group for exploiting her and, yes, at her for her gullibility.

In early July we went down to San Francisco. Barb joined us next morning at our motel and went with us to federal court to hear Ray argue an interesting case on Indian fishing rights. After the argument, Ray, Barb, Lauriel, and I went to the De Young Museum to see the Andrew Wyeth show. Silently Barb pointed out a quote to me: "I don't think something is really magical unless it has a terrifying quality. In fact, anything that is good is a little frightening and a little sad."

Tuesday night Ray and I went to Barb's Family. On Dana Street in Oakland sat a comfortable old house bare of furniture but clean, orderly, and pleasant. There were about sixty to dinner that Tuesday, approximately twenty members and the rest guests.

We were enthusiastically greeted by both young people and staff. Among the latter were an unreadable, attractive, fortyish Oriental woman, Onni, Korean founder of this outpost of Moonism; and Teresa, an Onni lieutenant, a handsome, vibrant, tough-minded person whose first sentence to us when she sat down beside us was "We need money." Dr. Moses Durst, another leader, who was later to become Onni's husband, had a pleasant but driven air.

The young members were to a person cordial and seemingly interested in us. Accustomed to the street-marching hostilities of the young, we were impressed by what appeared to be a genuine effort to close the generation gap.

Chairs and floor were crammed, and we were fed with amazing unflurry. There was lots of peppy, optimistic singing. As a group the young people were appealing, if somewhat startling. Attuned as our eyes were to casually threadbare clothes and long hair, their ties, coats, and prim long dresses looked nothing short of bizarre.

That evening an alert young man gave the introductory lecture on the Moon principles. I could only characterize what I heard as nineteenth-century moral philosophy, the kind of material students of an earlier period had to memorize by the pages. The assumption was idealistic—that love could effectively replace alienation. Christianity seemed to be part of the principles, though I got hints that later lectures would be more Asian.

The raptness in that room astonished me. I wasn't then experienced enough to realize that many young people, religiously illiterate from lack of training or personal disinclination, seize upon cultist truths as the only authentic religious words or experiences available. Now I watched young listeners treat bland generalizations like newly discovered grand truths. How hungry for something, for *anything* hopeful they must be, I concluded sadly.

As Ray and I drove back to my brother's we decided it *must* be from the living out of the principles, rather than the principles themselves, that the group derived its fervor and cohesiveness. Years later we knew ourselves to have been in the same position as Barb in her first days: at the center of Moonism is the requirement of secrecy and we had heard only a carefully devised elementary lecture.

We'd picked up certain other things, however: that Unification people didn't appear inclined to work for the disadvantaged but were power-minded. The conquest of the American establishment was their goal, that establishment which their peers had forsaken as beyond rescue. We also discovered the Family de-emphasized sexual love, regarding themselves as brothers and sisters instead. They allowed no drugs, alcohol, or tobacco, a fact paraded promptly before parental attention.

Each member belonged to a "trinity"—a small, three- or four-person group within the larger Family.

Ray flew back to Portland the next morning. That afternoon Barb and I had lunch on Telegraph Avenue, where individualism had gone berserk in daishikis, Civil War tunics, and bare feet, and then found a bench in the sun. We communed in what I thought was our good old way. Only with hindsight could I realize how I failed to read Barb's hints at impending denials and separations. . . .

Barb said the Family emphasized a different form of blood ties; for erring ancestors they had to pay an "indemnity." Somehow I just didn't click in to the separation implications of this Orientalism. I understood better Barb's saying she'd suddenly realized her own blood family wouldn't live forever; "I needed universal love beyond death, that's one of the reasons I joined the Family." With my mother's death only months past, with my dearly loved daughter sitting comfortably beside me, I related to the emotional need for *that*.

I'd always been fascinated by Barb's sense of adventure, her grit, her curiosity. Having felt that wartime women of my generation had lockstepped from their fathers' to their husbands' hearths without much independent experience, I had wanted something more for Barb: *first* the time to know and develop herself and her capacities, *then* her own family, if her stars so ordained.

I asked myself, now, how long would it be before she gave this experiment up? Fearfully: would she? Reassuring myself, of course. What would the six months I was hopefully estimating cost her? Could they even be enriching, supportive?

What *was* a religious conversion like? I didn't know. My faith—our faith, Ray's and mine—was grounded in a quiet, developmental Quaker tradition.

How genuine was Barb's conversion? I'd had no awareness she'd had other than intellectual responses to religion.

Would she be able to judge what she was doing? It's very hard to pass on to the young the meaning of silent group mysticism; Barb had come out of her years of Quakerism, relatively universal in conventional religion.

Above all, who were these people? What were their intentions? Was it a case of the right feelings directed at the wrong objects?

While I was in the Bay area Barb, trying to communicate to me the meaning of her experience, lent me a journal she had kept of her early weeks in the Family, a journal which had ended the latter part of April.

Still unaware of the word *cult* in its contemporary sense, I leafed through the journal.

With all kinds of hints shouting at me in those pages, I still didn't see beyond the triteness of the beliefs to some of the more disturbing implications of this apparently innocuous fundamentalist faith.

Trying to "feel" where Barb was, I made myself believe she was all right.

Only time was to tell me how miserably I'd failed to "feel."

APRIL 4.
Can people change? To what degree? The Family fills me with terror. I'm leaving Portland and all the meaningful roots in my life. I feel a need to bring with me all my present symbols of love, morality, purpose, talent. I pack my newest photographs, my last poems, and a foolish box of totems. And I need to store in my memory yesterday's water-bright, pierce and quiver mood of the Japanese cherry trees in the Japanese Garden with Mom. I think of her eyes watching.

My mother
So precious in flesh,
Every moment sustenance,
Tossing up love and fury,
Sadness and silliness
In a juggler's daring act . . .
Gentler than smile-wrinkles
Around her eyes.
My mother,
No idealized love
Relegated to distances,
Wishful thinking
Or censored performance.
Love so real it makes
Fears less single,
Womanhood reverberate,
My life expectant.
My mother
Whose selfhood and personal power
Seed my deepest intent.

As I pack, I'm filled with questions. How do I resolve *this* life, in which I long to be an artist whose apprehensions of truth are often solitary, with the Family's daily living, its never-alone-for-one-minute spiritual and daily communion? I ask, can these life-styles possibly synthesize? And how will the Family affect my connections with my family, Evan, the Marmadukes, Molly?

I'm afraid of the Family's appeal to a nonego center because *self* seems to form the necessary base for change and authentic transformation. I fear danger of loss of my own selfhood.

In this day and age, what huge, ludicrous skepticism fills me about *any* power which professes to be neither hypocritical, exploitative nor objectifying?

When I go down to Oakland and move into the Family, the first thing I have to ask is, am I doing this as an act of my will or someone else's? (How will I know?) Is this a sacrifice I make because it serves the whole or because, over and above everything else, it serves me?

I panic to think I'll never come home.

When I do, will I seem unrecognizable?

I need in my memory Mom's waiting and waving to the plane I go out on—even though I know she can't see me anymore. . . . Dad warned me I must treat this as a kind of field study, a sociological inquiry; he emphasized objectivity. Evan, being an artist, told me to keep on writing—"natural life raft in this dark ocean." Evan said, "Remember, we'll be in very different myths this next couple of months." How important that I hang on to this so as to prevent absolute absorbtion into any *one* philosophical system with all that denial of reality. There are multiple realities and I have to embrace them with all their diversity and ambiguity.

I remember my first introduction to the Family. I went on impulse to visit Joanna, who'd left Santa Cruz to join a mysterious communal setup in Oakland where there was a lot of talk in old-fashioned terms about love and duty to the collective goals. In that old house on Dana Street in Oakland and on their Boonville farm, I found a group of people, mostly my age, living in such a close way I couldn't believe it. When I heard all their old-fashioned rules of moral conduct, I thought *what absurdities* and then I went away. But afterward, I couldn't think of anything else except that weekend and those good, solid, happy faces. I decided I would have to move in sometime in the future, at least for a short time, and then finish up at Santa Cruz. But somewhere brewed intimations of a long-term commitment.

APRIL 5.
The Family was the beginning of the greatest ambivalence I've experienced. I told everybody I was going to write my senior thesis about the Oakland Family and I plan to. But it isn't only for cool scholarship that I go. Something more is entering my life than pure sociological research and I know it. I've expectations the Family will speak to the center of me, the nitty-gritty core, let me be far more than an observer. . . .

I'm seized sometimes with the desire to photograph my mother, to render a permanent image. Someday I want to render her without guilt—in our recollection to extinguish all guilt. She is a criminal without a crime. No guilt. No guilt, my mother. Habibi, dear one.

APRIL 7.
     I haven't left my Radical House here in Santa Cruz for Oakland yet. Tonight I went to a party with a friend, Cindy, in Ben Lomand, the mountains around Santa Cruz. It was one of those "nonhappenings" where everyone leaves asking what could have been done. We all operated like efficient vacuum cleaners sucking the vitality out of the air. Anything tried to electrify would have short-circuited, been too dangerous. Easier to sigh, yawn, think of leaving or sleeping, pretending to the mellowness that Santa Cruz is famous for. I didn't quite have the courage (which is to say, I didn't have it at all) to suggest charades, let out a dark secret, mention what I wanted to do before I died tomorrow, explain what country I'd like to be from, sing, mime, dance, share fantasies.

APRIL 8.
     I wake out of a fetal position, shift to a praying position. I smother a flood of tears as I wonder: can life really be all these brutal, mutually exclusive choices? I'm weary of Santa Cruz, but afraid to leave the familiar and afraid to embark upon the unknown. . . .

One gets older. Is that true? Am *I* getting older? But life seems a permanent state of siege. Do we move toward ambiguity or absolutes? Fanaticism, or skepticism and resignation? Faith or confirmed disbelief?

I called Joanna about moving in on April 11 to the Family. She sounded excited, but hinted at an odd spiritual ambience. She warned: "Be prepared and ready to serve the older brothers and sisters. Come positive, o.k?" I hung up the phone and wondered.

I pondered on the idea of *submission*. Question: will women in the Family be used to serve? I believe in serving but only through choice. I know the Family says that man and woman exist in unity centered on God:

Man	Creator	Woman
	Child	

I wonder, is this a fixed, exclusive model? How are alternatives treated, i.e., childlessness, singleness, homosexuality? Is there allowance for diversity?

APRIL 9.

I worry for a tightening in the head and throat, a hollowness in the chest called *not belonging*. Sometimes I want to be pushed by events, literally hurtled to get there, and not have to pull myself.

APRIL 11.

I'm in a state of readiness rather than reluctance, despite all the "not knowing" and the hidden end results. But still, when I stand up against counters and tables, my knees shake.

Here I am. I arrived in Oakland to the Family. It was a homecoming, a birthday with the presents not yet opened.

The Dana Street house is nondescript, wooden, has a small lawn on a cul-de-sac. It's well kept, but Spartan inside and out, with rows of neatly stacked shoes that are removed at the door. Yet even with few furnishings and paintings, there's a sense of life in it, a sense of intense, purposeful order, a sense even of roguish laughter and good times.

I'll sleep two blocks away at another church house on Regent street, six to a room, on the floor in sleeping bags. I'll get a lot of my clothes from a common room. And it looks as though we'll be fed—plentifully, but without much meat—by a kitchen crew that operates on a rotating basis. That means I'll cook, too!

In front of Dana Street, Family cars are parked every-which-way. They're in all states from shiny to decrepit—vans, trucks, motorcycles.

There's so much coming and going, but none of it solitary. In the whirlwind, I'll have to learn to trust. I must find a root to seed trust. Joanna.

I've come here to learn to be true to myself, which also means true to larger forces; I believe my writing will take on a praying aspect.

I've lived conscientiously in my life but now I'll have to live deeper than that. I know Evan will be the worst trial for me, the most struggle, because I love him so much and keep thinking about him.

To my surprise, the first evening lecture my energy was more on the explanation of the Unification Principle than on receiving or giving warmth to others around me. I'm acutely aware of my censoring process, yet I restrain a constant critical response to the lectures, restrain aspects of myself that might arouse a critical reaction from Family members. Is fear of rejection in me or the group? Is there as heavy pressure as there seems to be? Am I imagining it? Will the group discourage me from seeing my friends outside?

If I stay here very long some parts of me will grow, but I can tell other parts of me will atrophy. But which: the creative, curious, independent parts? I want to lose my selfishness, but not myself.

I'm finding that it's a lot more struggle to mobilize myself in anticipation of other's needs 100 percent of the time than my own needs. Heavy vibrations exist in the Family homes. I was meditating last night (wondering if that wasn't self-indulgent) but I could hear the door opening and closing on a trinity meeting. I sensed explosive spirits. Joanna, my friend and spiritual teacher, told me later they were exorcising evil influences and murmured something about Satanic forces. I listened to Joanna with outward passivity, but inside I felt crippled with fear. What am I involved in?

I tell myself I'll dismiss this project, I'll simply walk away from it. I'll get out. It's too harsh and emotional; there's too much faith in faith. And the conflict goes on in my head. Am I crazy? I'm terrified of the unfolding of some huge potential I sense. I'm terrified of my own unknown potential if I freely submit.

My trinity visited people to evangelize tonight. Varied reactions. I was self-conscious and felt pretty nutty. It was a relief to end up at Arlie and Adam Hochschild's from Santa Cruz days—I got to see their new son, David. Arlie's a splendid person and taught me so much in her sociology and feminism courses. She promised to come and look at the Family some night.

After we got home from several night visitations, I lay in my sleeping bag and shook with anxiety and panic. The cause and practice of these people is just too hard-driving, unrelenting, absolute.

APRIL 12.

Why do I begin to feel that so many of the books I've brought with me from college are looked upon critically by the Family? What are their priorities? I feel my books on sexuality are seen as pornography. The Family tells me that the only thing I need to read is *Divine Principle*. How much value does the Family place on writing? I don't believe all that much, except as Family-centered. But writing's my long-range goal. So I'm going to continue to record my thoughts no matter what happens, and not just thoughts that are positive and of high standard, as the Family suggests, but my honest terrors and insecurities, too.

Is the Family's zealousness repulsive or alluring? What about the question of personal anger? What do I do with it? What about people who come here and don't fit in? How do they handle that?

"Trust what you don't understand," I'm constantly told.

But there are people here who are more splendid than any I've ever met in my life—Evey, Daniel, Shelly. And Joanna, of course, who tells me over and over, "You're here because of God's will!" She keeps telling me I have a smaller viewpoint than God's viewpoint. How can I dispute that? She tells me because of that I must be prepared to *reorder* every single thought I've ever had.

I wonder how many of the people here now will be here a year from now? And where will they be sent? Will I be here?

What about leadership and the leadership principle? Nagging question: who makes the decisions in this Family? Everyone says the *Divine Principle* makes the decisions, but how does *Principle* do it unless through a personal interpretation by someone? It feels feudal. Would this Oakland house fall without the evanescent, Asian spirit of Onni?

APRIL 15.

There exists more power in this movement than I've ever experienced in my life. The Family is helping me to channel responsible anger and the fury to change, shows me how to transform human stumbling into rising. It's not impossible.

So many negative spirits enter into my job hunting. I keep romanticizing the comfort of life before the Family—past relationships, ocean beaches, dark rooms, embraces of passion, mother-ease, playing, meandering, music, records. But all of them were so self-centered, so within myself, or limited to a narrow group. I cry on buses, missing my old friends and landmarks. I know the crying is WRONG and weak. Sometimes my conscience feels pinned to the wall.

APRIL 18.

I can hardly believe in one week I've emptied myself of so many concepts, have turned my values inside out. I'm discovering the truth in the statement, "New wine for old bottles." If all of us can change ourselves, we can change society.

Damn it. Right now I'm sitting here agonizing over the fact that it's virtually impossible to write coherently in this journal. The Family schedule gives me no time for personal reflection, no time for sleep or aloneness; no privacy, no space. I feel guilty for wanting to write a letter.

I really wonder how selfish I am. Very selfish, if what I write is only for my own development or for the limited appreciation of those few who might love me and have a personal investment in me. But if I can see a more historical imperative to write, then maybe I can justify my writing.

I wonder about authority, and feel relief that I'm not in such a responsible position as trinity head or staff. Shelly, Martha, and Joanna leave for a late trinity head meeting and I feel shame. How could I glorify evading responsibility in a world which depends on every right action?

My standards for my life have been such narrow ones when I compare them to *perfection.* And all this time God loved me even while I refused the leap of faith that creates our relationship.

I can see now, many of the tests I set up to examine *Divine Principle* are old concepts; they don't strike as deep, however unused to *Divine Principle* as I am.

For a hurt, love back selflessly. Think first and always of others' needs. Love flows out, flows back; spirits lift, life grows rich, secure. *Divine Principle* works! Every day it works *as I accept its premises!*

Confession to Esther, an older sister today. Also to Evey about Evan. My life has been stained by so much evil. I'm guilty.

Four months after Barb was first introduced to the Family and a mere ten days after she moved into Dana Street, her journal begins to use specific Unification phraseology, to refer to Heavenly Father, Satanic forces, and Spirit World. And the strange word *Indemnity.*

APRIL 21.
There *are* Satanic forces. Lucifer *did* literally lead Eve into temptation, into the faithlessness that brought down the human tribe. I want to know more about this Devil and how he fits into my own experience of premature love, a love that for me was so intense it was all I wanted. How we two hurt, how we created disharmony. It's hard to accept that the person I've loved will only contribute to destruction unless I make conditions with Heavenly Father that he become my

brother rather than my lover. Was it all my fault? Was the Devil a bringer of seductive light?

Joanna tells me repeatedly there's a point where—using Principle—individual "lust" can be overcome. If I overcome Evan, I can serve with my whole being this wonderful Heavenly Father.

APRIL 23.
Spirit World must have called me to the Family. It's not what I wanted for my life, but after I left the first Boonville weekend retreat, I had powerful dreams that my life would collapse unless I joined with this Family.

Then Barb's journal became crowded with fragments of what I guessed was *Divine Principle*. The lecture notes seemed pieced together as best a neophyte could from the fast-paced format: Did they let her question? At first, there were interesting personal reactions pencilled on margins. Then I noticed those reactions disappeared. All that was left were the lecture notes, mostly incomprehensible to me. Overwhelmed by cult vocabulary, definitions, diagrams, Barb appeared to be trying to make sense of it all. After the first lecture, Barb's notes concluded:

God is dependent upon us and we are dependent upon Him. God cannot do it without us; we are like the key in the ignition. Nothing in the universe was created perfect; everything must grow and struggle, by conditions, toward a perfect end. An incomplete God called man to create His place in the human world.

The second lecture presented the deviation, or fall-of-man concept, which I learned later was at the heart of Unification. In these first pages of Barb's notes there is still no mention of the proposal that Reverend Moon is the Messiah who comes to undo the sexual sin of Adam and Eve and physically and spiritually save the world. Her brief introspection, after this generalized version of the fall theory, was mainly personal. She cited her confessions of sexual guilt over Evan, the Family obviously starting right in playing hard on former transgressions. She noted that she could not have been, by Family belief, ever truly loved before in her whole life. Only God truly loved her. Apparently she could not have had an unblemished ancestry, either. In the margin, she wrote:

Heavenly Father, why am I not humble? If Adam and Eve's love was premature, then there never have been children who were loved totally, including myself. Father, we are so stone-hearted. How awful that we have such difficulty feeling sorry for God at the fall of man. Father, I'm so sorry for my arrogance, my lack of sincerity.

APRIL 25.
Wandering in downtown Oakland still job hunting. Six months ago, Evan and I were walking into the furnace of our love. He didn't want me to have anything to do with the Family. He says he'll give me three months, then he'll come and get me.

(He tried. Barb talked to him by phone, but refused to see him alone without a chaperone. He refused to visit the Family headquarters.) Struggling to give up Evan, she tried to transcend her own personal, and—as she saw them—selfish feelings:

Depression is total immersion in self. I get depressed thinking of Evan. . . . I feel so guilty, selfishly fantasizing about him, hiding my innermost passion for him. But he's married. He was always unavailable to me in some complete way. And now God wants me to make myself inaccessible to him. Though he entered my life as teacher and friend, mostly he was the first man I ever loved physically. That was wrong according to the *Principle*. They tell me how much that hurt God. But I'm confused. Why did I feel so in love with Evan? Can I ever be pure in God's eyes again? How hard will I have to work to prove my purity? Am I willing to change my feelings for Evan if only God will accept me? Yes, if God will bring Evan to the Family as my brother, I'll try never to desire him again. If I can keep God in the center I'll rise above selfish love and depression. I guess it takes a push from a firm external source.

APRIL 26.
People's spiritual experiences here are amazing. I understand so much more my reason for coming. Why did I feel so much grief, sorrow, bitterness, separation before?
So one of my indemnities will be to make up for Evan. The day I felt the overpowering urge to see Joanna in the Family, Evan and I

were eating lunch down in Santa Cruz. A wind came up, sighed from
the north; I sensed Joanna calling me. Evan didn't want to take me up
to see her. He and I fought about the Family. But we drove to
Oakland anyway. Coming into the city, God emptied a rainbow into
a parking lot with graffiti-scrawled walls.

For the first time Barb's journal mentioned True Parents.

Everyone I've loved before could believe in True Parents, too.
The idea matches my dream, a God who can fulfill my hopes for
ongoing love. If God controls things through a perfect society, he'd
create perfect parents, too, wouldn't he? I know my own parents are
human, not perfect. Yet they can become believers some day, and part
of the perfect society we're creating too. I have a feeling of great hope.

Barb began to mention Messiah in her journal. But it didn't seem
to be an emotionally laden consideration for her. Apparently she didn't
have a concept of Messiah, except as a great teacher.

A**PRIL 27.**
   I may have a temporary job on the Berkeley campus.
Should be as good as that kind of job can be.

I must learn to feel natural witnessing to people on buses, street
corners and cafeterias.

I receive merit from these ancestors: grandpa's faith and sacrifice
through grandma's three-year sickness and death; dad's principled life
which has caused him loneliness and suffering.

I have these indemnities to pay: general family selfishness means I
must give all my material assets to the Family.

My own indemnity to God must restore Evan through me. What
a giving up.

I can't be desolate and empty but must be filled with a different
love.

God help me.

I'm really not caring for this journal even though Evan told me it
was dangerous to stop writing. I don't want to write, mostly because
my feelings are channeled into immediate energy demands. Every
instant of the day I'm serving and sharing, and struggling. Yet
somehow each day I have a sense of participation and completion.

At one point I thought I'd lost this record and I was upset. When

I realized and asked penance for my attachment to writing, I found the journal again.

Someday, maybe, I'll write. But I have to subdue myself.

First I need to free myself, empty myself.

I need to give myself up.

I gave the journal back to Barb and left the Bay Area.

In August 1973, Barb—her name by now changed to Lael—came home for a visit. Doug was there from Ohio; he went into the airport to get her. When he came out he was pale. As he climbed into the back seat of the car, he whispered to me, "She was standing at a window singing a song to herself in a loud voice. You've got to help me. I can't handle this." I understood his sheer social embarrassment.

In the front seat of the car Barb looked lean, tan, healthy. Yet this time we picked up a real change in her and not just in the way she was dressed—old-fashioned skirt and blouse, hair pinned up. We noticed her voice first, oddly hoarse, repressed, well modulated as a nun's. Her eyes were direct, but to our alarm and amazement, lifeless.

She could talk of nothing but *Divine Principle* and the Family, and the approach was now hardsell. She didn't want mere approval, she wanted us to consider joining her experience.

We also learned new and disturbing things about her life: she had just finished working forty straight days selling flowers, 7:00 A.M. to 1:00 A.M., running through factories, taverns, even into a circus, where (with a faint flash of her old humor) she said, "By mistake I came through the tent right under an elephant."

Selling on the street, we asked: what kind of full-time religious vocation was that? We figured if this kept up, in a year she'd gross the Family $40,000, no cent of which she'd keep for her own needs or even have any part in deciding how it would be spent. "Well, how *do* they spend it?"

Lamely, "We're printing thousands of copies of an eight-hundred-page explanation of *Divine Principle* and we're bringing some Japanese to the Bay Area for a conference."

After her restrained, almost careful manner, the next thing to hit us was that she seemed unable to think clearly, to respond with any kind of precision to the questions we asked. Where had her mind gone, her reason, we asked ourselves.

"It's like she's forgotten she has a brain," Ray complained, while I figured it *had* to be part of the fatigue and blurred, emotion-charged atmosphere she inhabited. She told us she had to bring a certain number of converts into the house. The practice was, no time off unless those converts came in. Fury, fury in me. Barb had the perfect exploitation-prone personality: hardworking, anxious to please, perfectionist.

"Lots of people in the house don't go home anymore," she told us (but we picked up no warning). "They don't feel they have home ties anymore."

Doug and Barb—often ones to pull and haul—were in constant debate. I tried to tell myself new brooms sweep hard, but I certainly sympathized with Doug's opposition to her insistence.

We didn't know what a later age of parents has been told: keep the disagreement quiet, appear to approve, don't put the enthusiastic neophyte on the defensive. Would that kind of deception have been possible for us anyhow? Accustomed as we were to open dealing with our children, I doubt it.

We had a confrontation, Ray, Doug, Barb. Around the kitchen table, Ray said he was beginning to see the movement as undemocratic. "This slavish leadership principle's bad. It doesn't allow for individual growth, development. And there's no millennium, Barb, and no possibility of a perfect society. To see only the positives without the negatives gives a truncated vision, reduces a person's ability to cope with real life. And the same goes for trying to live inside a rigid thought system. It's possible you're being badly exploited by a clever man. It's possible that in simply raising money for your own movement, not having a constructive outreach program for the poor or needy, you're badly exploiting others."

I agreed. I agreed with every rational word. But watching Barb's face, my heart ached for her. She'd come home to offer us her bright new vision of life and we were having to say no. As the visit wore on, I grew more troubled and anxious. She grew quieter and quieter.

Sunday morning I needed to try to reconcile the painful warring elements in myself. I stayed in bed and read the cult's *Principles of Education*. I found I simply couldn't keep my mind on the stuff; either some spiritual sensitivity was lacking in me or the concepts and language were trite and fuzzy. I lay trying to figure where I was. I faced the enormity of the loss of the essential Barb as we knew her. I had to admit that, in truth, parents feel personally repudiated when a child turns wholesale against their views, their way of life, and their goals, the ones the child has been consciously or unconsciously taught. Was it harder on me because I was the mother, she was the daughter? Somehow, I reasoned, there was apt to be more guilt about the offspring of the same sex; fathers must feel more responsible for the socialization of sons.

Later I had a frank talk with Barb about old times. I told her that to evangelize by letter or in person the way she was doing seemed a direct form of tyranny to lots of people, and old friends wouldn't know how to deal with it except to let her alone. "I've been too driving, too intense," she admitted, going off to the Marmadukes.

Again my heart turned over for her, for what reception might be ahead of her.

Monday late afternoon, Ray and I were to take Barb to the airport. Behind closed doors, we conferred briefly. We agreed that the main thing wasn't us, it was *her,* for her to be all right. She seemed to be dealing with the loss of Evan; she'd handle this Moon thing too, find a way out, a person with her independent mind and spirit.

But still, driving to the airport, we were terribly worried.

The three of us had dinner and Barb seemed to come suddenly popping out of her strange new skin, natural, alive, and familiar. "Do you think I've changed, I'm strange the way Doug said I was? I didn't mean to be, especially with him."

She opened up to us then, that old loveable, spunky, perceptive, very human daughter. "When I first went in the Family," she confessed, "I thought I'd have to shout obscenities just to relieve the bland, enthusiastic goodness. Yet when I come out in the world, everything's so awful; there's so much conflict and turmoil."

Tears of relief came to me when she talked like that. I knew how much she wanted to be a good person but my spontaneous reaction was to put my arm around her and reassure her, "I don't think people *want* to live with an angel."

Anyway, we had her back for an hour before—again like ignorant idiots—we kissed her good-bye.

When she walked into the tunnel to the plane, she turned, grinned at us, and then did a momentary jig.

I'll always remember her doing that.

As the plane flew out, through the blur, Ray took my hand. We walked into the airport waiting room together.

Barb: In the Unification Church— I Am Reborn

"I would rather be ashes than dust. I would rather that my spark should burn out in a brilliant blaze than that it should be stifled by dry rot. I would rather be a superb meteor, every atom of me in one magnificent glow, than a sleepy and permanent planet. The proper function of man is to live, not to exist. I shall not waste my days in trying to prolong them. I shall use my time."
—JOAN LONDON, *Jack London and His Times: An Unconventional Biography*

APRIL 1973-JANUARY 1977.
   The Unification years meant one essential thing: I was reborn. I experienced myself as a transformed, totally reconstructed person. In the transition period, I died to my old self, Barbara, and

became Lael. My new identity was shaped by action, for life in the Church *is* action. As a new person in a new Family, acting upon new hopes, anxieties, and goals, I began my life for the first time. What was the process of this rebirth?

The seeds were planted when I first *named* all the love I had experienced in my life, *God.* But as Barbara, meeting the Unification Family, my love was uncharted and without direction. Through the Unification concept of Truth and God my love found embodiment in an individual, Sun Myung Moon, as a divine object of worship. Reverend Moon offered my life hope, power, and authority. Barbara was forced to die; only Lael would live forever.

Reborn, I was several different persons depending upon my "Heavenly" task. I participated in five major missions or activities: Center Life, Recruitment Workshops, Flower Selling, National Campaign Activities, and Devotion to Moon. In center life, where the new Truth was structured in community, I grew from "infant" to "child" to "parent" as I gained responsibility. In the recruitment workshops, where I learned the theology, I was a "visionary" along with all the other chosen brothers and sisters. As a flower seller, I was a "soldier" for God. As a national campaigner, I was a "crusader." And in devotion to Sun Myung Moon as my Messiah, I was a "saved" person, who had sinned.

The only reason I could ceaselessly recruit, fund-raise, campaign, give over my possessions and submit to a rigorous and self-denying spiritual discipline was because "Father" (Reverend Moon), as God's Son, became my total love. Love-God-Moon was the energizing dynamic shaping each day of my four-year commitment to the cult.

After first joining the Unification Family in Oakland, California, in April 1973, I worked for the U.S. Forest Service and donated all my paychecks. I was also trained in the techniques of street proselytism or "witnessing" at this time. My mother and brother visited me for one of our weekend workshops in October of that year.

Between August 1973 and February 1977, I sold flowers sporadically in the San Francisco Bay Area, as well as around the country. The greatest portion of my time was spent "on the road." My selling teams combed territory as far-reaching as California, Oregon, Washington, Idaho, Utah, Arizona, and Texas to Arkansas, Louisiana,

Oklahoma, and Ohio, Kansas, Michigan, Illinois, Wisconsin, and surreptitiously in Canada.

I set out with an Oregon-bound team on my first out-of-state flower trip in December 1973, while the rest of the Church members drove to Washington, D.C., to march (with hundreds of "Forgive, Love, Unite" posters) in support of President Nixon after the Watergate disclosures. My team and I stayed briefly with my parents.

Beginning in January 1974, I lived—regarded as a great honor—with my flower team in the Avalon mansion, the Berkeley home of Dr. Durst and Onni Soo Lim, leaders of the West Coast movement. I was a servant for Reverend Moon and his wife the week they came to Berkeley for the "Day of Hope" tours.

From May to June, 1974, I recruited new members from the streets and campus of Berkeley while living at the Hearst Street mansion.

July to September, 1974, I sold flowers on teams around America. September 7 found me with twenty-eight others on a New York-bound missionary truck caravan to campaign for Moon's Madison Square Garden Rally. I spent one frenetic week pamphleting on Flatbush Avenue in Brooklyn.

From November 1974 to spring of 1975, I fund-raised with several teams on flower trips in the south and midwest. In December 1974, I flew up for another brief visit with my family in Portland.

I was assigned the tasks of cook, hostess, accountant, lecturer and recruiter at the Oakland Dana Street center in summer of 1975. My parents visited me there for two days, which turned out to be our last time together for over two years. My weekends were spent with new-found guests at the Boonville training center. I was promoted to a seven-day staff workshop leader in Boonville in July 1975. I didn't leave the farm gates until January 1976.

From January to May, 1976, I was assigned to travel on two flower teams in Detroit, Dallas, and the south.

June 1, 1976, signaled Moon's Yankee Stadium Rally, which my flower team attended. On that same day, my captain, Yacov, was "kidnapped" by his New Jersey parents for "deprogramming," but he escaped back to the Church.

I was moved to the all-women's Washington Street house on Pacific Heights in San Francisco for the summer. House teams witnessed from a bus on the wharf and in the Cannery. In August, l was sent to

Ohio to regain a staff leader, Michele, who was legally constrained and taken by her father in San Francisco. After my unsuccessful mission, I spent a week in Boonville in training with several "fugitive" members who feared their parents would attempt "deprogramming."

From September to November, 1976, I went out flower selling in Canada, interrupted only by attendance at the September 18 Washington Monument Rally of Moon. After returning to Berkeley in November, my team captain and other staff members were legally "kidnapped" and "deprogrammed" from the Church.

I inherited the responsibility to "captain" the flower team from December 1976 until February 1977, when I returned to San Francisco for a court trial. March 9, 1977, marks the beginning of the end of my "reborn years."

Life at the Centers

"Thence did I drink the. visionary power;
And deem not profitless, those fleeting moods
of shadowy exultation."

—WORDSWORTH

Center Life Schedule
(Monday through Friday, without deviation)
5:00 A.M. - Wake up, dress, fold sleeping bags
5:15   - Chanting Condition
5:45   - Exercises
6:00   - Clean-up
6:30   - Bible reading
6:45   - Liquid breakfast in small groups
7:30   - Lecture practice/Prayer
8:00   - Business meetings: Flower selling/Witnessing for that day
8:30   - Clear the house, everyone out to *work* for the day
5:00 P.M. - Find a guest for dinner program
5:30   - Bring guest home
6:00   - Singing, dinner
6:45   - Lecture program/Slides
8:00   - Refreshments/Weekend sign-ups and membership forms
9:30   - Clean house (On Friday, drive to Boonville with guests)

/   61

10:00	– Family meeting, small group study, or selling flowers in bars, or visiting potential recruits
11:00	– Prayer meeting
12:00	– Fast break for fasters
	– Write in diary, read *Divine Principle,* write letters
12:30	– Ready for bed, lights out for Family
12:00–	
2:00 A.M.	– Staff meetings

Like the proverbial Goldilocks, I tasted and tried center life in many "seatings."

I first moved into the Oakland Regent Street house for two months. I lived out of my backpack. The brown-shingle, six-bedroom house bulged with forty brothers and sisters. With never enough closet, bathroom, or sleeping-bag space, the first lessons in life as a spiritual "infant" were: DON'T BE NEGATIVE and USE CONSCIENTIOUS COMMON SENSE!

I was assigned to a small living group of three (a "trinity") and received my initial spiritual care and training from Joanna and an elder sister, Shelly. To them I confessed. I told them how selfish and wrong I felt I'd been in past intimate relations, how I hadn't been a perfect daughter, how I'd sometimes disappointed or hurt my friends. I felt guilt that I couldn't love ideally, that I was less than free.

From them I learned the proprieties of being reborn as an infant before a new God. They taught me how to approach this God. They showed me how to relinquish my ego, and become a total dependent on other hands. Every detail was attended to: how to pray and chant; how to serve my elders; how to approach Onni to please her; how to take notes in lecture; what to share and not share in group meetings; how to feel about Reverend Moon as Father and Messiah; how to recruit new members; how to fast; what to wear; how to part with my belongings and bank account; how to write letters; how to relate to brothers and to non-family men; what to think about world events; how to eat; how to sing; how to overcome sickness; and what to think of my parents and former friends. They taught me that *any* doubts are unfaithful and must be erased.

After two months I graduated from "infancy" to "childhood." I moved to Dana Street, Onni's home. I was assigned a new trinity leader, named Martha. She was a severe ultra-puritan who felt justice overruled kindness. When my Forest Service job ended, I joined Martha's witnessing team. Finding new recruits and caring for them as potential Family members was the surest way to grow a child's heart to parental size. To take responsibility for other peoples' salvation and growth proved more difficult than I thought. But after being nurtured for a period, it was now my turn to nurture others.

Martha believed the quicker the ego was cleaved away at the root, the quicker one's heart grew. One Monday in July 1973, while riding to campus to witness together, Martha told me I mustn't let my laryngitis (from enthusiastic singing in training session) interfere with talking to strangers.

"Martha, I have to whisper." I apologized.

"No, you don't! It's just your concept!"

"I'm sorry, I can hardly talk. I don't mean to be negative."

"It's SATAN controlling you. If you *yell* 'OUT SATAN' all the way to campus, you'll be fine," Martha ordered.

"Martha, but . . ."

"Out Satan! Out Satan! Come on, Lael, Out Satan!" she screamed. She started pounding me on the shoulder.

I joined in, my throat straining, "Out Satan, Out Satan!"

"Louder, come on!"

"OUT SATAN! OUT SATAN! OUT SATAN!" we screamed together, our faces getting flushed.

"Don't stop, Lael!"

After several weeks of witnessing at Dana Street, I gathered in and cultivated a crop of prospective members who attended the Dana Street weekend workshops. We called workshops "training sessions" because they trained "character." My spiritual growth proceeded through practicing "caring for others"—often people I felt nothing in common with except the vision the Church promised all people.

This theological "vision" penetrated me each workshop. Through continuous lectures on moral principles and the *Divine Principle,* through group experience and testimonials by elders, I accepted along with younger members several startlingly new and foreign speculations about spiritual reality. I began to accept them as revealed Truth. My new "vision" consisted of: the acceptance of an organic, invisible spirit world of ancestors—evil or righteous—who were influencing me; the necessity to replace atheistic communism with theocracy; the authenticity of original sin and my own fallen nature; the acceptance of deliverance, transcendence, and purification through Reverend Moon and his wife as my True Parents; and the yearning for a child and husband, an Ideal Family centered on God.

Divine Principle was continually reinforced by community life, especially in Family Meetings. These were a time for brothers and sisters in the centers to share their realizations of God, their conquests of their own selfishness, or their dreams. Sometimes Onni would speak words of fire. Because of this, the call for Family Meeting struck like lightning.

"Quick, pali-pali!" *(Pali* meaning *hurry* in Korean.) "Onni's coming tonight for a Family Meeting. Clean up now!" Teresa ordered. Teresa, who was responsible for preparing the worshipful atmosphere, assigned an older sister to prepare fruit and Ginseng tea for Onni and Dr. Durst, tasks accepted with honor and fear. Tensions ran high to meet Onni's standard of perfection. Windows were opened because we all knew Onni's "spiritual smell" was very sensitive to "low spirits" from recently departed guests still dwelling in the Satanic world. Hair combed, faces washed, shirts tucked in, the Family gathered in full circle around a pillow or sofa prepared for Onni. Teresa would lead us in singing before the magisterial arrival.

Onni and Dr. Durst would sweep in. Onni's presence commanded full obedience. Meetings would usually start with a ritual passing of fortune cookies, which we read out loud. Seen as a barometer of our spiritual states of mind, the ones I saved were memorable: "Great thoughts come from the heart," "Life to you is a dashing and bold adventure," or "He that falls in love with himself [which I publicly read, "God"] will have no rivals."

One Family meeting scarred my soul. An elder sister, Amy, had left the Family months earlier to take care of her daughter. Teresa met Amy one day and invited her back for an evening. Pressured to come, Amy sat as guest of "honor" across the long banquet table in the dining room. The atmosphere was strained as Family members waited for Onni's cue to know how to treat Amy. Was she a prodigal daughter returned? Should we sit in judgment and condemn her selfish departure?

"Amy, why you left?" Onni bore in.

"Onni, because I couldn't give up my daughter and many pleasures in life," Amy was shaken but forthright.

"Amy, you come back now to Family. Stop your evil ways! You make promise to me this moment!" Onni spoke the verdict.

"I can't." Amy bowed her head.

"Why you can't?" Onni yelled.

"Because I'm too selfish," stated the "fallen" sister.

"Amy, listen. Stop your flirt with Satan. You dying out there. Promise me you come back, become righteous sister. Repent!"

"No, Onni, I'm sorry, I want to keep my daughter; I'm too selfish for your world."

"Amy, you no good daughter of God. You don't give your life to God, He kick you out forever! Bah!"

Amy's attachment to her physical child, born outside Church blessing, was the most extreme of the problems of attachment. *Principle* dictated that in three years' time, each must be willing to give up all attachments to one's mind, body, and to physical "things," of a personal nature. When a new member moved into a center, musical instruments and conservative clothes were kept for community use, but property regarded as less utilitarian was often sold in rummage sales without the owner's consent. Books and backpacks were "stored" and disappeared forever. Valuables like jewelry were given to "Heaven" in the form of offerings to Onni or Dr. Durst as "Heaven's representatives." Cars were often turned over to the Family, as well as bank accounts, in the constant effort to wrest material ownership from Satan and return it to rightful ownership in God's lap. It was advised that even physical children be cared for elsewhere.

I changed trinities again, and left Dana Street. I joined the flower-selling company in August 1973 and moved in with an "army" of elder brothers and sisters—Yacov, John, Denise and Gerald—who lived at Dr. Durst's Kingston house, the house he had owned with his two sons and former wife prior to his meeting Onni. My memories of the cozy Kingston house include clandestine outings with John for omelettes at three in the morning, learning to address Mose Durst as "Dr." in the interests of future diplomacy, "whisper" exercises with Yacov under the stars at 5:00 A.M., returning home from selling flowers in the bars to eat cakes, cookies, and casseroles baked by Denise, who mothered us with ardor.

Once Yacov, Gerald, John, Dr. Durst and I converged on the kitchen from our different directions for one of our clandestine snacks after a hard day. At the same time, Denise woke with a shock, suddenly remembering she had baked a rebirthday cake for Gerald, but unable to remember, in her sleepiness and exhaustion, what she had done with it. She found us—midnight bandits all—huddled round the refrigerator.

Whirling around, opening shelf doors, unconscious of her disconnected movements, she finally discovered the cake still in the oven. As she grabbed the hot pan, it flew out of her hands right into Gerald's arms. Frosting splattered as the cake slipped through his clutches onto the floor. Our stealthy, guilty midnight mood erupted in laughter! "Anyway, happy rebirthday, Gerald," read Denise's disappointed face.

I also lived at the Hearst Street mansion, a stately old Georgian exfraternity house near the University of California campus; at The Gardens, elegant and palatial home of Onni and Dr. Durst, for a few months; up in the Boonville trailers; and at the dignified Victorian Washington Street center in San Francisco.

The most complete responsibility in center life I ever assumed was during two months in summer of 1975 when I moved back to Oakland's modest but historic Dana Street center. Jonah directed that house with bursting momentum, consistent as a reliably wound clock. My duties as his "object," or assistant, included cooking for thirty each day and night, buying food and provisions, and in "spare" hours leading a recruiting team in downtown Oakland in which our goal was a "date" for dinner each night. (I still recall those unsuspecting sidewalk innocents on whom we lunged in desperation a few minutes before dinner.) I also hostessed evening lecture programs, gave lectures and slide presentations, kept the finances and the family history, answered telephones, drove flower-selling missions at night, conducted prayer meetings and trinity meetings, group-assisted at Boonville on weekends, and, above all, served Jonah with total obedience.

Jonah treated me with stern instruction, ever ready to correct. He'd catapult out of the house for meetings at The Gardens with Onni, sticking his head back in the door to yell about all the errors in judgment I'd committed that day. With no chance to plead for justice, I'd trot to Onni's prayer room to faithfully pray for inner strength to humble myself to his holy tyranny, to feel "married for eternity" to his will. I tried to sense our bond as unending, the only way I could force myself to submit temporarily. After unlocking it with a hidden key, I'd slip into the Dana prayer room. One for each center, this one was immaculate with quiet light, translucent curtains gently blowing, photos of True Parents and Jesus, mementos from Korea, holy books, and the fragrance of fresh-cut roses. These moments were the few times when

Reverend Moon's wife, my True Mother, emerged as more important to me than "Father" himself. I had been told that her course in restoring the world set the example for all sisters. She lived an absolute shadow existence to Reverend Moon, an obedient birth-giver to "perfect" children, one after another. Kneeling under her unreadable face posed beside Father's, I identified with her intense struggle to endure her life.

At Dana Street, while I was assistant, our main mission consisted of recruiting eight hours a day in places like the San Francisco wharf, Golden Gate Park, on Berkeley's campus, or on the new subway system, BART. Working with a small team of partners, we would approach and invite to dinner as many bright, capable passers-by as we could manage to engage in conversation. Onni instructed us to avoid talking too long to any one person, especially to avoid talking philosophy about the Church. She herself had set the standard when, in the early movement, she had reached out to one hundred people in one day. "Make friends, offer them whatever they are seeking, pray for Heavenly Father to guide them to dinner," Onni would teach. "Sisters get handsome men, brothers attract pretty girls. It's good if they come because they like you. Once in God's house, they learn to love God instead." By spoken and unspoken understandings, we knew what we were looking for: capable, healthy, restless, young, white people like ourselves, preferably lonely and traveling, uprooted. They might respond to our approach: "Beautiful day, isn't it? Been traveling long? Where are you from? Have you ever met our Family? We live on a huge farm together. You should come visit us; you're always welcome. By the way, are you hungry?"

Two Family buses, called the "Coffee-Break-Bus" and the "Elephant Bus," were strategically located in tourist areas as recruiting centers for "hitchhikers with knapsacks." Our teams would look for young prospects, bring them back to the bus for coffee and doughnuts, and introduce them to the Family. Our psychological approach was irresistible. Members of the Church "radiated" love and kindness to strangers. Many conscientious, open people felt obliged to respond to us on a personal and social level because we made it seem too cruel to resist.

After a full day of recruitment, reaching out to people we believed we could save, our dinners at the center consisted of more intense relating to individuals. We fed them, entertained them, and suggested to them an "amazing set of ideas that would change their lives and make them happy." We insisted they stay with us. The success of the day was measured by how many guests "signed up" and *paid* for a weekend training session up on our isolated 680 acres of land, the Boonville farm.

After guests left the centers at nine-thirty at night, the house was cleaned. Moneymaking teams prepared to "blitz the bars." Everyone else visited prospective "spiritual children," or held trinity meetings to read "Master Speaks," a series of tracts based on Moon's speeches. Prayer and chanting was at eleven sharp. Anyone who had fasted, to bring more people or money in, would break that fast at midnight with soup and ice cream. By 12:30 younger Family members were in their sleeping bags, men side by side on one floor, women on the next level in strict segregation. Carpet cleaning or auto repair crews might come in at four or five o'clock after working all night.

After midnight, as center assistant, I planned menus, incorporating Boonville farm produce into rice, soup, or potato combinations for next night's dinner. (Breakfast had been juice, coffee, oatmeal; lunch was peanut butter and jelly sandwiches, raisins, carrots, cookies.) One-thirty A.M. found me still making lists of workshop signups and fund-raising accounts, and trying to locate used clothes in the "extra clothes room" for new sisters.

By two o'clock, Jonah would either stagger in or bluster in, depending on Onni's mood, from a staff meeting at The Gardens. Over his milkshake or a stack of gooey jelly and peanut butter sandwiches I'd prepared, I would try to guess from him the content of the meetings. I later read through a staff brother's notebook and learned what a tight ship Onni ran. The following are quotes from Onni, as recorded in his notebook:

"If one person doubts then no good. If on staff and drop out, this creates disunity because can't trust you. Such people are betrayers. You know heavenly secrets. If you go away, you dangerous because you know too much. You can't zig-zag. If you fight it out, you can overcome." (2/13/74).

"You staff have Satanic evil mouths. Have to knock off—don't say too much. And when you talk to people, talk only about their needs, their benefits, find out what will get them in. In witnessing, if people get negative toward you, just say that we support all churches." (2/3/74).

(And a few days later): "We never tell any lie, never give any untruth. Who accuse us of that?" (2/21/74).

"If you don't listen to me [Onni], no way for you to be restored. Bind with Onni. Do or die for purpose. Get rid of own ego. Our own will or desires must be last." (2/14/74).

In January Onni had given instructions to Teresa about a sister who had complained of seeing evil spirits: "Teresa, must ask Abbey honestly heart to heart, pray together. Then talk. If no good, then chase evil spirit out of her. If not we'll send her to hospital. She should do laundry each day."

Onni had said of a brother, a young insurance salesman noted for his spunk and independence of mind: "Never let Don drive again. I don't like him. Smash his ego. Or put him in Heavenly jail to change his attitude!" (2/21/74).

Other provisos: "Everyone *must* raise hand and share experience at Family meeting. If you can't raise hand you are living selfishly. No good." Or: "When you go out and witness, witness to the people for Dr. Durst; they respect Ph.D. bag. But when people come into Family to stay, then you witness for Onni." And, "No one want elderly people around for dinner because they are not needed." (2/20/74).

Onni also made clear in staff meetings: "No German travelers for workshop; they too scientific and heady. And black people don't fit in so well. Hard for them. Not right time in God's providence for them. Father says if whites don't accomplish *then* use blacks to shame whites in America, but not yet."

Talking with Jonah late at night consisted of my seeking his advice about "spiritual problems" of various Family members within our household. Jonah was quick to tell me that each person just had to "fight it out." Even physical sickness to him was "just in their heads," was "laziness or arrogance." By the time I got around to questions about my own concerns, he was snoring over his half-munched sandwiches, his head tilted on the sofa next to mine. Still, these squeezed-in, one-way conversations, free of obligations, were somehow priceless to me because delightful human chinks emerged in Jonah's armor and let an occasional boyish need for mothering show through. At such unguarded times, he'd reveal to me his shortcomings of faith as well as his hidden gratitude for my effort. The last weekend I worked as his apprentice (before he pushed me up to a full-fledged group leader of weekend workshops in Boonville), he wrote me a note suggesting my endurance hadn't gone unappreciated. His grandfatherly character, earning him the affectionate title "Gramps" by all his brothers and sisters, showed through:

Dearest Lael,

You are . . . Father's small bug, powerful as any live wire, joyful, colorful as dancing fire, most precious, most needed. Heavenly Father loves you. True Parents love you. Onni and Abba love you. I love you. Thank you for your work, dedication, and support. In gratitude,

Brother Jonah.

In the mad pace of urgent accomplishment in the centers, physical health was viewed as of little concern. Sleep, especially, was viewed as an indulgence since God never slept in His efforts to save mankind. Sleep, more than food, thus came to represent the most sought-after "privilege" of a future life in the Kingdom of Heaven. The staff averaged three hours a night; newer Family would average six. Recognized but unspoken was a state of constant exhaustion in all righteous children of God. Whenever drowsiness befell a member other than between the prescribed hours of 2:00 to 5:00 A.M., the cause was attributed to evil spirits hovering on the shoulders, pulling on the hair, closing the eyelids, and otherwise attacking the insincere. And so each person had his or her own pet "disaster" to narrate about being "hit by sleep spirits" in some critical moment.

Such episodes were the most common inside joke about Family life.

Daniel's job as an engineer trainee at an engineering company in San Francisco required total alertness. A "heavenly child" disguised in a shirt and tie, he brushed elbows with the corporate elite of America. After an unusually late Family staff meeting he planned one day to rest over lunch hour. His resting place? Curled up under his desk behind the wall divider, alarm clock set! Another time, during an executive board meeting, Daniel rested his head on his hand looking down as if scrutinizing his notes. In his dozing, he caught everybody's rapt attention by drooling on his paper.

Staff members fell asleep in prayer frequently. While still manager of the Ideal Sandwich Company, in which the members stayed up all night baking bread to sell the next day, Evey Eden knelt next to me in prayer. As I was praying according to the petitionary outline—one ear tuned to her elder example—I heard pleas coming from Eve which weren't written on my prayer sheet. "Heavenly Father, please give us hundreds of tuna and avocado sandwiches for tomorrow. We don't have time to make them," Eve breathed soundly next to me.

Yacov was often heard by his cross-country flower team praying in his sleep to find places to dump huge boxes of old flowers or to "discover industrial parks in which to sell."

Len Foster, a flower team captain, was famous for a flower run made in his sleep. Unconscious, he jumped behind the wheel of the van, dreaming he'd let his team members off on different street corners and had to go retrieve them. After driving around for half an hour, still dreaming, he routed his way back to the coffee shop and his waiting assistant under the impression that he had collected everyone. The assistant, worried and upset, jumped into the van and asked where Len had been for so long. Len sleepily replied that he'd been picking up his crew, of course. Eye cocked to the empty van, the assistant shook Len to rude awakening. "But where are they? Where's the crew?" With a jerk into reality, Len realized his crew was still waiting out on dark streets while he'd been driving around aimlessly in his sleep.

Mark and Jonah were notorious for falling asleep at traffic lights after all-night carpet cleaning jobs. Not until morning traffic piled up behind them, horns furiously honking, would they realize it was daylight and they'd never made it home!

Two universally sinful sleep practices included putting your head down during lectures to new guests whom you were trying to "infect with enthusiasm," and sleeping in Family Meetings, even after taking No-Doz, five cups of coffee, and beseeching your spiritual children to poke you with pins.

But perhaps the sleep episode evoking the most opprobrium was falling asleep hunched over during group prayer meeting. At the end, when the rest of the Family stood up, there you were, one lone heap, bottoms up.

The most thrilling and dramatic days of center life were the holidays. These celebrations were fleeting moments of delight interrupting the hustle and exhaustion in the routine of street witnessing and flower selling. Four times a year—God's Day, True Parents' Day, Children's Day, and World Day—we vacationed from our mission whirlwind.

I remember when 250 Family members gathered January 1, 1975, to celebrate the holiest of the four holidays, God's Day. Signifying a time of renewal, repentance, and gratitude to God and Reverend Moon, we pledged our lives at midnight service the night before the rejoicing. Brothers and sisters gathered in formation together, each one burning in the fireplace a list of sins he had committed last year. Then facing the altar or center table, the sisters stood in hand-sewn pure white skirts and blouses, the brothers in dark suits. We bowed down three times on our knees touching the floor, our hands to our foreheads in front of True Parents' picture. Onni and Dr. Durst in front, with white robes and gloves, set the example. I promised, reciting from memory something like this:

1. As the center of the cosmos, I will fulfill our Father's will (purpose of creation) and the responsibility given me (for self-perfection). I will become a dutiful son (or daughter), and a child of goodness to attend our Father forever in the ideal world of creation (by) returning joy and glory to Him. This I pledge.

2. I will take upon myself completely the Will of God to give me the whole creation as my inheritance. He has given me His Word, His personality, and His heart, and is reviving me who had died, making me one with Him and His true child. To do this, our Father has persevered for 6,000 years the sacrificial way of the cross. This I pledge.

3. As a true son (or daughter), I will follow our Father's pattern and charge bravely forward into the enemy camp until I have judged them completely with the weapons with which He has been defeating the enemy Satan for me throughout the course of history by sowing sweat for earth, tears for man, and blood for heaven, as a servant but with a father's heart in order to restore His children and the universe, lost to Satan. This I pledge.

4. The individual, family, society, nation, world, and cosmos who are willing to attend our Father, the source of peace, happiness, freedom, and all ideals, will fulfill the ideal world of one heart in one body by restoring their original nature. To do this, I will become a true son (or daughter), returning joy and satisfaction to our Father, and as our Father's representative, I will transfer to the creation peace, happiness, freedom and all ideals in the world of the heart. This I pledge.

5. I am proud of the one Sovereignty, proud of the one people, proud of the one land, proud of the one language and culture centered upon God, proud of becoming the child of the One True Parent,

proud of the family who is to inherit one tradition, proud of being a laborer who is working to establish the one world of the heart.

I will fight with my life.

I will be responsible for accomplishing my duty and mission.

This I pledge and swear.

This I pledge and swear.

This I pledge and swear.

After the God's Day pledge service, we squeezed trinity by trinity into every available vehicle: old tour buses, dented Dodge vans, farm trucks, sedans. The serpentine motorcade of divine but dilapidated vehicles coiled its way through the predawn streets of Oakland, Berkeley, and San Francisco. What began as a dignified procession metamorphosed after a few miles into a wild and challenging chase for the honor of driving directly behind the Lincoln Continental bearing Onni and Dr. Durst.

Fenders scraped, bumpers were occasionally grazed as Family members jockeyed to cling to that sedate lead car which seemed oblivious to the dangerous race going on behind it.

"Big Mick's catching up on our left," copiloted Michele. "Don't stop singing!" she insisted, unifying the spirits of brothers and sisters in the van. Steering our bulbous ark, Yacov slammed down on the accelerator to block Mick. Bumpers screeched momentarily and Big Mick was "up the creek"; Yacov kept him from passing. In the still of night, our motorcade raced on, training for battle and celebrating the present in the eye of its own cyclone.

Between two and four in the morning, we drove through the territory Reverend Moon had assigned Onni to conquer. We stopped off at both Holy Grounds to pray and rededicated our efforts to God and the Lord of the Second Advent. (The California Holy Grounds, Lake Merrit in Oakland and Twin Peaks in San Francisco, were 2 out of 120 spots Moon had blessed around the world to herald the physical transition from hell to Heaven on Earth.)

At dawn, after the tour, the Family slept briefly in order to re-energize itself for the eating and entertainment to follow. Elder sisters had labored into the morning hours preparing mountainous quantities of Jewish and Korean dishes for voracious appetites: matzo ball soup, bagels, lox, pastrami, salami, egg rolls, cheesecake, matzo brie, yogurt, rice, kim chee, chop choi, boolkoki, cake, ice cream, candy. Fruit, cookies, sweets were stacked in layers of seven (the numerological symbol of perfection) and placed on the center table where full settings had been elaborately laid for Reverend Moon and His Bride. Onni and Dr. Durst represented Them at the celebration banquet.

Once the Kingdom of Heaven had arrived on earth, three days would be officially scheduled for each holiday, but until that time we were only allowed one day. While elder sisters frantically served generous plates of food, Family members danced, read poetry, staged mime, and sang original songs like the following:

We're building a Kingdom
Where love and beauty abound
And truth is within everything that you see,
Just my Father and me;
My brothers and sisters are Kings and Queens,
Loving each other, forever devoted—
Oh, what a world it will be.
The morning is sunlight, the dawn lights the wings of our hearts,
We're flying together as one Family!

Sometimes Onni surprised us with her graceful apple-juggling acts, which she had learned on the faraway streets of Korea; Onni with her flashing-eyed face, shoulder-length black hair, dressed in a flowered pink pantsuit, and blouse. Sometimes her husband, Dr. Durst, performed a dance accompanied by fiddle or piano. With his special comic grace, what he lacked in finesse was made up for in Brooklyn-Jewish chutzpah! After exuberant sharing of talents, Family members huddled together with popcorn and fruit to watch rented movies, *Brother Sun, Sister Moon, Lost Horizon, Man of La Mancha, The Ten Commandments.*

But always the respite was brief, and before evening we all went out to gather in new guests for dinner. Inspired by the holiday spirit, our only urgency was to expand the Family "pali-pali."

Flower Seller

"Ten thousand difficulties do not make one doubt."
—NEWMAN

Occasionally people called me a hustler.

But when they did their meaning was affectionate; their tone was hearty, humorous, almost admiring. For four years which I could only describe as sacrificial, I felt sincerely at home selling flowers in earthy bars, down-home cafés, elegant nightclubs, and bustling casinos all over America and Canada. As a "church girl" I loved to ease into the ribald but cozy truck stops from Motor City and Saginaw to Toronto and Kingston, to Las Vegas, St. Louis, Kansas City, and Albuquerque.

"Hey!" they'd shout at me. "It's Liza Doolittle! Come here! You've got yourself a room full of suckers."

I learned to be eloquent and inventive for my cause. If it was hard for people to refuse a smile, it was even harder to refuse the elephant-sized, newspaper-wrapped bundles of bud roses. Especially coming in out of a blizzard.

Professional men in America's industrial office centers often pointed half-accusing fingers at me, embarrassed about the "job" I'd pulled on them. After they bought, they'd laughingly direct me on to others. Salesmen themselves, they responded to my exuberance and life, were often supportive and sometimes eager to help me. Because I'd been trained that every flower I sold meant eternal life for the person who bought, I loved the bright-coaled feeling which flared up from the genuine if momentary transaction.

As I breathed in and flashed back the life in these encounters, the giving out of my own spirit was far more reward than the cash. Besides, I knew God would love every hardworking person unknowingly bringing about my explosive secret, a restored earth.

No matter whether the flowers wilted or not.

Pumped up by Onni's urgent admonitions and well-wishes, teams of six or seven people would load up in Dodge vans prepared for two-month vigils away from the California church centers. Inspired by our leaders, we ourselves wanted to make the millions of dollars required for maintenance and purchase of hotels, resorts, palatial residences from Chicago to New Orleans, training and living centers, college campuses, yachts, even (we hoped) the Empire State and Pan Am buildings some day. Instilled in us was the firm belief that Moon must reclaim all ownership of money and land from Satan's stolen stockpile.

As the years passed and I became a seasoned seller, I felt like a soldier fit for any battle. I was ripe for any daring entrance or hustled exit, fortified by my own, absolute belief, which gave me a sense of personal power. By now I wasn't afraid of rebuff. I had incorporated into myself the Church's theology of persecution, and was half-proud to be thrown out of places now and again as a test of my faith.

My flower career began in August 1973 with eighteen other Church women packed into a Dodge van. With buckets full of sloshing water and sweet williams, daffodils, and carnations, we drove every day to Daly City to stir the slumbrous neighborhoods. Rows and rows of housewives answered our knocks and pleas. Interrupted only by a prayer and one grapefruit for lunch, we kept trotting from 9:00 to 5:00, but our sales never matched our effort. Finally we withdrew forces from residential areas and rendezvoused in commercial centers.

Scouting and mapping industrial parks, shopping centers, business streets, and office plazas by night, we would deploy Church members to sell in teams by day. The entire Bay Area served our purpose. Our strategy? To give love and cheer to all the people we sold to. And to Chant-Pray-and-Run all day. We would chant our monetary goal, pray for success, and run between customers as we charged down the street.

I learned this strategy from Evey, to whose team I was assigned. Evey's team was assigned to sell in the most crime-ridden, impoverished sections of Oakland. What we sacrificed in material harvest, we gained in character as we tried to really love the rough-and-tumble and the poor. Evey, with her gentle, yet determined attitude, always showed us that if we had hoped that the poorest can give, then our expectations could be sky high for the rich. As a team, we gained competence and were soon selling in the lucrative areas of San Francisco and Palo Alto. We were ready to go on an extended flower trip out of town.

As we headed towards Oregon on that first of many such trips, I began to keep journals of our adventures.

DECEMBER 18, 1973.
The end of a two-week period away from Oakland Family as a mini-unit flying by God's love up north. Our flower team was led by Evey. I wonder if it's unprincipled to love your team captain so much? I guess I'll have to learn to work with other people eventually. Rather than any one person, I'll just have to develop an unshakable bond with Heavenly Father. As a team, we loved Oregon's people, their simplicity and rusticity. We stayed at my parents' home in Portland while selling in town. Evey, sick with a pneumonia infection, recovered in my bed. It was a blessing for my mother to learn Principle from Evey. Perhaps my need to see my physical parents is faithless. I had to trust Evey to be spiritual parent to my parents. I hope they understand the urgency of our selling mission.

I stayed two more days with my mother and father and Doug, my brother, while my team drove on south. We challenged one another's ideas. Their intellectual, subjective minds are so arrogant. But I see much of this in myself, too.

The following day I wrote how reassuring it was to be reunited with my True Family. A lot of the Church members had been to Washington, D.C., to take part in a demonstration at the White House to show God's love for America and for President Nixon. "Project Unity" had called for American citizens to forgive our national leaders and bring this country into unity through love, despite Watergate. At the White House demonstration, accompanied by only a few Secret Service men, Nixon had been drawn across the street into the Church crowd. As brothers and sisters were holding hands and kneeling, they said Nixon looked surprised and joyous. (It surprises me even now how readily I accepted Nixon simply because we were told that God needed him, when, before joining the Church, I hated him.) President of the Unification Church of America, Neil Salonen, arranged an interview for Reverend Moon with Nixon. I wrote in my journal:

Now is the time for our Father to speak ... Reverend Moon must become advisor to Nixon or this country will fall. America is the representative democratic nation and must stand firm to world review. To maintain foreign confidence, we must keep Nixon in office in the face of impeachment considerations. Total disintegration will come to America if Nixon is ousted. As a Church, if we really love Nixon and demonstrate this publicly, Nixon will want to follow our Father's advice. God can transform Nixon through Father. After all, Nixon's corruption is the sin within each of us.

Before our next flower trip, I attended several Christian churches in the Bay Area and witnessed to the congregations and ministers. Just before Christmas I noted in my journal: "We must love Christians, however adamant and set they are in their views about Jesus. But what irony to hear Christians yearn for the Second Coming and not be able to tell them He's here. Jesus must have felt this way in the Jewish temples."

CHRISTMAS DAY.
A woman leader from the British Unification Church came to talk to us about communism versus democracy, saying that the European movement is embarking on a painful period where people are getting assassinated and must go underground. The work of communists, she said. In her own words, "People are looking to America as a free country. Will it be the land of doom or salvation?" When I heard, a month after joining the Family, as Joanna and I sold flowers on a street corner, that the group supported the Vietnam War, I was shocked. I couldn't sell anymore that night. Thinking the group was a nonviolent revolutionary community, I felt I'd been tricked. But I've since come to understand the necessity to oppose atheistic communism and keep the world safe for God-centered democracies. My viewpoint has greatly enlarged.

As the British Unification leader talked that Christmas night, I prayed for Reverend Moon's meeting with Nixon and my own attempt to understand Watergate. I also prayed to bring in more spiritual children, to restore health to Onni, end communism, and to sell more flowers on the next trip. Soon afterward, I was on Evey's team heading north again. I wrote:

JANUARY 3, 1974.
　　All of us confronted our less-than-complete passion to sell flowers in the rain of Yuba City. A hard run. Our bar run started in Chico and ended six hours later in Redding. The bars are a world of hard-faced waiters, cracker-barrel philosophers, speculators, frauds, doubters, wanderers, . . . and an occasional pure soul. I've got to love them all. We plugged and pushed through the cold and called home at midnight. Onni said her spirit was with us. She said patience was a virtue unless you're a flower seller; then it's a hindrance. We've got to be aggressive for God! We drove on to Ashland under a ghostly moon and slept in the van, shivering until prayer condition at 5:00 A.M.

On January 6, we sold in Olympia, Washington, which felt like a tomb. With so few people around, we had to sell door to door in residential areas. We rented a cheap motel because the flowers would freeze if we slept in the van. The flowers appreciated the warmth and didn't mind the cockroaches. We appreciated the security and warmth after nights in the van parked behind hotels, where we slid into the lobby to use the bathrooms or sneaked into empty rooms to shower in stealth.

On January 8, with Evey's team in Seattle, we ran into some sellers from the Unification Church International team. Two young men, from France and Germany, they were very cautious with us. In their serious manner, they warned us about the dangers of communists. Not wanting to tangle with the International selling team, Onni ordered us— her own personal guerrilla force—out of Seattle.

January 10 we slid our way to Everett, where we sold dead carnations and roses. In Everett we had to get out of the van to push it out of an icy drift. Once the van got started, Paul, the driver, couldn't stop it and we had to bale in, one by one like box-car hopping. One sister didn't make it! What a sight, seeing her skating behind, scarf flying, long skirt parted showing her flowered long johns!

But ahead loomed potential disaster. Unable to stop the van, it was bearing down on an old lady pushing a shopping cart into our path. Paul ordered Evey out, "Quick, hustle her across the road!" Evey skated to the granny, grabbed her arm, and whisked her out of the way. Into the van Evey hopped, willing and laughing and brave.

The next night we reached my parents' home in Portland and

quietly sacked out in the basement. Everyone felt so at home there. We had early prayer condition and breakfast with my parents, who were glad to see the traveling vagabonds again. They warned us of severe flood conditions and critical gas shortages ahead.

On January 17, we ended up far short of our goal. Paul suggested it was because we sold dead roses all day that were holding together on faith alone. (We also sold limp white carnations that we scotch-taped together.) But Evey said no. We were to blame, for being insincere and missing prayer condition that morning.

On pure inspiration we went to Reno. We found brittle people, mesmerized by money. No spirit in them, like eggs without yolks. The casino throng was dead weight, sorrow for our Father. Plunk, plunk, plunk—silver dollars entered our pockets slowly. We battled hawklike casino bouncers, police, and rich bores who didn't want our precious flowers.

A few days later Evey's team was taken to the police station in Brigham, Utah, for violating the Green River Ordinance. We fought blizzards in Pocatello, Idaho, didn't get our flowers by air, and had to sell little American flags and fortune cookies. I got more than a few double-takes with that combination!

In Boise we were physically chased away by local Unification Church brothers. There was no end to that sort of adventure while on the road. Evey's team, on which I usually served, sold as New Education Development rather than Unification Church, and came to be known as the "Oakland Raiders." Using fly-by-night guerrilla tactics, selling without permits, we became infamous within the national Church. We aroused their anger and envy; Robin Hoods are always more attractive than pious saints. "We're the greatest, there's no doubt; Heavenly Father, we'll sell out!" became our favorite team chant.

On our three-day drive back to Oakland, Evey testified about her sincere love of Onni and True Parents. She was obviously preparing us for a special event coming up.

"Onni's secret," Evey confided, "is her ability to *jump it* and respond to Father immediately without thinking." This explained Onni's value to Reverend Moon. At a moment's notice, Reverend Moon could place a call from his base in New York to his "woman soldier" Onni on the West Coast. He would demand thousands of dollars, pioneers for national Mobile Fund Raising teams, people to participate in East Coast publicity campaigns. Onni answered his requests promptly and faithfully. Her devotion to him as the True Parent was limitless. And so was her ambition to be near him in the Kingdom of Heaven.

Finally Evey disclosed the secret she was preparing us for. She reported that Reverend Moon was coming to Berkeley for the Day of Hope tour and our team would work together serving the Messiah while he visited the Dursts. This, she said, was the ultimate honor.

Whenever Reverend Moon passed between America and the Korean "fatherland," or was on speaking tours, he would stop over at the Avalon house, The Gardens. Onni and Mose Durst's East Bay home was replete with pool, sauna, seven bedrooms, four-car garage, cabana, bay view, elaborate courtyard and grounds, and contemporary furnishings with Korean screens.

JANUARY 21.

Our team arrived at the Avalon house today. We rushed to The Gardens to serve our True Parents. Evey served Onni so Onni could concentrate on preparing for Father and Mother. An older sister, Marilyn, and I will clean, help cook, and do their laundry for a week. The others will cook or be on security teams. My first special mission! I'm nervous, expectant, hopeful to do right, grateful for such an unbelievable blessing; aware of my undeservedness, ever willing to restart from any mistakes. I'm so thankful to be under the guidance of Onni. Perhaps I'll see her in a different light. I so want to humble myself to her in a natural and devoted way. I'm really tired of my fear of her moods. I don't understand her Oriental ways, but I know it's because my thinking is too worldly, not heartistic enough, not vertical enough with God.

Today is preparation for our True Parents' arrival. Father, Mother, and Mrs. Choi have their own china, food, laundry soap, new linen, and mattresses; we can't mix their things with anyone else's because it would cause impurity. Scurry and pray to set the right atmosphere. Deep reverence for the sacred person yet to come. I want to trust in his Lordship. I want to understand the meaning of serving a Messiah, the most valuable individual in six thousand years of human history. Never, ever think Father doesn't deserve all the intricate treatment and attention. That's Satan whispering in my ear.

Working, serving and cleaning at The Gardens with Marilyn is a blessing. I can really accept her criticisms as instructive, not judgmental. I want to give everything of myself; especially, I want to show the Berkeley Family that Oakland Family has a higher heavenly standard.

Onni's dishes which seem jewels to us at Dana Street when we serve a symbolic plate every night for her, are simple compared to the dishes of True Parents. Just as we reserve our nicest room at Dana Street for Onni, even when she isn't there, Onni vacates her best rooms for Reverend Moon and his party, keeping the humbler bedding for herself. Onni is so exuberant to have Father, Mother, Mrs. Choi, Mr. Neil Salonen, Colonel Bo Hi Pak, and Mr. David Kim, at The Gardens which Oakland Family, by its selling devotion, has made possible.

The party arrived at 4:00 P.M. Father was so singular and commanding in His entrance—a man who, in all heaven and earth, has God within his temple, who must see everyone as a mere child, even his wife. The women all hurried around beside Him opening doors and preparing His way. He is a round-faced, moonlike, full-bodied man of great presence. Though we bowed deeply to show humility and unworthiness, we must keep our distance in His service. Mother, his wife, follows like a shadow, delicate, smooth-skinned. Onni absolutely, but with beautiful spunk, attends our True Parents.

The assigned sisters joined forces to serve dinner. Every item in the kitchen for our True Parents is specially marked. Each bowl, napkin, jelly spoon, is treated with utmost reverence. Our Mother and Father are so regal, serving them comes naturally. By watching I'm learning for eternity the standard of how to serve any center person.

JANUARY 23.

Today I was given the privilege of washing by hand Father's shirts, using His special detergent. I stood in the laundry room and scrubbed the collar, knowing He would give God's prophetic message in it to California tonight. Tears flowed from my eyes into the water. I prayed they wouldn't stain Him. Remembering my past life before rebirth and how much I'd hated housework—preferring to ride my horse, read a good book, go caving with friends—all I could do now was say over and over, "Without esteem, without renown, I only wish to follow." If it meant serving God, I would wash Father's shirts locked in a laundry room forever.

On February 11, President Nixon embraced Reverend Moon after the Family had demonstrated for several hours in support of Nixon's State of the Union message.

February 17, 1974, was the first birthday I had in the Church. Because it was my physical birth, rather than spiritual birth (the day I joined the Church), I fasted in order to pay indemnity for my Satanic blood lineage—having imperfect parents. All day I thought about Onni, trying to envision her as my spiritual Mother, second only to Reverend Moon's wife. I wrote in my journal: "I must never betray Onni. I should love her and always find out before anything is done what Onni wants. I should never sleep until I know. I am a disciple of the Messiah. Heavenly Father killed all but eight people in the time of Noah. In our final Judgment, there is no guarantee of Heaven even though we are in the Family. I must be prepared to die, too."

At a fund-raising meeting February 18, we were told that as a flower company, we are urban guerrillas and must never breathe a word to new guests about our financial activities. Neither should we reveal our trip destination to other Family members. While on the road, we are to say we are a New Education Development mobile fund-raising team scouting new areas for youth centers. In police relations, if caught, we are not to implicate the movement. Rather, we must carry *personal* I.D. and make up a *personal* story. Appearance: no levis, only clean clothes. Boys are to wear ties, sisters long skirts or slacks, nondistinct, neat.

Once more Evey's team set off to Oregon and Washington on March 20. The first day of driving was a fierce battle to stay awake. I wrote in my journal that a Spirit Man was "sitting on the heads of everyone on our team." We believed legions of spirits battled around us in a war between God and Satan. We wrestled each other and read the Truth out loud.

After reaching Portland, Evey let me off downtown and spurred me to "sell out!" Staring up in a quandary at a narrow, three-story brick building, I suddenly remembered from high school days that this was the Arlington Club, sacrosanct for men. Women were not only not allowed membership but weren't even allowed to set foot inside.

My old feminist convictions rumbled inside me, reinforcing my indomitable Church spirit. The challenge to "crack this case" sent me sleuthing a basement entrance. I went in, ducking pipes and plumbing, and wound my way up the stairs, only to find myself off the kitchen on the second floor.

No one was in sight.

I tiptoed out to the hallway and into the patriarchal Gothic library. Suddenly, faced with four senior tycoon-looking gentlemen behind four solemn *Wall Street Journals*, I felt my spirits drop from Brobdingnagian size to Lilliputian.

Gathering up my courage, I sprang forward, knocked on the first newspaper, and said, "Hello, sir, we're having a special Portland rose sale for our youth guidance center. It's only for today and you could make someone very happy. A dollar a rose or ten dollars a dozen. What color do you want?" I beamed warmly.

The first gentleman, taken by total surprise, bought a single rose; each surprised gentleman thereafter bought one in reflex. The domino theory was at work!

Ignoring the mutterings in my wake that ladies weren't allowed in the club, I sold half a dozen roses in the billiard room, then sailed to a luncheon table of earnest businessmen. I was so quick with my offers they had no time to refuse. I sold two and a half dozen. Then I swooshed to the bar, where the bartender bought a dozen on condition that I leave promptly. He gave me a royal escort out the front doors.

On April 23 we went to Marysville, Oroville, and surrounding ranch towns in northern California. Onni set $300 a day as my personal goal, saying, "Satan will sometimes prevent you but if you try and try you *can* do it." She said I could sell a flower a minute if I prayed hard. Onni warned our team to show only positive love for each other, to forgive and forget the negatives. She sent us off with figs, dates, and candy. "Onni is our local Messiah. And to me after all these months, Evey is too!"

After selling up north, we sold again in Portland, but didn't visit my parents. I jotted down in my journal:

One of the most poignant days was leaving Portland to go back to San Francisco. I called my physical parents. My mother started to cry and her tears were the accumulation of a whole ancestral line. She felt abandoned by me, her only daughter. Dear mother, when will you come home to God? My father had heard our Father, Reverend Moon, speak at the Hilton Hotel. He said that the talk was bombastic and the message diluted in translation. My dad just doesn't understand that the Last Days are drawing near.

When we arrived in Oakland, we dedicated and sang a song to Onni. She sent us into The Garden swimming pool, clothes and all. We witnessed the rest of the afternoon.

After a deep prayer that night to open our hearts, I experienced deep, penetrating colors, as though my mind and body were on different energy levels. My Spirit Man seemed to be leaving my body. I came running down the stairs and held onto Evey, feeling ungrounded. I prayed to know if that was Spirit World, or a result of my seven-day water-only fast.

On the first anniversary of my having joined the Church I wrote: "I am one year old in the Church and ready to spread my wings and fly to Heaven for Father."

From July to September, 1974, I spent sunup to bar closing every day selling flowers in the midwest with a new team captain. Gerald had replaced Evey this trip. I missed her terribly.

On July 30, feeling lonely, I called my mother from the Chicago O'Hare airport. Our conversation reminded me of a cat and dog circling each other curiously, suspiciously. She sensed I didn't need her in the primary way that I used to, and I sensed her unwillingness to adjust to my missionary zeal. I longed for God to bring us together.

An elder sister, Michele Tunis, was also having difficulty with her parents. On August 3 in Lake Winnebago, our team slept outside under a raw, moon-swelled sky. I woke to find that Michele had gone to New York to see her parents for a few days. It was always a trial for her to visit home. Her parents subjected her to ceaseless interrogation about Sun Moon, support of Nixon, finances, conversion from Judaism to Christianity, her change of manners and personality and supposed loss of freedom. "Some day all our parents will know why we have been impelled to act as we do."

Gerald was definitely a different leader from the sacrificial Evey. He believed in ultimate pleasures every once in a while as motivation. On August 1 in Minneapolis, Gerald treated the team to a banquet at the Jax Cafe. The sky was the limit! We had escargots, clam chowder, Caesar salad, Mandarin duck, lobster, steak, shortcake, cheesecake, cream and coffee. The dining was a relaxing communion.

While in the restaurant I recognized Senator Hubert Humphrey. I went out to the van to get red roses for him. We approached his table forthrightly, introducing ourselves as Unification Church members and followers of Sun Myung Moon. Humphrey said he personally knew "Moonies" on Capitol Hill who were gracious in the Senate offices. Later, when Michele called Onni exultantly, Onni chastised her for *giving* the flowers away. She said Humphrey should have contributed money. Then he might have gotten a "blessing from God."

On August 2 we went to Milwaukee. I did a few black bars, mind-boggling places packed with loose hands and words. At 1:30, while I was waiting to be picked up by Gerald, a drunk tipped over my coffee, picked me up, and held me high. I yelled to be let down, and was. I huddled in a corner and read St. Matthew. I felt almost a physical calm wash over me as I opened my Bible.

I'll never forget a bar in Oshkosh on August 3. It was my last one and was called Lucifer's. Roses in hand, I stepped into the big lounge, a liquid red radiance. On one side was a wooden statue of Lucifer. To an accompaniment of weird, spidery, languid music, naked women danced in the redness. I hopped from table side to table side, and was lucky to be met with nothing worse than stony looks.

We traveled across the plains to Wyoming. Outside of Laramie I prayed for an informative dream. That night I dreamt my mother's voice said to me: "I know we all need True Parents. I understand for the first time why you love Reverend Moon and his wife so much. He is the Messiah, isn't he?" I also dreamt that my resistant father actually went on TV acknowledging the spirituality of Reverend Moon.

On August 8, we prayed in a staid Episcopal church. The janitor answered our plaintive knocking and let us in, uncertain as to our intentions. We sang and prayed aloud with great urgency that Nixon wouldn't resign the presidency. We also prayed to accomplish our monetary goal for True Parents. We shed sincere tears of anguish and hope. The janitor, who was a Pentecostal, said he'd never heard prayer of that intensity before. He wanted to come closer to our understanding of God.

On August 9 Richard Nixon resigned from the presidency. Onni said it was the blackest moment in history for America, that only God and our Father really knew its devastating impact.

The beginning of 1975 found me back in dangerous Detroit selling dead stubby roses. I had joined a new dynamic team. Yacov, the "business whiz" of the flower drivers, was my daring captain. He worked me harder and sent me into riskier places than ever before. I began to feel guilty even for hunger and fatigue. But as I relied more upon approval from him, my daily money totals started to skyrocket.

One freezing night in January, while Yacov was repairing the van signals, I was let off for a three-hour selling run until 2:00 A.M. Carrying four enormous bundles, I hobbled from rowdy bar to bar. Hungry and exhausted, running on nerves and adrenalin, I was selling roses in the broken-down Telegraph Bar in Detroit when I shuffled over to ask two drunken billiard players to buy a flower for their girl friends. In response to their mocking questions, I began carrying on an animated, in-depth explanation of the creation of the universe. Suddenly I was startled by raucous laughter, and emerged from my stupor to realize that I was muttering and gesticulating to thin air: the billiard players had walked away five minutes before. The whole bar, meanwhile, had seated itself for a bird's eye view of this amazing soliloquy by one spiritual but bedraggled Liza Doolittle.

Another wintry night, in Chicago. Steamy glasses, chapped legs and face, the wind walloping me from every direction, my carnations freezing in the breeze. I sold "singles" in the Hyatt-Regency. The manager threw me out and said if he saw me there again, "Ralph would finish me off." Dinner was of humility and grace: bologna, mayonnaise, and soda crackers. Next night we sold our dead roses in bars that were the Black Hole of Calcutta. We traded dead buds for a big, fat pizza.

Yacov calculated there'd be a lot of loose money in the bars after the Superbowl in New Orleans, so he sent half his team down. As we frantically mopped up the water leaking from the roses inside, we had to convince United Airlines that our enormous coffin-shaped flower box was filled with Michele's personal wardrobe.

Taking plane and taxi, we landed up in a flophouse off Bourbon Street. Up the creaky old steps we stole, hoisting our suspicious body-length cardboard box.

"Let's divide the roses and go. We'll make a million on these baby yellows," Gerald said.

"Father be with you," Michele whispered to me as we crept down the hotel stairs. I felt like I was on a parachute jump into hell.

But money was easy, and in an all-night blitz we collected $1,000, Michele pulling in the biggest catch from Joe Namath and his friends—$60!

Down deep, we knew nobody would remember their $10 and $20

contributions for one rosebud after morning hangovers. But God would know.

Although our team generally spent most of our hours selling to sauerkraut-beer-and-weiner-type people in factories and bars around America and in commercial areas, we occasionally rubbed elbows with the caviar crowd. One of the strangest incidents in February 1975 occurred the night we spent at Elvis Presley's Graceland mansion in Memphis.

Our leader, Yacov, had fallen asleep after thirty days of four hours of sleep a night. He struggled into consciousness when he heard the commotion in the van.

"Michele, what's going on? Where are we?" he barked.

I leaned over to explain. In Memphis, on an impulse, Colleen had gotten the gate guard at Elvis Presley's mansion to phone up to the house because she had suddenly remembered that a certain man named Doug, purported to be Elvis's financial manager, had once briefly been a member of our church.

Miracle of miracles, it was this same man who seemed to be answering our call right now, his broad telescreen surveying the white Dodge van at the foot of his drive.

"Hey, you say you're from Berkeley? I used to belong to a church in Berkeley and roamed around selling candles in a van like yours. What church you from?" Doug queried.

"Unification. Did you live at Euclid Street?" asked Michele, jumping ecstatically.

"Yeah, that's where I lived for two months. Hey, wait there. I'll be right down to get you." Doug slammed the receiver in haste.

"I don't believe it! I don't believe it!" exulted Michele. "Did you know that the Unification Church, through Mr. Sudo, the education director in the New York region, has been trying for years to get Elvis to sing for a publicity rally for Father?"

Yacov, coming to his senses, shrugged philosophically. "Well, maybe this wild excursion could have a point after all. What got in you to come here?" He couldn't suppress a playful smile, a smile I adored.

Doug was driven down to the treble-clef-inscribed gate in a black limousine, hopped out to join us in the van, and pointed our way up the drive. "Follow him," Doug said, pointing to the chauffeured black Lincoln Continental. "Hey, what a cozy van! I see you're selling daisies for the damsels. You're Gerald? You know how I know you're from the Unification church? Your socks don't match."

Doug cautioned us to be quiet "because Elvis is on the third floor and he hasn't seen anybody for weeks. He hasn't made any public appearances because he's trying to lose weight. His grandma's in the kitchen. She fixes Elvis black-eyed peas. We can eat German chocolate cake. I'll show you through the house. Come on."

Bewildered but encouraged by Doug's seeming confidence in total strangers, we obediently followed, praying that God might lead us to a Big Donation. Every room in the house dazzled bizarrely with shaggy red and black carpets and pillows, peacock feather wall and ceiling covers, mirrors, gold and silver plating everywhere. We stared at the overpowering but nauseating decorating job.

"Wild, huh?" Doug chortled at our rubbernecking. "Actually, Elvis is a real family guy. Casual. When his friends are around he floats in and out in a pair of pajamas. He won't come down, but have some cake and watch TV."

I tagged after Doug while Colleen and Michele made friends with grandma. "Doug, why did you leave the church?"

"I got tired of being told what to do every minute. I read the *Divine Principle* and sold lots of candles, but then this job with Elvis came up. In a choice between Moon and Elvis, I took Elvis," he was frank.

I was shocked. "But didn't you ever think Reverend Moon was the Messiah?"

"Well, what's a messiah? You know some people think Elvis is a kind of messiah figure. He's got a bigger following than Moon and he sings about God and Jesus. Seriously, if a messiah exists on earth today, I'd say Moon is one candidate. Still, I don't know. I got Elvis to read chapter one on the Creation lecture that Moon wrote but I can't get him interested in chapter two. That's the part about sex being evil, or Lucifer seducing Eve, isn't it? Pretty farfetched," Doug shrugged.

I felt sorry for Doug's astonishing negligence.

Stuffed with cake, Gerald asked, "Doug, you think we can sing a song for Elvis?"

"Whoa now, we're not to bring him into this, O.K.? He'd whip my britches. And you've already blown *my* sneakers off by being here. But I wouldn't have passed it up. I always wondered where that church would get to. And now if it hasn't come by to haunt me," Doug chuckled.

Gathering around Doug to say good-bye, each of us knew his time would come, that time when frivolity would end and he'd have to reckon again with the true God.

In March 1975, in a van christened "Resurrection," we set out again to conquer cities across America. Burning to save denizens of drizzly bars, five-and-ten's, subways, Texaco stations, perspiring delicatessens, before we started we prayed. "Heavenly Father, we surrender to you. Mold us into perfect beings so we can accomplish for you. This we want and this we pledge." We were brothers and sisters, familiar, but with new hearts—Yacov, Daniel, Michele, Ann, Colleen, and Lael. Each of us was ready to span canyons, zoom zealous with desire to accomplish our material and spiritual goals. I was grateful to work close to Yacov, my favorite brother.

The fun began on that particular trip when we opened our "Ideal" box of green, white, and pink carnations at O'Hare International Airport where they'd been sent us by the Oakland Church. The day? St. Patrick's Day. Daniel, as a top leader put out to sell for the first time in full business suit and a pair of white tennis shoes, bolted out on a bar run carrying only pinks. Amist the barroom clamor for green, Daniel raced to a hardware store and painted his blooms with green, sticky spray. Wild with anticipation, he dashed back into the bar and tried to sell. The odor was putrifying; the carnations were stiff, blotched, and lumpy. But there stood Daniel, grinning sheepishly, half-tickled at his own novice inventiveness, eager, but deep down awkward, almost shy. "Top o' the day to ye!" he roared. Then a few bars down the block, he took an accidental dive down the dim stairs into a cozy, all-too-intimate lounge and, picking himself up, debated whether to fly out of the crowd unexplained or to imply he'd arranged the entrance as a selling ploy. Pushing aside his immediate craving to crawl inside the pocket of the nearest coat and hide forever, he smiled weakly and gestured to his smelly blooms. Everyone bought, out of sympathy and discomfort.

Dallas brings memories of a Daniel's three-ring circus again. He made himself welcome in the Petroleum Club at its happy hour, oiled up his sales pitch, and plowed in among the Texas "black gold" magnates. Posing in tennis shoes in the midst of tuxedos, he introduced Michele as his wife. They'd just managed to convince a wealthy businessman to host our stay in Dallas when all ended too abruptly as Daniel's charade as a San Francisco corporation head taking a few weeks off to contribute to the "kids of America" collided with Michele's version that they were staff members of a Jewish Youth Crusade!

During Daniel's same bold hour, I ventured into Dallas's Fairmont Hotel to do what I could in the World Champion Tennis Tournament banquet. With elegant long-stemmed red roses cradled in my arms and a pageant-style dress to cover my jeans and hiking boots, I swung merrily through the millionaires and earned $10 a rose from Lloyd Bridges, Charlton Heston, and someone looking exactly like Robert Redford, if it wasn't Redford himself. It wasn't long before I got the boot, but I went away with booty of my own.

Later that Dallas evening, we lost Michele. Yacov had delivered her to a lifeless shopping mall, with plans to pick her up in a few hours. She never showed up. In frantic search, Daniel called Onni in Oakland just at the moment Michele was calling Onni from the Dallas police station. Michele had been followed and kidnapped by two goliath Lebanese men. They'd dragged her into their green Chevelle, taken off her glasses, and blindfolded her. Hauling her by the arm, they'd taken her into an elevator and yanked her into a room where she waited, praying to Heavenly Father for safety. Suddenly a heavy-set man entered the room and studied Michele. "Hey, this one, this is the wrong one!" So her original captors in great disgust took her into the car again, blindfolded her, and drove her in circles. When they pushed her out, she was in the middle of a downtown Dallas street, where a policeman took her in when she tried to explain her story to him.

Dallas always yielded sky-high excitement. One evening I was dropped off at a country club where they kicked me out four times for soliciting on private property. Determined to try one more time, I went in a back door, only to find myself unexpectedly in the men's locker room. With only one direction to go to get out, I yelled on my way asking if anyone wanted roses. To my amazement, my agitated request started a stampede; everyone in that locker room seemed in trouble with wives or lovers! In boxer shorts and briefs (later I had to repent to God for having seen them), they bought my roses out, fifty dollars worth. Roseless, I ran to meet Ann across the street. Her story was no less stunning. She'd walked into a liquor store and the manager had grabbed all her bundles and thanked her. Shocked, Ann had demanded $50, which he paid her promptly, expressing his gratitude. It seems God—in the form of Ann—had beat some legitimate florist to the punch. Little did the manager know his ordered flowers were right then speeding to his store. We didn't stay around to see him when he found out.

That entire trip had been a long shot for the "B.D."—Big Dona-tion. We'd prayed for a million dollars and chanted incessantly from Dallas to Little Rock. One day, on a hunch, Ann suggested the team drive to Arkansas to visit her dad's best war buddy, Bob Golden. Bob operated the Stern Variety Store chain and was a wealthy man, had just been divorced, and would probably welcome company. Like a dove out of a magician's hat, we jumped at it, betting that with the Holy Spirit's assistance the Big Donation would come from Bob.

For five hours we took shifts, driving like mad, each shift chanting over and over, "Bob Golden, Bob Golden, Bob Golden, Give Heaven Your Money!" By the time we met the solitary, grandfatherly figure in the Stern Distribution parking lot, we'd no doubt we'd set the proper spiritual conditions for success.

We piled out to greet him, full of hugs and handshakes. He donned the red, white, and blue carnations we presented him and toured us through his plant. After showing us through executive offices filled with bears' pelts and sailfish, he drove us out to his son's farm some miles away.

While driving, Bob shared with us his ideas on how to rekindle the world with a passion for Zionism; Ann had forgotten to tell us Bob thought we were a Zionist youth group. Bob obviously warmed to what he saw as the Yiddish character of our team, and it was true, almost everyone on the team *was* descended from lines of rabbis and cantors except Colleen (blonde and Polish) and me (roundfaced and Scottish). Nevertheless, both Colleen and I wholeheartedly joined the "Shaloms" and "zoom-golly-gollys" in the backseat with everyone else, suppressing our grins as best we could.

Out on the farm, Bob introduced us to his son and daughter-in-law and to Rodney, a fine-feathered duck who immediately imprinted himself to Colleen (even when she went to the bathroom). Naomi, Bob's deerlike little granddaughter, padded shyly after Yacov.

Driving back to Little Rock, Bob picked up some southern fried chicken for us, and we returned to his singularly modest apartment. Each one of us was beginning to feel guilty about spending an entire day with Bob, however kind and lonely he was, rather than out fund-raising. We grew anxious to pose the Big Donation question to him and justify our time off. Nervously we gulped chicken down like savages, then coffee, then cake. Daniel, unable to handle the strain of our money machinations, proceeded to get sick and retreated to the bathroom.

Yacov, Colleen, and I retrieved the van while Ann and Michele took Bob aside to discuss his giving a contribution to our Jewish youth group. We knew we'd made him love us; we knew his life was winding down; we knew his ideals were lofty.

All the ingredients were set.

Bob wrote New Education Development a check not for $10,000 but $100, and sent us off with ephemeral hopes only for future success. We drove away, our emotions bittersweet. But Flower Teams didn't succeed by regret, so, after a time, someone began to sing. One by one the rest of us joined in.

In the lake district north of Chicago, fall, 1976, Yacov steered, mapping the route of a pioneer bar-run. All of a sudden he pulled into a dimly lit parking lot, skidding to a halt.

"You're not going to believe this. Anybody want to come?" he shouted.

When your center man—especially Yacov—shouted, you followed.

Streaming after him, we found ourselves unexpectedly in an antique player-piano shop. An old, weathered hut, its interior was crowded with player pianos.

Without a word, all seven of us scurried for a separate seat. Legs pumped. Fingers fumbled in masquerade antics. A recital of cacophony followed: "Oh, What a Beautiful Morning," "Papa, Won't You Dance With Me?", "Beer Barrel Polka," "Oh, Suzannah," "Red River Valley," "Up on the Roof," "Sewanee River"—all in one great jubilee. The owner, failing to uproot us, shouted out, "It's closing time!" Finally he turned off all the lights, but the crazy orchestration continued.

When he locked the door from the outside, Yacov leaped to the rescue. "We'll be trapped in a giant music box!" he yelled. "Let's get outta' here!"

Novelty stimulated sales. As the surprise factor waned with repeated visits to a city, our team sought new territory. Chicago, Detroit, Kansas City, and St. Louis seemed depleted as we got the "boot" more often. Canada was the wilderness we sought to explore.

In Detroit Yacov put me on a plane to Toronto in October 1976, for a scouting mission. I arrived, rented a van and a motel room, and spent hours driving and mapping this two-million-person city. I circled in red every inch of prime commercial-industrial area. I applied for an international import broker's license to receive flower shipments by air from San Francisco after midnight. Pretending Canadian citizenship, I opened a bank account, set up a P.O. box and a telephone answering service number. Then it was time for Yacov to send part of his Detroit team across the border. Our only worry was interception by the Royal Canadian Mounted Police or import duty officials. We didn't want to get caught and deported, as another team had in Manitoba.

For three weeks I ran a "holy brigade" of sellers within English-speaking Ontario, while Yacov drove the bilingual members of our team in Montreal. ("Voulez-vous achetez des fleurs?")

Oktoberfest in Guelph, Kitchener, and Waterloo, Ontario, promised a perfect arena for our enterprise—rathskellers and circus tents of inebriated crowds, singing and craving to buy roses to decorate their bottles. After getting bounced twice from the Coronet Club, an energetic sister, Ellen Galligan, and I once more crouched table to table selling bouquets, watchful of the authorities. Finally the pub security intervened, furious at the knowledge that any money we had extracted from the crowd depleted their own profits. The R.C.M.P. was called in to investigate. Ellen and I were saved miraculously by a brawl that distracted their attention, allowing us to sneak away.

Our teams united again after a lucrative selling spree, and returned on order to Oakland to celebrate Children's Day with the Family. This was my last trip with Yacov.

Yacov and Evey, whom I had grown deeply attached to over four years, were legally kidnapped by their parents in early December after our Children's Day celebration. Hoping they would both escape their deprogrammers, as Yacov had done one time before, and return home, Onni appointed me as temporary team captain in Yacov's place.

But my heart was paralyzed. I feared the deprogrammers would crush their spiritual lives.

December 1977, the coldest winter in Michigan history, found me leading my flower team into an arctic deep freeze. Snowbound in Grand Rapids for four days (in a storm that caused southwest Michigan to be declared a disaster area), we'd done the same bar runs twelve times. We had thoroughly worn out our welcome; I'd been bodily thrown out of one Mexican restaurant.

Time to set our wagon in motion and head on, that is if we could spend more time in motion than in digging ourselves out.

I decided to chance driving to Muskegon, a small port town on Lake Michigan. The town's folks had supported our efforts in the past through hail or monsoon. A bar run there might work out.

Two hours later, we crept through the silky white streets of an abandoned city. Not a light shone in store or restaurant. Sculptured snow "grotesques" loomed up, nearly covering residences; brooding ghosts and frothy sprites captured bushes; elongated icicles fell upside down out of roof gutters. The world was motionless, noiseless.

"Let's do it!" I shouted, remembering Yacov's gift for spontaneity. In a flash, we all lined up behind the van's back bumper; the streets provided a fantastical playground for skiiing behind the van. But without skis.

Shoulder to shoulder, feet flat, I yelled to the driver, "Hit it!"

"Wheee! We must be going thirty."

"My soles are going to burn."

"Better burn for Heaven than Hell!"

Behind Fences: Boonville

"To beguile many, and be beguiled by one."
—SHAKESPEARE

Weekend Workshop Schedule
Saturday/*Sunday*

6:00 A.M.	- Staff wake-up and chanting
7:00	- Staff meeting, discuss groups
8:00	- Family and guests awake
8:45	- Exercises/*Singing*
9:30	- Breakfast in groups
10:15	- Introduction Lecture
11:45	- Hike, lunch in groups
1:00 P.M.	- Dodgeball
2:00	- Creation Lecture/*Ideal World*
3:15	- Group meeting
3:45	- Creation Lecture/*Man's Responsibility*
5:00	- Group meeting
5:30	- Deviation, Fall of Man lecture/*Testimonials*
7:00	- Dinner, create songs in groups
8:30	- Song Festival, Campfire/*New recruits decide to stay for seven days or return to S.F.*
9:45	- Staff testimonials
10:45	- Group meeting
11:00	- Family to bed
	- Staff meeting to discuss recruits
12:00	- Staff prayer

/ 97

Boonville marked the spot where I first plunged into the Family's ideology and communion. My two Boonville weekend workshops in October 1972 and February 1973, when I was still a student at Santa Cruz, had influenced me to join the Family by .April 1973.

For many months after I became a Family member, the weekend workshops were held in Oakland, not Boonville. But by 1974 and 1975 the Family was again holding weekend training sessions for new recruits on the Boonville farm. From July to January, 1975, I lived on the 680-acre farm after being promoted to a staff group leader for the seven-day and weekend lecture workshops.

My duties on the farm were always punctuated by center life or extended flower trips. But basically I served as counselor, group facilitator, cook, farmer, and "elder sister" to young members.

The Boonville week I remember most vividly occurred in August 1976 after my return from Ohio, where I had tried to rescue Michele Tunis from deprogramming by her parents.

I was headed toward Boonville with Daniel in a VW bug that was struggling up Highway 101, coughing and snorting. The sky was mother-of-pearl moments before the dawn of the day above Tiburon.

"Are we going to make it?" I ventured, looking sleepily over to Daniel.

"What do you mean, 'are we'? You've got to have more determination than that!"

"Daniel, Father had better watch out or you'll be replacing Him in a year or two," I teased.

"Why do you say that?" Daniel coaxed.

"Because you're determined to win," I explained, sensing as I always did that Daniel's goodness, idealism, stamina, inspiration would be well received by the world, that God endorsed his every action, and that Daniel knew this.

I cherished these moments with the "perfected" and half-worshipped older staff members, because they were a rarity in the mad pace of Unification center life. You stole those times between keeping schedules, attending new guests, seminar sign-ups, making money, cooking, trinity meetings, serving center man, witnessing, lectures, laundry, transportation headaches, counseling everyone with "spiritual difficulties," dealing with public relations, heading off persecutions. To capture Daniel—head of a center, director of training sessions—was like having a gem in my palm.

My mind drifted back to another day I'd spent with him in the offices of his short-lived dream baby, the Ethical Management Project. Started in 1975 with Onni's blessing, Ethical Management was to have been a series of symposia on energy, crime, law enforcement, mass transit, urban housing, business ethics. One evening before Onni had abruptly shut it down as extraneous to God's plan and sent its young innovator Daniel out to humble himself on the streets selling flowers, he and I had been in the midst of arranging files and drawers. Daniel had bent over and confided, "I got a letter from my dad. It really got to me, down to the bone. I'm not sure what to do about it. He thinks Father's a charlatan, he thinks I'm wasting my life. He lies awake nights worrying over me, grinding his teeth . . . literally. You know, I do still love him." Shyly Daniel had handed me the worn sheets of his father's letter— obviously read and reread. But in the same clutch he'd also handed me a poem that he had just written, telling how much the Church meant to him. Some of his lines haunted me. They expressed both his tenderness and his strength. "And the fury, the power, will gather your soul. . . . Now singing the silence, the gentlest song. . . .'"

Temporarily snapping back to the present, to the highway and the driver at the wheel, I studied Daniel, imagining from what he'd told me of himself what he must have been like before joining the Church. In college, restless and hungry for resolution, he'd sought relief from the world's cruel confusion in a fantasy: running to the Olduvai Gorge to let out a convulsive primal scream.

What, I wondered, had brought us all together into this life? A shared "karass" as Kurt Vonnegut described a spiritual network? Vietnam war generation and political disappointments? Lack of intimacy born of the "free love" ethic and the ambiguities of sexual preference? Too many choices, too many disintegrating guidelines?

The Church Family, I reflected, offered first of all a sense of belonging to a romantic and intense "world" that needed each and every one of us. It offered us "forever" and "future" in a world of "instants" and "obsoletes," guaranteed us success and recognition by future generations. Brothers and sisters, we were bound in eros, in the instinct for life, but shielded by Church-ordained safeguards against any expressions of sexuality. Tired of competitive scholarship, we welcomed community emotion. The Family represented unified nonconformism spiced with the distinctiveness, notoriety, self-definition, even deviousness, revolutionaries traditionally thrive on, all within a context of disciplined commitment.

It had provided other things, too: an outlet for idealism and self-sacrifice on the one hand; on the other, opportunity for greater power, value, purpose, and courage than one person acting alone could achieve.

The most important thing the Church offered was the heroic and perfect "Father," a visionary who possessed the singular key to God's heart, who could deliver security, happiness, hope, peace, justice, prestige, eternality where authority figures in our former life had disappointed us.

Too frightened to overturn all authority for a limitless freedom, we had found another authority instead. We had entered a microcosm where the complexities of adulthood were postponed and we didn't have to assume responsibility for ourselves. Someone had taken us into His hands, defined us, given us endless rules to live by, held us as "slaves of love" by our own hope and by our need for security. Simple, clear answers to unanswerable predicaments, tangible absolutes, and clearly prescribed courses of action instead of relativity, doubt, mystery, ambiguities, anguished skepticism.

The Church promised its collaborators perfect spouse, perfect family, perfect self unified in perfect oneness with perfect leadership and God. A perfect kingdom to come through a presumably perfect revolution. . . .

"Hey, you still there?" I broke my reverie. "What's going on up at the Boonville Sheep Barn?"

"God's charging ahead. Forty guests signed up for this week's seminar. Lots of group leaders are needed; Onni told me we *have* to get everyone new to move into a center. We decided you're going to be leading a group this week," Daniel informed me.

It was a promotion; I was excited. Besides, I wanted to get a look at Daniel's experimental Boonville seminars, which were growing famous. He conducted them in the gritty and primitive Sheep Barn. With goats and lambs looking on, Daniel lectured not on *Divine Principle* by Moon but on a diluted set of aphorisms about truth, beauty, and love, the purpose of God's creating the universe, the causes of crime, and the return to a lost but intended perfect society. Daniel's preliminary course was proving to be a very successful catchall for young travelers looking for friendship and community. He managed to claim the new seekers' idealism and good-heartedness for the community. He was especially tender to agnostics and offered no clue to Reverend Moon's role.

"Guess who's going to be leading groups?" laughed Daniel.

"Who?"

"Rick, John, Pat, Bertha, you, myself and none other than the man from the trenches, 'Michael Hon-ul'!" Daniel shot me a grin.

" 'Michael Hon-ul'? Who's that?" Then, "You mean Yacov?" I pounced.

"None other! We'll have some fun. You know he and I haven't really worked together on the farm." Daniel was expectant. "Yacov had to change his name. Onni gave him 'Hon-ul'—it means 'heaven' in Korean. You were there when he was kidnapped just before Yankee Stadium, weren't you?"

"I spent all night calling his parents and the N.J. police, who were sure *I* was crazy. But his escape down the fire escape in his socks and T-shirt was better than anything Houdini could have thought up, believe me."

Daniel and I turned silent, sharing the secret joy of knowing Yacov, whom everyone gravitated to because of his firm and funny ways.

"What about that 'Hon-ul'?" I asked. "Don't they think he's safe by now?"

"His mother was on television in New York last week criticizing the Unification Church for squeezing the life out of her son. She may try to nab him again," Daniel warned.

"They'd never be able to deprogram Yacov; he's completely solid when it comes to his commitment to Onni and the Father." But I waited in secret anxiety for affirmation from Daniel, who'd been brought into the movement by Yacov.

"Don't underestimate the power of Satan. We've all done little things that set conditions for Satan to invade," Daniel warned. "Sin just isn't worth it."

My mind flashed to the last flower trip with Yacov; I wondered what Daniel was intimating.

At Cloverdale we stopped for the main staple of Unification Church members, coffee. After Daniel's third cup, I joked, "The world will be out of coffee before we ever reach the Kingdom of Heaven. Slow down."

"Just nervous, I guess," he confided.

"You mean *you* get nervous too?" I exclaimed in shock. "I thought senior staff members always had everything under control. You don't mean you make mistakes, too, do you?" I never ceased to wonder what went on in the insides of more perfected people, those center people our faith demanded we see as perfect.

"Let's just say Teresa and Onni tell me I make mistakes, they keep me *very* aware that I do. And then," Daniel added slowly, "sometimes my own heart feels closed and far from God."

"Yours, too?" How treasured was Daniel's confession, how it spoke to my own experience, gave me hope for myself. "Younger Family members walk around thinking the staff are paragons of virtue and act in total confidence. Do you think Onni's perfect?" I asked. He hesitated. Then I dared to venture, "Most of the staff think she is."

"She must be, then," Daniel stated with cheerful finality, adhering absolutely to the line that the Oriental woman was infallible. "If I ever wonder, I'm just too arrogant with my own ideas, I guess."

He'd said it in a way and manner I must believe, I *would* believe, too. But something in Daniel's face made me remember a time when I'd asked Teresa a question about Daniel's advice to me and she'd snapped, "That Daniel, you can't pay any attention to him. He never knows what he's talking about—always doing his own thing."

"Daniel, we're going to be late. We've got to wake up the staff before everyone else gets up and wanders off," I prodded.

"Keep your eye out for decent-looking hitchhikers. Maybe I can catch some spiritual children to bring along," Daniel said as we crawled into the car.

Mendicino County undulated before our eyes, pastoral and biblical, its hillsides of live oak, meadowlark, deer, and sheep. We had the hills almost to ourselves; only a few farms, a school, and the Mendicino fair grounds were visible. The Unification farm swelled Boonville's village population figures every weekend. Someday we hoped it would be the site of Ideal City, an international community of God-loving leadership and harmonized daily life.

"You're going to be my object this weekend," Daniel said, rolling the car window up against the summer dust. (That meant I must follow him absolutely.) "You can help lead singing and set the best example responding to my lectures. You've got to really love this group, whoever is in it. God wants you to grow to be able to take care of hundreds, maybe thousands of people someday. We're so blessed to know the complete truth and know a Messiah walks on earth right now. Good luck, though; we'll work close, O.K.?" Daniel was brotherly in his glance. "Now get out and open the gate."

About two hundred yards from the highway down a rutted road, edging a tiny apple orchard, stood a cyclone and wood fence. It had a gate that was padlocked, and was obviously more than a deer fence, though this was its purpose as explained to guests. You could look at that fence and gate two ways: it kept people herded in, enclosed, because permission had to be sought to get in and out, or it kept the outside world from encroaching on the dreams of the dwellers within. Ten acres of lush vegetable fields surrounded us as we passed through the gate; the road dipped down past a pig hut to Soda Creek. Across the river lay a rudimentary "village" consisting of two modern trailers and a rebuilt chicken barn (gloriously titled the "Chicken Palace" or "Hen Castle") used for weekend and week-long lectures and song practice. Past this trailer and shack settlement we drove through valleys and rises, beside rock outcroppings, grazing cattle, stubby sheep, and windward over-looks. Perched on a rise was the old sheep barn, soon to be Daniel's weathered domain. Nearby were a worn kickball field and lined-up, cockeyed latrines—the only vestige of civilization in what was a carefully isolated place, and to many one of disrepute and mystery.

Rick and John came galloping toward us up the road, hearty and comical and filled with joy at our arrival. They were relieved their center man had finally appeared to give them instructions. Rick, a biochemist, had given up his profession to join the Unification Church. John was a billowy, competent, idealistic general practitioner, who served unofficially as the Church doctor and fix-it man. Bertha and Pat, hugging each other in the morning muddle, waved to us as they sauntered from the women's lean-to toward the latrines. Suddenly a brother with a tousled head and bulky sweater emerged from the tiny hindquarters of a Chevy camper.

"Michael!" I yelled, relieved to remember his new name, "welcome back from the wars alive!" We shook hands, he winked.

"I've got to get staff meeting going," Daniel worried. We gathered together, mindful as always that staff meetings were privileged, were a time for passing judgment on each performance.

Daniel prayed. We raced through the list of which people were in which groups, and finalized our weekend schedule. Assistants were parceled out among the leaders. Responsibility was assigned for song leading, calisthenics, food preparation, seating assignments, and campfire plans.

Away from Onni, Daniel dared trust his staff even if some were novices. "O.K., everybody's going to get one hundred percent of their people to move in, right? We have to have total concern for the guests;

don't think about your own capability—God's with you. Really support my lectures, that's crucial. Father be with you all," Daniel dismissed us.

With a few moments to spare before calisthenics, I jogged to the cliff overlooking the mountain range and prayed. Very much alone, my knees wedged between two rocks, I begged God fervently: "Make me faithful, Heavenly Father. So often I've tried to capture You as a feeling and You seemed real only so long as the feeling was there. But, Heavenly Father, I know You are always there and absolute, and when I don't feel You, it's only because of my own fallen nature. I hate what Adam and Eve and Lucifer did and the depravity that is in me because of my stained inheritance. Forgive me. I've been on a liquid fast for a week and I promise to continue it so that every new guest in this training session will respond to You. I'll take care of the new heavenly children in my group and promise to be humble to You, True Parents, the truth, and to Daniel. I pray for a perfect week. In the name of the True Parents, Amen."

That day, after Daniel's electric lectures on creation, sin revealed through selfish love, and the spiritual world determining the physical world, all the groups had lunch in the cornfield. Afternoon meditation followed, then dinner by the creek, then campfire and singing. Around the campfire testimonials were given by Family members about their own salvation from corruption and misery. Group prayers were offered to the obsidian sky.

And so the women trotted to their far-off leanto, the men to bed down in the barn loft. It was time for the staff to meet, discuss, and conclude the day.

We met in an ancient, drooping canvas tent propped up by spindly poles in the middle of a sheep field. Glancing in before we entered, I saw that Daniel and "Michael" were sprawled out, Michael resting his head on Daniel's stomach. That companionable pose made me suspect the tone of this staff meeting might be drastically casual. John and Rick had just stepped in, arms laden with honey and tea, napkins full of prunes, apples, and granola. Unable to resist impulse, Pat, Bertha, and I suddenly dove laughingly into the party, upsetting the brothers' primitive serving plans.

"Hey, let's get serious." Daniel struggled to a sitting position, his exertions belying his simultaneous bearlike tickle of brother "Michael's" ribs. "So, how were your group discussions today?" he tried to be sober.

"Well, our discussions weren't too deep. I mean it was hard really getting the feeling of hurting God in the 'Cause of Crimes' lecture because we ate peanut butter sandwiches in the corn patch right afterward," Pat snickered, aware of the gravity of the meeting but unable to control her amusement.

"Yeah, whose idea was that, to eat in the middle of the cornfield? It was wild. I couldn't even see who was sitting next to me," remarked Rick in his proper British accent.

All eyes turned to Daniel and "Michael"—a lot of us were familiar with some of their raucous schemes before they'd met the Family. The suspense all of a sudden erupted into laughter and groans as John tipped over the pot of tea, and hot liquid spilled over blankets, stocking feet, prunes, and granola alike.

Propelled by guilt over a feast denied the other campers, we hastened to clean up, believing Satan might even be accusing us of greediness by causing that spill.

"All right," Daniel started over again. "We'll go around the circle and each person, starting with Lael, will evaluate how everyone acted in their group and how the lectures came across."

Order restored from the shameful fun, summarizing began. Daniel scolded me for my reluctance to give testimonial of my conversion when he'd invited me to speak at the campfire. "God only gives you as much responsibility as you can handle. You let your ego and lack of confidence get in the way. If you don't jump for the chance to serve, Heavenly Father will never ask you again."

Properly rebuked and miserable, disappointed and defeated inside, yet forced to be outwardly grateful for punishment from a superior, I stayed up most of the night watching the fog leapfrog down the mountain and repenting for my timidity.

When we awoke the next morning, all the staff members assembled for our ritual chanting. Onni had set a 24-hour indemnity condition in which different teams of people throughout the Bay Area took turns chanting every minute of the day. Struggling, as always, to stay awake and to maintain a unified rhythm, we chanted:

> Glory to Heaven and peace on earth: Bless True Parents; success in their mission; all trainees move in; 600 children move in right now; restore material foundation; bring multimillionaires; end persecution now; all negative parents, negative media, negative people repent! *All parents become positive, serve God, serve True*

Parents; serve this Family; bring Onni and Abba one righteous, capable, healthy baby boy; reborn ourselves; elevate personal character."

Our half hour of chanting over, our second day on the land began.

At Boonville during the week-long workshops there was a period reserved each day after working on the land. Called meditation hour, this was a time for individual prayer, showers, phone calls, letter writing, playing musical instruments, counseling, reading, or hiking within a prescribed area. No talking was allowed; new guests weren't permitted to talk to each other (to prevent new men and women from becoming intimate, and to prevent "negativity sharing" about the workshop). One sensed in newcomers the great struggle to submit the will to the "other."

One of my duties as a staff person was to report on people who talked during meditation hour or ventured outside the boundaries of the designated areas. I was also given charge of monitoring the pay telephone, which could be turned off and declared out of order anytime. I was often instructed to pray with new guests, hold their hands during calls from the outside "Satanic" world, advise them exactly what to say to their parents, friends, or bosses, deflect any notion that the workshop was evangelical or religious in nature or connected to any international organization. Many a time I held at bay an onslaught of suspicious and "Satanic" parents questioning the accuracy of their children's innocent descriptions of the farm. Although they did not object to the wholesomeness promoted by the Church (habits and appearance were cleaned up, health-threatening drugs were discontinued, promiscuity was inhibited by promises of delayed monogamy), they did object to being replaced by surrogate parents and seeing their children removed from the sphere of socially useful activity and used as pawns for the financial and political betterment of the Church.

In Boonville I also screened the mail, since many new recruits obviously were not "solid" enough to receive mail that would draw them emotionally back to lovers or family. This mail was simply held back.

During meditation time I seldom meditated; for the staff there was little time for such self-development. I remember vividly, however, one Monday in August 1976, after three years in the Family. At the close of group prayer in a field, everyone scattered for individual activity. Just once I decided to take fifteen minutes for myself, to drink in the natural splendor around me. In a setting wholly without privacy, I told myself I would appreciate the world for God, as His grateful child, not for myself. Letting my spirit soar through the scalloped clouds, dance in the cattails, hunt mistletoe in the live oak, I momentarily returned to a former self, exulting in the moment and the existential world around me. I was seized with an intuition of the danger that lay in total abandon to the natural forces within my body and around me. This was the first time in three years of Family life that I had allowed myself to stop to absorb the "here and now" rather than be racing for the mission in a place called "other" and a time called "tomorrow." As I ran back to the staff trailer, I knew I had "spaced out," as we said in the Church.

But in the main, I accepted that my life, thoughts, and emotions in Boonville were seldom my own. There were too many people who needed guidance and counseling to spend my time so selfishly as to write a letter, practice guitar, talk to a fellow sister, or read a book. (Anyway, there were few recommended books except *Divine Principle*.) Every moment was a moment to be saving someone's spiritual life from Satan, who was constantly trying to "press on our throats." After all, there were so many "heavenly manners" to be inculcated and passed on; we were creating an eternal tradition. (But such tradition was secret, since we never let out to newcomers the very guarded and ultimate truth that the Master was right here on earth in the form of a Korean in a business suit named Sun Myung Moon. That was a revelation available only to the elect who had earned it by sincerity, righteousness and—above all— obedience.)

Prayers were also formed by strict guidelines. Private group prayer was fervent, hysterical, fist pounding, and competitive, each person struggling to show himself more righteous and tearful than the next. Public group prayer and chanting were rigidly formularized; individual prayer and chanting highly structured by a right and wrong way to get God's undivided attention. One time I was even chastised for praying too long and passionately after the lecture presenting Jesus's life as a tragic, lonely failure. It was just before lunch, everyone was hungry, and I was informed that I should have been briefer.

Despite the required self-sacrifices, I finally reserved a special Boon- ville space for myself—a wrinkle in time—between the hours of six and seven Sunday mornings to write poems to God. These I gave to my favorite people, to Dr. Durst, Yacov, Daniel, and John.

#1
Prayer of poppies,
Field filling.
The Heavenly Father
Knelt down . . .
Plucked me,
Pressed me
Beside His heart.
Perhaps He has a plan-perfect
For each His own
Child
Am I.

#2
Eons ago—
When sun glazed the earth's potted crust
And grain danced a sword-dance with lark,
God watched and prepared.
The wind scorched and blew
While stillness soaked the air in hushed
Love-wait
For the advent of His children-creatures.
Hand in breadth,
Two came forth in the palm of love,
Mewing and alive, a special existence—
More than cell, compound, reflex—
Sentient beings with fireworks.
They grew and grew
Until, lo, they knew too much too soon,
And left.
They left their Father tonguetied.
So our Father watches still . . .
But no more silent tongues and hearts.
His voice resounds in the dance of His Son:
Watersmooth, bride-bound, bond-perfect,
Lustrous,
Faith deep.

All for True Parents:
National Activities

" *I hear my Father; I need never fear. I hear my Mother; I shall never be lonely or want for love. When I am hungry it is They who provide for me; when I am in dismay it is They who fill me with comfort.*

When I am astonished or bewildered, it is They who make the weak ground firm beneath my soul: it is in Them that I put my trust.

When I am sick it is They who send for the doctor; when I am well and happy, it is in Their eyes that I know best that I am loved; and it is toward the shining of their smiles that I lift up my heart and in their laughter that I know my best delight.

I hear my Father and my Mother, and They are my giants, my King and my Queen, beside whom there are no others so wise and honorable or brave or beautiful in this world.

I need never fear, nor shall I lack for loving kindness. . . ."

—JAMES AGEE, *A Death in the Family*

THIS COULD BE THE DAY OF YOUR REBIRTHDAY! Thousands of street posters urged New Yorkers to attend the Madison Square Garden rally, September 18, 1974.

Reverend Moon had ordered Onni to send thirty people from Oakland to assist in the New York City ticket blitz. With hurried preparation, twenty-nine of us set out on Friday, September 7, in a rickety old farm truck led by a cherry red VW bug. Calling ourselves the "Oakies from Oakland" because of our costuming and caravan, we would constitute only a tiny minority of the thousands of Church members streaming in from many countries for the great public rally where Father would speak. Before we departed, Onni warned us, "Take care of each other. You are Heavenly child first, and Spirit of Oakland next. Do not walk alone at night in New York. Unite with other members of Church, but you come right home to Onni!"

As a mass of brothers and sisters dwelling in a cozy, cramped fort, we hurtled onwards to crusade. Food, clothes, shoes, cameras, books, and rows of sleeping bodies were crowded so close together at night we had to time our breathing and our turning over. By day we wrote songs, read the Bible and *Divine Principle,* played charades, and heard Yacov give history talks about Korea. We stopped to stretch in games of "Red Rover," and boisterously sang "Swing Lo, Sweet Chariot" in a gas station while changing a flat tire. Our group prayers were so intense that if we'd been in the Ark, we'd have rocked the boat.

It took us four days to the Lincoln Tunnel. We arrived in Manhattan at 3:00 A.M. September 11. Bedraggled, we unloaded into the Taft Hotel, six to a room, and set our alarms for forty-five minutes of sleep.

Dressed in a casual tailored work shirt, looking well rested and confident, Reverend Moon addressed two thousand of us in New York Episcopal church at seven the following morning, Wednesday. We divided after his inspiring pep talk into ticketing teams. Members of different regions of the country mixed together. My commander was from the Arizona Family; for the first time I was without Oakland Family comrades.

Before noon my team set out on the streets of Manhattan and Brooklyn. In Oakland we avoided criticism by denying our connection to Moon, but we couldn't do this in New York and at the same time promote Father's rally, so "negativity" from the public was a new and constant torment. "Why did Moon waste so much paper defacing New York streets with his posters?" "He's just a rich tycoon." "Isn't he a fascist?" "Doesn't he support Park in South Korea?" Or, "How can he want love when he owns a company that makes M-16 rifles?" One Church brother was scared off with a pistol. Another's leaflets were taken from him and tossed over a parkway.

Still, I persisted in believing New Yorkers were excited by seeing unselfish, clean, dedicated, international youth all over the city working for a man they trusted completely. Self-consciously, I walked with an awkward sandwich board at a Wall Street rally. I concluded in my journal: "Our Church speakers held the financial section in their grip, sent them away awed, wondering, baffled, their consciences stimulated."

SATURDAY, SEPTEMBER 14.

We must constantly be on guard so that Satan cannot attack through breakdown of center man's authority. Above all, become a melting pot of love for True Parents." And more, "No matter how tired my bones and my back, I get new spirit from the black people; they respond much more than the whites, although the business-suited young ones are militantly anti-Moon. I cried today with a black Pentecostal woman on the street corner and with another black fundamentalist who shared with me his grief over Christ's suffering, but tragically never opened up to listen to my offer of salvation through Reverend Moon.

SUNDAY, SEPTEMBER 15.

Our team leafleted at Shea Stadium. Father should stand on a baseball mound at halftime and simply take over. Easily, at each game, He'd get 20,000 people, We gave out tickets across from Staten Island in the sunset and talked to some stubborn, close-minded Jehovah's Witnesses who couldn't see the real Truth at all.

MONDAY, SEPTEMBER 16.

An exciting day. So much sizzling about the Messiah. Articles about Moon's coming rally were in the *New York Times* and the *Post* and on TV. Everyone is having to examine their moral spiritual standard in New York. They can't beat us, so why not join us? When people are hostile, we mustn't be defensive, but rather show open innocence. After all, we're giving people every chance to redeem their lives by hearing Father speak. Unification teams are even going out to black and minority congregations offering donations for every person the minister gets to come.

TUESDAY, SEPTEMBER 17.

The days grow more tense; Satan is desperate to stop Father. But the banquet held at the Waldorf-Astoria by Father for 2,000 was televised and successful.

WEDNESDAY, SEPTEMBER 18.

Father speaks. The lonely cry of God is heard. There was a full house—21,000 inside Madison Square Garden and at least that many milling around in the streets outside pouring out of public or Church-provided buses. We Church members were herded into a gigantic elevator and told to run and find seats scattered around the stadium in order to both inspire and control the crowd. Each member looked over the audience prayerfully. Reverend Moon stepped on stage and took his place behind large glass bullet protectors. By his side was Colonel Bo Hi Pak, his interpreter. Father apologized for adding more noisy youth to the New York noise; he apologized for the posters. He invited the opposition to express itself: "Anti-Moonies speak out now. I will talk one to one. I respect you. This is a land of freedom."

At this point some people stood up to yell accusations. Specially chosen trained security men of the Church grabbed them and took them, fighting, out of the crowd. I don't know what happened to them after that. I felt surprised and concerned. Something seemed wrong to me. The air was tense and electric. Then, in his deep tremolo, Father sang a suffering lullaby to calm the atmosphere and soothe God's broken heart for those who could in ignorance reject the Messiah.

After things quieted down, Father spelled out his blueprint for America and the world, saying that, since age sixteen, he'd been chosen as God's tool. He declared that throughout history those who brought new ideas from God, working against Satan, had been persecuted, but that he would obey his mission even with his life and even if America failed to understand or accept him. He explained that history was not a crucifixion but a restoration, that although Satan presently possessed the physical earth, the Lord is coming back to claim the body of fallen man, and the time has come to accept God's Son in the flesh. God's ideal is to find one perfect man, wife, child, and family. Ever since the fall of man, marriage has been a tragic sin, not blessed. But God will fulfill heavenly maternity with the coming of the Messiah who will make possible sinless True Parents. However, Father said, the leader can't bring the Kingdom unconditionally. Man must change and help himself. He closed with "God Bless America."

That night my journal continued: "To prove our word to New York City officials, in a herculean effort we stayed up all night to remove our posters of Father. Father said that New York will wake up to a ghost town without posters and young, smiling faces on street corners, and will wish us back. Father is a teacher of guts and raw courage."

SEPTEMBER 19.
We climbed into vans and hurtled our weary bodies but bright spirits to Belvedere, Father's home, to hear him speak at our big celebration victory.

Across the street from the stately, rolling acres on which Father's large gray mansion sat overlooking the Hudson, crusaders were parking legions—hundreds and hundreds—of vans from which we poured to gather at the side of Belvedere house to hear him. Nearby in the vast gardens that our members keep up with immaculate care, we saw Father's rock, a huge boulder where he prays. Beside it was the platform where he stood, solid, titanic, an immovable arm-chopping force. Colonel Pak translated. Rev. Moon said in his first three years of responsibility to America, his first problem had been attracting numbers of people, that a blitz wasn't easy to carry out, nor to take a movement to fifty states. "When we carried this out the mass media wondered where we got the money. We've become the multimillion-dollar church by reputation. This because of such hard work. I never granted interview to any reporter, so I remained a person in mystery. They must use their imagination. . . .

"Next year Yankee Stadium, then Washington Monument. The time bomb is ticking and the situation is urgent. God blessed us for only so long. I have a master plan and will push no matter what. Can I trust you?"

After Father's talk McDonald's hamburgers were trundled in for the brothers and sisters; some also shared bits of raw tuna from the fish which Master had recently caught from his ocean yacht.

Onni sent dozens of Oakland members to campaign for the expected 200,000 people needed to fulfill Moon's prophecy of a mass pentecost for America at Yankee Stadium, June 1, 1976. I had been fund-raising in the midwest with Yacov's flower team when Onni called our team to New York to hear Reverend Moon speak again. A series of extraordinary events followed.

After two years without seeing his parents in New Jersey, Yacov delivered our team to their front door to spend a pleasant day visiting and swimming. Treated with hospitable grace by his parents, we learned that a game plan had been worked out by Onni and Dr. Durst, who insisted on seeing the team at their suite in the New Yorker Hotel that night. Reluctantly they consented to let Yacov stay behind alone and visit a few more hours with his family.

Yacov, with his brother-in-law, escorted our van to the proper turnpike entrance to downtown Manhattan; we were to visit the Dursts in the city, then come back to spend the night at Yacov's house in New Jersey. At the New Yorker Hotel we picked up money to purchase new shoes after months of pounding pavements selling roses. By midnight we returned to the New Jersey suburbs. When we pulled up at Yacov's driveway, two formidable men moved out of the shadows to block each door of our van and prevent us from getting out.

"Norm," I whispered to our driver, "open your window just a crack. Find out what they want. Cover the money bag, quick," I ordered, assuming my position as second-in-command after Yacov.

As Norm craned his neck, the deep voice threatened, "Get your gear from the driveway and get out quick. If you have any questions, call the local police."

"Oh, my god," I tensed. "They've done something to Yacov! Norm, would you stay back and sneak around the house to see if he's tied up in there?"

"I could make a break for the front door and just barge in," Norm volunteered—the kind-faced giant of a brother had been a strong farm boy who'd spent his life plowing fields in upstate New York.

"No," I reconsidered in lightning decision, aware of my responsibility to the whole team, including Norm. "Everybody start chanting right away for Yacov. Norm, hop out; gather up our things. We'll get right out of here and call Onni from a pay phone. Make sure we aren't followed," I snapped, sounding a good deal more commanding and less frightened than I felt. I had suddenly inherited the serious role of team leader.

A few twists and turns down the road, I spotted a solitary, dimly lit phone booth. Dropping my dimes, I finally got through security in the New Yorker Hotel to Onni's suite. "Onni, this is Lael. We got to Yacov's house and were ordered away. I'm sure they've kidnapped him. I'm sure they're trying to deprogram him. What should we do?"

Onni's voice was shrill. "That's Satan, we'll smash him. Lael, listen. You know where the other flower teams are staying? You take your team there. Go now. We'll hunt for Yacov."

"Yes, Onni. But I'll call the police and Yacov's parents and try to get information. I'll report a kidnapping to the newspapers. He'll escape, I know it," I tried to reassure the easily upset Onni.

Filled with church rumors of atrocities committed by deprogrammers, I feared for Yacov's spiritual life and spent the remaining hours of the night praying for him.

I also called Yacov's parents and tonguelashed them with God's words.

"Hello, this is Lael. I don't mean to wake you at four in the morning, but you've got to tell me where Yacov is. I can't believe you'd do such a horrible thing."

Yacov's father spoke kindly, half apologetically. "Yes, Lael, well I assure you, he's safe. I can't tell you where he is, though."

"I know you're a man of conscience. What are you doing to him— taking God out of his life? I can't believe you'd resort to such cruelty," I pressed hard, in tears.

"You see, it's not that we have anything against you. You were very sweet all coming over to the house this afternoon. I'm sorry it's come to this. But I can't help you. Speak to my wife later." He hung up.

My pleas for help to the local newspaper and police were met with evasiveness. Since I knew Yacov's parents were prominent in the community, I assumed I was dealing with outright persecution.

Yankee Stadium wore a Janus face to our team. We were hopeful for Father's speech, yet filled with a deep sense of loss. As we distributed tickets without our Yacov, our team pulled close together for consolation.

When the hour came, Church members led songs, marched, and paraded outside Yankee Stadium gates. Our work was often interrupted as we ran into beloved members who'd joined in Oakland but had since gone on overseas or national missions. The spirit was strained, but high.

Moments before the stadium gates opened, black clouds pressed down and let loose a downpour.

We all wondered, would the flood prevent the crowds from coming? *Could* God be so unjust, after all our struggle to draw people to this cosmic event? We piled into the grandstands, waving our American banners and singing Church songs.

One mishap followed another. Balloons were released before intended; wind blew and rain drowned us; the amplification was faulty. A restless, piecemeal crowd of curiosity seekers munched caramel corn and shouted for Cokes in the middle of Father's speech. Stunned at the thought of God's dismay at such pandemonium, we asked ourselves if we were witnessing success or miserable failure. (Though by now, from long practice we suspected we must view it as absolute success.) Uncertainty over Yacov's plight fueled our apprehensions.

Taunted by gangs of young street kids on the way to our vans, our various flower teams drove to the New York Hilton to meet with Dr. Durst and the somber Oakland staff. Gathering upstairs in a quiet, black convention ballroom, we settled down to pray.

Suddenly I saw a messenger slip into the room and deliver something to Evey. Evey, in sudden tears, raced out of the room. Intuition seized me; I was sure she'd heard something about Yacov. But what? I glanced at my team. My heart thumped; I longed to be released from prayer to rush after Evey.

Soon the whispers passed like electricity from person to person: Yacov himself was downstairs in the Hilton lobby!

Released, we tumbled into the escalator. Looking up at us, smiling and waving, was our brother Yacov! In a new white trenchcoat, new shoes, new shirt and tie, carrying a Bible under his arm, he was a dazzling sight. The pig-pile of staff brothers and sisters nearly knocked him to the floor. Dr. Durst, tearful with joy, affectionately mussed up Yacov's hair.

I longed to hug Yacov too.

"Let's celebrate Yankee Stadium and Brother Yacov's return! I know a great deli across the street; treat's on Heavenly Father!" Dr. Durst invited. Fifteen of us clasped hands and formed a running line through a red light, then filed into the already packed Stage Deli. Unconscious of everyone else, exhilarated by reunion and the "chosenness" of our company, we set up two long tables and played musical chairs to get next to Yacov and Dr. Durst.

"What happened?" "Where'd you get those duds?" "How'd you know where to meet us?"

"You'll never believe what happened; I can't myself. But first, how was Yankee Stadium? How was Father? I prayed the whole time I was in the warehouse for victory to God," said the mission-minded Yacov with characteristic energy.

We all leaned into the conversation as Dr. Durst explained, "I've never seen such unity in the Family. That alone made Yankee Stadium a victory. God was really testing our endurance through the rain and noise. But we'll find out exactly how it was tomorrow at Belvedere when Father speaks to us."

Finally Yacov succumbed to our pleas for his story: "I'm wearing this outfit because I had on only a T-shirt and shorts when I climbed down a fire escape of the warehouse where I was taken. I did have some money on me, though, so in my stocking feet I thumbed a ride to an industrial park and dived into the first shoe and clothing store I saw. Then I went to a movie, because I didn't want to appear at Yankee Stadium and risk recapture. I bought a Bible and at the suggestion of a cabdriver came to the Hilton to read until I could get in touch with everybody again."

"How did your mom and dad nab you?" I asked. "All I know is, our team pulled up at your house at midnight and were met by a couple of monsters who told us to get lost. I called your dad and he wouldn't tell me where you were."

Yacov answered, "After my brother-in-law and I led you to the freeway, we stopped for some milk and bread. It was all planned; our stopping gave the kidnappers time to pull a van into our garage and get ready to grab me as I stepped in the door. When I walked in I thought they were burglars and yelled for Mom and Dad, who suddenly appeared at the top of the stairs. When they didn't protest, I froze, was grabbed, and was led to the van in the garage. By then I knew *exactly* what was going on." Yacov took a breath.

"Next thing, we were going into this warehouse. It was set up with little rooms, some with several people in them. Up walked one of my former spiritual sons. He was the one supposed to 'break me,' I guess. I ended up in this little cubicle with bright lights. There were a lot of intense questions thrown at me; tapes about Father and supposed discrepancies between the Bible and *Divine Principle* were playing. I just kept chanting and didn't let anything in. But nobody hurt me."

Suddenly I nearly lost the thread of Yacov's story for a minute; an awful wonder had hit me. Why had he bought a Bible? Why hadn't he been quicker to get in touch with Onni after his escape? Had Yacov been sitting in the Hilton doing some research on his own? What, I wondered in dismay, *had* gotten in, despite his chanting?

When I came to, Yacov was finishing his story. "They tried to keep me awake all night, but the funny thing was, I kept making the security men assigned to me feel guilty for dozing off. *I* stayed in the subject position; I wouldn't let anyone smoke in my presence, for instance."

Yacov looked so firm and we were all so relieved that we laughed hilariously at the thought of his lording it over his captors. "You should have stayed and been like Peter; he converted his jailers. Just think, you might have a whole new trinity of spiritual children by now!" Evey teased, herself honored for bringing in more recruits than any other Family member.

"In the morning Mother came to visit me in my little room; my guard left when she came in. I wouldn't talk to her, because my civil rights were being taken away, so she rushed out of the room to call my dad. I was alone; furthermore, all night long I'd been studying out an escape route. I locked the door and climbed out the window onto the fire escape. But as I tore down it, I realized the escape ladder stopped on the second floor. I was stopped there when a man across the street pointed out a ladder to me that continued around the corner of the building. I dropped to the ground without even looking back!" Yacov smiled a heroic grin.

Bathed in our spiritual victory and Yacov's personal victory, it didn't seem the right time to bring up how pained and anxious his father had seemed on the phone the night before. I told myself Yacov's parents deserved their defeat.

Four and a half months later, September 18, 1976, Yacov's flower team was called from Michigan and ordered to attend "incognito" the Washington Monument rally. We arrived on the by-now momentous scene, brothers and sisters from all over the east diligently distributing tickets. The day of the rally, we gathered with chickin'-lickin' picnic-mood crowds for Moon's speech, for the New Hope Singers, and for the most grandiose fireworks display ever put on in America. The thrill of the pyrotechnics lighting up Washington Monument, the Reflecting Pool, the dignified Lincoln memorial, ignited every cell of my body. Father, I was certain, would truly redeem mankind this time!

Onni and Dr. Durst invited all us vagabond Oakland flower sellers, who'd so materially helped finance the big fireworks, to spend a night in the stately Hayes-Adams Hotel where they had a triple suite.

After a mighty McDonald's banquet, we rested while Onni, Dr. Durst, Teresa, and Micah dressed to go out.

"Make sure everything's in perfect order when Onni and Abba get back. Lael, you're the eldest sister so you have to set the standard," Teresa ordered.

"Yes, Teresa, thanks for reminding me." I managed a few obse-quious words, trying not to count on one hand the times in three and one half years Teresa had said something affirmative rather than admonitory to me.

I'd just dropped off in exhausted sleep when the door banged and I woke with a start. It was Teresa coming back for a final check, Teresa whose presence always made me feel I was being escorted by tumbril to the scaffolding. "Lael," she barked from the bathroom, "the sink has a hair in it and the toilet seat's up. Do you remember what I told you?"

"I washed out the sink and straightened the towels right after you left, Teresa," I tried to justify my effort—I who had always been a tidy, even compulsive housekeeper. "But maybe someone used things after I was in there."

"You know what it means to be in the Abel position; it means you're responsible for everyone else's actions, too. You can't blame anyone else, ever. We're going out again, so why don't you clean up Onni's room. Thank you." As I heaved my weary bones out of my sleeping bag, I tried to remember that Teresa only repeated her own treatment by Onni. As usual, I worked myself into believing I was too arrogant anyway.

The following day, before our teams left Washington to start fund-raising again, Onni suggested a hike to Baskin-Robbins for ice cream; once there, she ordered a second round for the brothers. On the way back to the vans and the hotel, the whole pack of us got sidetracked by a frantic game of Frisbee. The men took off their suitcoats, the sisters rolled up their sleeves ready to outwit the men. Eager to prove themselves an aggressive, soldierly, competitive lot, fashioned after Onni and Teresa, the sisters put up a hard match! While Onni and Teresa watched, talking more important business from a park bench, Micah, the director of Boonville training camp, emerged a hero after diving head-first into a hedge to retrieve the flying disk. Dr. Durst burst forth unexpectedly from low-hanging branches behind trash cans; Yacov kept being tackled by the sisters; John pranced regally through every onslaught.

Onni stood up. Enough pleasure and tension releasing for one day. God was happy, her look told us, but not happy enough. More money must be harvested. And those of us trained to find our sole value in the money we earned weren't fulfilled unless we were out on the streets harvesting it.

Who Is Not With Us
Is Against Us: Persecution

"He is either a 'member' or he is not a member. He is either part of one's own mob, or he is outside the mob. Woe to him, above all, if he stands outside the mob with the mute protest of his individual personality!"
—THOMAS MERTON, *Disputed Questions*

As disciples of Reverend Sun Myung Moon, the Lord of the Second Advent, we rejoiced that we were chosen, "worthy to suffer shame for his name" (Acts 5:41). We believed that no matter how heavily our Enemies persecuted us, the Unification Church was of God, and could not be overthrown. We identified these Enemies: Communism, the liberal press, Christians and Jews who didn't recognize Reverend Moon's messiahship, and negative parents, congressmen, academics, and deprogrammers.

As Church members, we encountered "persecution" and believed that the *Washington Post* and the *New York Times* often hired Satanic or Communistic writers. We were accustomed to picketers who accused us of "brainwashing" and "deception." They stood in front of our centers in San Francisco and Berkeley at dinner time or before lectures to recruits. But what struck closest to home were the "kidnappings" and "deprogrammings" of our own staff and membership.

Every night at five, rain or fog, a few stalwarts of "Eclipse," the local anti-Moon organization, strode in front of the San Francisco Washington Street center with placards. In an effort to warn guests who had been invited to dinner but deliberately not told they were to be fed by the Unification Church, these "renegades for Satan" gave away our secret, our connection with Sun Myung Moon. Their signs read THIS IS THE HOME OF SUN MOON! DON'T BE BRAINWASHED! BE FREE!

It was usually my job as a staff member to escort invited people to the steps before they were snagged by the Eclipse wolves. I'd laugh and joke with the guests, saying things like, "Meet our local persecutors! They seem to think we're brainwashed. Do I look brainwashed? They seem to think this is Reverend Moon's home. I've lived here a long time and I've never seen Reverend Moon hiding in any of our closets."

One night in early September 1976, as I walked in the door, Shelly, who tended the reception desk, signed people in, and collected donations for dinner, grabbed my arm.

"Stick around. Something's up," she hissed.

"Is everything all right?" I paused for her to welcome a guest.

"Hello, what's *your* name? We're *so, so* glad you came. What a *nice* camera! Who invited you? Would you sign here? Also, *any* donation for dinner really helps buy rice, granola and simple stuff. *Thanks!* Have a *wonderful* evening." After the effusion, Shelly leaned over and whispered in a businesslike way to me, "Take this and go right up to my room. Yacov and Amos are up there. They'll tell you what to do. Also, grab that tape recorder on the way." Without question I followed Shelly's instructions; she was centerperson while Teresa was out.

Heavy with intrigue, I bore under my arm a paper file tied shut and wet with rain. The file and tape recorder I couldn't explain.

"Good, you got them!" exclaimed Amos abruptly, obviously facilitator of some cops-and-robbers scheme.

"Can I ask what's going on, or am I just the archangel, the messenger?" I joked. "You two look like Sherlock and Watson."

Amos lectured even when he wasn't lecturing. "The file was left outside the doorstep by an Eclipse creep who must be eating our dinner disguised as a guest right now. Shelly found it and checked it out—lots of names of ex-members, phone numbers, lists of Church license plates. They apparently follow us around."

Yacov shot me a dark look. "Keep the material and get rid of the file case."

"Yeah, Lael, *burn* the file holder. I wonder which is the guy, and who's taking care of him tonight. Hope it's an older brother or sister in case he pulls something."

Although I managed at the time not to admit to myself that I was performing Amos and Yacov's dirty work, I still vividly remember my reply. *"Burn* it? Isn't that extreme?" Then, at their looks, "O.K. I'll handle it." I even managed to feel important for the assignment. "What's in the tape recorder?"

"Bob came home with a woman guest from North Carolina. She taped their conversation on the bus and when she came in the house she kept taping conversations with members in the kitchen."

"You know who comes from North Carolina, don't you?" Yacov tested me.

"Marilyn, Laura, Mitch ... Oh, so you think some parents have hired this lady to inform on Church activities before they try to get their kids deprogrammed," I concluded resolutely. "Or maybe she's with Eclipse, too."

"Possible," Yacov said, retaliation in his tone.

"Your job's to erase the entire tape so she has no evidence of anything. We'll quietly put it back and she'll leave without knowing we did it," Amos informed me. "I'll let you work in my room while I get ready for law class tonight."

"But is that legal? Isn't that her personal property?" came out of me.

"Look, she didn't get permission to do her taping. If that's true, do we need permission to eliminate it? Of course not," Amos countered.

He banged out of the room.

"This persecution business is eerie," I turned to Yacov. "Satan is certainly real. And parents are certainly desperate."

"The paranoia's real on both sides. Our parents aren't crazy, they even have sincere intentions. They're just ignorant of the Truth and of Father's mission." Yacov amazed me by granting any good motives to our enemies.

"Yacov, do you feel like a fugitive? I mean, do you think your parents might try to nab you again?" I sought reassurance.

"Sure they will. But I look over my shoulder every minute of every day, and Onni's probably going to keep me on the road or underground. I wonder if I'd listen if they got me again?" Yacov sounded reflective.

"Of course you wouldn't!" I declared as I turned to leave the room. Before I shut the door, I saw Yacov had neither changed his pose nor motioned good-bye.

By January 1977 the fear of deprogramming as the most insidious of persecutions gripped the entire Family. Yacov and Evey had been kidnapped and successfully deprogrammed in December. Both extremely staunch staff members, their separation from the Church, which signified to us the death of their souls, plunged the staff into dismayed mourning over God's loss. We couldn't fathom their public statements about brainwashing practices of the Church. No one could understand the departures and exposures by Michele, Mitch, and another brother, Larry, as anything other than the workings of an all-powerful and threatening Satanic force.

Onni feared that Yacov would try to influence, possibly even kidnap, his flower team because of the devotion he had once inspired in us and we in him. As the powerhouse behind money-earning for the Family, our team was greatly protected by Onni, and I was in a mood to practice her caution because I'd inherited the leadership of Yacov's team.

Though I didn't suspect my parents, when I came down to Washington Street on January 3, after God's Day celebration up on the farm, I learned that it was now Teresa's job to make sure none of the flower teams were too visible until we could get out of the state again to resume our selling missions. There were, Teresa said, reports of deprogrammers in the vicinity: Dr. Durst had seen Larry driving by Hearst Street; Teresa had bumped into Mitch while getting an ice cream cone; Michele and maybe Evey and Yacov themselves might be scouting around. . . .

That same gray, cold January afternoon Onni arrived at Washington Street. She kept me up in her room while she made several inscrutable phone calls in Japanese and Korean. I prayed self-consciously, on razor's edge, while I waited for her to tell me what she wanted. "Come. You come with me. Get keys for car from Amos!" Onni took my hand, the first time she'd ever made a familiar gesture toward me. She seldom expressed even simple affection physically and did not welcome it from others.

She hurried me down the stairs and onto the street. I knew she appreciated the rolling evening fog that provided a cover, though both of us were painfully aware it could also hide enemies.

"Get into the car. Drive."

The car kept stalling and I knew I was fumbling. My mind raced to all my evil ancestors who seemed chronically to keep me apart from Onni. "Where shall we go?" I asked, feeling stupid and unfit, as I always did around her.

"You know Japanese Cultural Center? Go there. Shiatsu Massage, off of Fillmore." I was expected to know how to get there—everyone was expected to know any detail which would fulfill Onni's wants in any situation.

We parked, locked up, and walked into a comfortably modern

Japanese massage and sauna business. I stood beside Onni as she made her requests in Japanese.

A young woman came into the room, beckoned to me, and led me away from Onni, for what I assumed would be only a moment.

Ordered by a tiny Oriental woman to take off all my clothes I complied. Uncertainty—the usual feeling which kept you always off balance over Onni's exotic aspect and unknown past—gripped me. What was Onni's intention? Was this some kind of test of faith? Was it a way to hide me from kidnappers? Had she seen my parents? Was it just frivolity? When I realized that the last thing in my mind was that it might be an act of pure kindness, I felt how desperately I wanted it to be so. And with that realization came another. For four years she had been a stranger to me, was a stranger still. After the shock, I reflected on my apparently unconquerable mistrust of Onni. By now I knew that her giving was seldom free of expected favors. Was she buying my faithfulness at a time in the Church when faith was beset on all sides by the loss of so many staff members?

Anyway, where was she? Where had she gone, leaving me stranded here?

What I had, of course, was simply a full body massage.

Onni and I remet in the hallway. "You like?" she asked me, but before I could respond in grateful relief, a phone call came in to her from Teresa. Onni told me she was going to be picked up to be returned to Washington Street immediately, but I was to go right on outside and drive to Dana Street to join my flower team. Amos would give us instructions.

My team was gathered at Dana Street. The curtains were closed, all lights were off, doors and windows were locked. A call had come in from Washington center. Cruising cars had appeared around every Church center the night before. We were not to answer the telephone after the one that told us that fact. Helpless prisoners in our own house, we shivered in consternation. The nibbling neighborhood raccoons making nocturnal raids on the garbage cans drove us wild with black fantasies of kidnap.

There was a soft knock at the door; I peeked through the downstairs curtains. A long, lean shadow stood on the front porch. Was it Yacov back to regain his old team? While I was hesitating, Amos shouted furiously, "Let me in!"

Literally shaking with relief, I let him in and quickly bolted the door. "Amos, Onni's fear of deprogrammers has me and my team climbing the walls. When are we going to load up and get out of town?"

"Right now. In fact, I've come to *rescue* you," Amos replied with forced gallantry, something he wasn't good at. "Your team of seven will join Harvey with his team of seven. You'll all drive out to Oklahoma City together where you'll pick up your van—it's getting fixed from the last accident. You'll sell flowers in Las Vegas, Albuquerque, Bakersfield. Harvey'll go on to Kansas City; you'll head ultimately to Detroit, O.K.?"

"Amos, that's fourteen people trying to sell out of one van," I protested. "It'll take all day just to drop everyone off on one run."

"Well, Heavenly Father'll help you. This is the best we can do. We've got to get you people out of town; I smell a rat and we can't afford to lose you," Amos tried to cheer me.

"Before you leave," he said later, "everybody's to sign retainer forms giving power of attorney to Ralph Baker in case anyone gets kidnapped on the road. That means Baker will automatically represent you if you get captured," Amos was confident.

"Shouldn't we have met the lawyer first?" I asked, standing there wondering about the legal ethics of a mass signing for the services of an unknown professional.

"Don't be faithless, Lael. Sometimes I wonder about your inability to trust orders. You've *got* to trust me because I'm your center man and for all the other flower teams, too. Have you forgotten God works through me?" Amos was belligerent.

I covered my frustration.

"Is everyone who stays in town threatened by deprogrammers? How can we stop the kidnappings?"

"Don't worry, we're working out a way we could injure ourselves if there's any chance of being hauled off. That way we could get to a hospital and call Onni."

"You mean hurt ourselves?" I was shocked.

"Better physically hurt than spiritually dead."

That was too heavy for me. "Why don't we all just get out of town?" I asked, overcome with anxiety.

"Calm down. Heavenly Father works through Onni and she won't let Satan defeat us." Amos took my hand, pulled me along. "Come on, we've got a world to build. It doesn't get done by thinking; it gets done by moving."

Betty: In the Cult– Visits and Nonvisits

"Thou waitest for the spark from heaven! and we,
Light half-believers in our casual creeds
Who hesitate and falter life away,
And lose tomorrow the ground won today—
   Ah, do not we, Wanderer, await it too?"
   —MATTHEW ARNOLD

OCTOBER, 1973.
   Only a few years ago you could live in this country and know practically nothing about cults; as I've written, that was our state. When Barb went in her "group," I'd promised her I'd come down

for a weekend seminar in the Family. In that first year, I was ambivalent, sometimes lulled by her seeming sense of joy and purpose.

On Friday, October 12, 1973, my son Jeff and I set out by car for Oakland. Ailing from fatigue and anxiety, I'd nearly called the trip off; Ray urged this. But both Jeff and I shared a similar curiosity, a similar willingness to expose ourselves one time to what we suspected might prove to be a strange and hard experience.

We tore into Oakland, trying to make the nine o'clock lecture at Dana Street. Barb was waiting for us, seemingly calm, ready with a hug.

The lecture began at once, to about thirty people. I can't reconstruct it in any comprehensive way except to say it was called "Dimensions of Life" and featured Dr. Mose Durst, introduced as a professor at nearby Laney College. There seemed many wise individual sentences; picking up good kernels like a busy chicken, I waited for the lecture to make me feel filled up.

Durst said truth's standards were universal, eternal, reasonable, constructive, instructive, and practical; enthusiastically he drew diagrams on the blackboard.

"If a man," he said, "centers on working for a larger whole, he's a part of truth. If he works for himself, he's separated." Psychologist Jeff at this point whispered in my ear, "A very efficient precept for absolute socialization of people."

Durst talked a good deal about the ultimate centering force. He also talked about feelings. "If you embrace without feeling you get nothing back. Eighty percent of our energy is probably defensive." I couldn't find a thing to disagree with in those points; I just simply couldn't see how they were astonishing enough to form the basis of a new religion.

Durst's last sentence was "The ultimate spiritual experience is working from conscience and love for others." When he sat down I continued to struggle with my first mystification: what *is* so unique about this as to totally co-opt the lives of these starry-eyed young people?

Everyone then sang fervid songs about comradeship and the world getting better; high school Sunday school camp echoed in me.

We drove up to a city park and visitors and members played kickball. I—being over-age—was allowed to sit on a blanket on the grass. People played hard, especially the group members, with quite a lot of fierceness behind the good-natured yelling. (I didn't know it then but sometimes these games are played to incessant, unnerving, benumbing chanting.) When it was time for sandwiches, we women were the carriers and servers.

We rocketed back in our ragged fleet of cars, everyone bellowing songs. I tried not to perish from fatigue, remembering a good friend of ours who had visited Barb and laughingly reported, "Oh, those kids are just Quakers. But I told them their movement wasn't for anyone over twenty-five; the rest of us didn't have the stamina."

Yet even while I was amazed, repelled, amused, confused, anxiously disapproving, on other levels I was aware that I, too, was susceptible to a truth and practice which would solve problems and make people feel better. I, too, was responsive to the overflowing good fellowship. In our world everyone hugging and approving of and rooting for each other? Wouldn't that be *something!*

In the plain, clean, sunny room of the old Dana Street house I looked around at some of the young Family members: Martha, a trinity head, a blond girl with an aspect of hard living behind her; Esther, an anxious-looking Jewish girl of lonely aspect; Shelly, a buxom public health nurse who declared she wanted twelve kids; Daniel, a remarkable leader—I'll get to him later; Mark, a reserved, tender young man; Micah, a tall, dour Jewish boy I discovered on Sunday standing behind me as I took undecipherable notes. When I glanced around, he asked me, with dark meaning, "Writing an exposé?" Dora from Boalt Hall law school, over precise for most tastes and Cyndi, a neophyte with haunting dark eyes, had come together. And then there was the young bedraggled hippy woman visitor who hadn't much of an idea what it was all about and nobody was going to tell her because they didn't want her; she hovered around the edges like a moth at a lamp.

From time to time members dropped off in clearly exhausted sleep. In consternation I noticed they were mercilessly prodded awake by their brothers and sisters. Why?

Daniel gave the afternoon lecture, "The Essence of Principle," an apparent effort to raise pathologically low spirits and elicit personal commitment. Daniel was a handsome, energized, humorous young man of intense and emotional oratorical style. "God is heart and energy. Somebody told me God is dead. I can't believe it. I never got to know him. Everyone says they want to be mellow, avoid the hassle. But if we give everything we have, then everything responds. Our lives are much bigger than we realize."

Listening to him, I was aware that here was an eager young man on his way to power in a hurry; at another address and part of town, I'd be listening to a future corporation president. Yet there was something indescribably appealing about him even when he artlessly admitted to stratagems: "I make myself be fascinated by a person, then my response fascinates them."

Occasionally Jeff whispered to me: "All Barb's life she's been on the hunt for an abstract ideal. It's made her critical of the chaos of reality." And, whispering, we agreed: "You can't comprehend this place without experiencing it."

At the end of his lecture Daniel drew one of the ubiquitous charts, this one called "Correlation between Spirit Man and Physical Body," and I struggled to make myself accept that he, too, was one of these chart-happy people who put God in little circles along with truth and beauty. We broke into small groups, our group of women trotting upstairs behind Martha. I don't remember how she exhorted us—in the same nineteenth-century moral philosophy vein, I believe. Barb sat beside me treating all she heard with respectful attentiveness, absolutely tuned in to what was being said. On all sides people told me, "Lael is endlessly giving." Everyone remarked on her energy and inventiveness.

I'd arranged to go to dinner with my brother Scott, his wife Lauriel, and friends. Now I had a rude awakening, one that exposed the priorities in Barb I hadn't yet come to grips with. I discovered Barb had decided on her own that I must stay at Dana Street, had deflected several of Lauriel's frantic phone calls, and then cancelled me out on our dinner plans. When I asked Barb, she gave no explanation except a shrug and the comment that "where I was was better for me."

After dinner, after singing, after another brief lecture, fun night was staged. Drawing on my antiquity, I again declined to be part of our small female group charades. I remember Jeff was the hind end of a blanket-covered "horse." When his head came out, his face was hot and annoyed.

Jeff and I began our farewells about eleven; driving into Oakland we'd agreed he wouldn't spend the night with the Family. "I'm not up to that much pressure," he'd said.

"But, Jeff, you're going to spend the night, aren't you?" Micah asked.

"No. I'm too tired from the drive; I'm going to get some sleep."

By now we had eased our way out on the porch steps. A circle had formed around Jeff, tall, dark, determined faces. Suddenly, beneath the cordiality, I sensed something harshly, chillingly different. I stood aside, waited unbreathing.

"We think you ought to reconsider, Jeff. It's important to spend the night."

"No, I don't want to."

A long, considering, ominous silence. *What would be happening now if I weren't here?* my startled mind asked.

Reluctantly they let Jeff go after Micah's warning that "warm-ups" were at 6:30.

"We'll come tomorrow as early as we can," I called firmly. I remember the thick, intent hostile quiet that flowed after us.

Jeff was understandably furious. But after both of us had cooled off, we had to admit that all day our emotions had swung back and forth like pendulums, first longing to be part of the warm-seeming human community, then repelled by either the arbitrary, banal philosophy or the pressured group methods.

"It'd be impossible for me," I concluded, "unless, of course, I just decided to fool myself and jump in anyway."

"Which is what I suspect Barb did," Jeff finished for me.

Sunday morning at 7:00 A.M. the phone rang at my brother's house. "This is Micah, where's Jeff?" the curt voice asked. "He's sleeping." Micah's tone was even more abrupt. "Tell him calisthenics have already begun."

Daniel's fervent Sunday morning lecture, on the life and death of Christ, explained why Christians have collided with Moonies theologically. Jesus, Daniel said, had been rivaled by John the Baptist, denied by his father, unloved by his natural family, his mother and father were not even united. "They took him to Jerusalem and left him three days. His brothers didn't like him. His mother didn't understand him. Eventually the priesthood and finally his disciples deserted him."

I watched Barb; she was crying.

"Jesus's death," Daniel said, "wasn't a celebration but a lonely and ugly human tragedy and the world was *not* saved by it."

It developed, of course, that because Jesus should have gone on to marry and found an Edenic family, now a new messiah must come to perform that rite. I waited for someone to say something further. No one did; the lecture left the matter hanging there. By now Barb had of course told us of a leader named Mr. Moon, a Korean evangelist, but we had little or no knowledge of Unification's specific theology. Would *he* fulfill such a marriage and "save" humanity? My generation wasn't used to the idea of a messiah on every street corner. Preposterous, I told myself. These people wouldn't believe anything like *that;* bland as their concepts seemed to be, they wouldn't embrace *that.*

But they certainly intended to make some changes in the world, by the way Daniel was getting carried away. "We could march into downtown Oakland, we could part the Bay like the Red Sea, we could explode the country. If our hearts are pure, everybody will be hit by us. Brothers and sisters, we're a battering ram; we can steamroll the world with love."

At last the undercurrent of manipulation and force was too much for the Quaker in me. I got up, rushed out, walked blindly up to Telegraph Avenue, sat on a wall, and cried. "I can't go back there," I kept saying to myself. "But I have to go back for Barb," I answered myself.

I managed to walk back as far as the car, and crawled in. All around me the raggle-taggle fleet of cars was loading up, taking off for another one of those frenzied ball games and female-basket-borne lunches.

Barb found me; without comment she came in and wordlessly put her arm around me.

"I come from a peaceable sect, Barb," I told her, "and I can't see how it's going to do the world any good to steamroll it with anything, let alone say that kind of oppression is love. At this house I can see how you support each other, I can feel it, but God preserve me from living in a city, a state, or a country run by you."

Without response, she drove us around by the house and Daniel, waiting alone at the curb, got in beside her. I told him how I felt; he didn't say too much, only that souls were numb and it took strong emotions to unfreeze them—"get them moving." He said he didn't have any problems at all with an autocratic, materialistic leadership.

At the park Daniel and I sat on a blanket and talked while the avid kickball game resumed; Daniel kept a sharp eye on it, applauding audacity and verve. "Look at Jeff. He's a fighter, he doesn't turn his back on the ball. We watch the visitors, see which ones show a strong spirit."

Good God, I felt suddenly, I *am* in a religious boot camp.

Still, Daniel was warm and appealing, this bright, attractive, well brought-up young zealot come of what he said was a perfection-driven Jewish family (he couldn't explain why so many Moon members were Jewish, only said the biggest fear of Jewish parents was that their children were turning Christian). Daniel had gone to an eastern university, had been an athlete, hung out with a bunch of rock musicians, gambled. "But I was always searching."

He came west and eventually joined the Family, then a lonely band struggling under the Korean woman, Onni. "I've always wanted to do the very hardest thing." (I sensed that Daniel, like Barb, was a continuous self-tester.) "In that little Family I was the spiritual 'baby,' I was given the worst jobs and I accepted them, but inside I was seething. My biggest necessity was to subdue myself." Daniel said his greatest inspiration was Moon himself; he indicated he'd prefer to be involved with the eastern leadership. "But the thing I really want most to do is have a family and rear my children in Principle."

Daniel had held two responsible jobs and, though not actually trained for either of them, had apparently been very successful. "The Family gave me courage," he said simply. But the jobs were hard on him in other ways: "I'm with people who don't live by Principle. What do they talk about at the office water cooler? The secretaries," the wistful young Puritan confided in me.

"And how does your family feel about all this?"

"My father's come to accept me with as much respect as anybody he knows."

But at mention of his father, I noticed the challenge of the kickball game grew overpowering; Daniel suddenly jumped from the blanket and made a mad dash into the melee.

Somewhat uncomfortably, Martha sidled into his place. When Daniel returned they spoke of their similar upbringings; Martha said she'd gone to Vassar and Daniel was surprised. Startled, I realized these people apparently really knew little about each other, presumably had little interest in each other's precult lives.

After lunch our small groups met once more. Sitting upstairs in a circle on the floor around Martha, we touched, in a guarded way, on the occult, on spiritualism. Principle, I'd learned, taught that every person has a Spirit Man. At the point of physical death, the spirit continues. I waited to discover if there were a selection process at that end, and could discern none. Fair enough, I thought, that's a plus-one for them. Now Martha said the Family didn't believe in the Immaculate Conception.

Plus-two, I concluded. But then someone alluded to clouds of Satanic spirits separating us from God, and I wiped out all my mental plusses and thought wistfully, *If only they wouldn't substitute their own impossible mythologies for the ones they are throwing out.*

The weekend was winding up downstairs in a series of testimonials; the young people who spoke were illumined by a very special beauty.

"Barb, I'm going now."

"Wait, I'll have to ask Micah if it's all right."

"Barb, it doesn't matter *what* Micah says, I've promised to be back at Scott's and I'm leaving."

We embraced people, said good-bye. As we went out, Daniel was shouting, "If our spiritual ears were really open, our individual heart-beats would be like a roar. . . ."

Next day, on our way down to Santa Cruz and the Radical House to pick up Barb's remaining things, she jumped out at the gas station to invite the young gas station attendant to visit the Dana Street house.

The Radical House lived up to my previous forebodings; it was a depressing place, disheveled and dark. As we carried Barb's boxes down from the attic, regret tore at me.

On the excursion back from Santa Cruz, Jeff, Barb, and I talked of nothing but the Family; any other conversation with her was impossible. Jeff, smarting and frustrated, presented reasoned and temperate arguments against coercion, evasion, authoritarianism, and the limitations such practices placed on individual growth and understanding, just as Doug had done.

I raised with Barb the question about the way some of the Oakland church leaders had, in a small-world coincidence, come into my brother's law partner and possibly compromised their integrity in trying to buy a small college campus. Scott's law partner had said to him, "I refused their business. I'm worried."

Whatever had happened, Barb said firmly, was all right. No member of the leadership would do wrong, go against the interest of the whole.

"But how do you *know?*" Jeff persisted, close to desperate. "They don't tell you anything they don't want you to know. How do you account for the fact that Moon's been so wealthy ever since he's been into his religious movement?"

"I know how sacrificially he lives," Barb answered serenely. "And besides, we believe our leaders are closer to perfection and deserve the best."

Impatient snort from Jeff.

Talking about Daniel, Barb said he'd been in the hospital with an injured back. "Did the Family pay for his hospitalization?" I asked.

"Oh, no," she answered guilelessly, "they asked his family to."

"But, Barb, he has a good job, he turns over everything he earns to the Family so he's penniless, and then they won't even pay for his hospital bills," I exploded.

Maybe, she retreated, she'd been mistaken.

Late that night, we drove her from Scott and Lauriel's to Dana Street. Still struggling to make myself somehow understand, I don't remember much about that parting.

Jeff and I got home after a grueling trip. All the way back we compared notes and shook our heads over our occasional responsiveness to the heady brotherhood, the hopeful values expressed, the sense of limitless individual possibilities. If you stayed in it long, that atmosphere could suck you right in, we concluded. After that weekend, I tried never to forget that fact.

Once more we dissected and tried to comprehend how the high energy, the purposeful excitement, above all, the continuous if self-conscious encouragement and "love" could prove irresistible. We didn't have an answer; there was something overridingly mysterious about it.

We carried Barb's boxes downstairs and stored them. It was months before I could make myself go through those college belongings, wash them and hang them in her closet. They hung there, untouched, for three years.

A few days after getting back, I tried to write Barb my religious views and the philosophy and ethical system Ray and I had tried to rear her with. I ended the struggling, long letter:

Desperate people make desperate choices, Barbo. I believe you were desperate when you went to Dana Street. Your world had been shifting crazily for several years and you were so hurt, so confused, so alone you wanted anything which promised that pain's quitting. But when desperate people grab causes, religions, their own need brings harshness, assertiveness into their beliefs and ways of treating people. And if they come to religion out of a desperate grasping, don't they turn into zealots? And aren't zealots arrogant, relentless, hostile? Don't they feed on their own feelings of election and someone else's damnation? I know you too well and love you too much to feel that's the kind of person you want to become, Barbo.

In early December 1973 I fell and broke my right arm. One morning Ray and I were in the den downstairs, where I was forlornly holding my cast and he was fighting flu, when the telephone rang. It was Barb. "We're in Portland, at Good Samaritan emergency ward. We've been selling flowers up the Willamette valley for a week, sleeping in the van in the cold, and Evey, our team leader, is really sick. We need a place to come in out of the rain for four or five days, a place to put Evey to bed."

Faced with our own troubles; our joy was mingled with dismay. Hugging Barb with one arm at the door, however, all things seemed suddenly more possible, though I knew by now there would be few concessions made for a one-armed natural mother and a sick natural father.

The six team members insisted on bedding Evey down in the coldest bedroom. ("It's the biggest—she's the leader," Barb said firmly.) The four girl team members were to sleep on sleeping bags at Evey's feet; the two boys would sleep in a nearby bedroom.

With Evey deposited, coughing, with us to soup-carry and pill-administer (aided by faithful phone calls that team members made to Evey every few hours), out into the dank, blowing cold the team rushed to its flower selling. Barb showed me her arms. They were hard and muscular: "... In order to save time we load up with as many bundles as we can so we won't have to run back to the van very often."

Every day they sold all day in the Portland downtown and industrial areas, then, as night came on, they hit the taverns, not returning to the house till 2:00 A.M. In conversations at breakfast it was clear they had developed a hard-boiled commercial attitude; people who'd been drinking, for instance, bought more easily, and men were the best targets for flower-selling girls.

It was around this breakfast table that I first heard the word "chutzpa"—Yiddish for high spirits, effrontery—applied to my daughter. Barb, it seems, was without hesitation or fear. She'd gotten illegally into high-rises and corporate headquarters, talking with bank presidents and industrial moguls all over the country. "But lawyers," her teammates teased her, "she's got them all figured out—she's got a sure touch with them. They always buy from her."

There were elements of the team's hardheaded canniness that—for a so-called religious movement—astounded and concerned us, to say the least; there were other elements which absolutely enraged us. (When asked at the hospital emergency ward if they had any money, the team said no so that Evey was treated as an indigent patient. At that time, by their own smirking admission, they had $3,000 in the van.)

As she recovered, I had a chance to get to know Evey better. I came to love her. She was a Detroit lawyer's daughter from a liberal political family, had been educated at the University of Michigan, was a skilled weaver and craftsperson, had spent a summer digging and cement-laying in Two Sun Arcosanti, Paolo Soleri's famous city project in the southwest. The side Evey showed us was bright, warm, idealistic, and infinitely faithful. No matter how heavy-lidded and dull-eyed with fever she was, every morning at five she crawled out of bed to have prayer meeting in the living room with her team; she ate breakfast with them when she could hardly whisper. Over my protest, on the blowiest day of them all, she went downtown to buy a dress to take back to Onni, the Oakland leader.

Mr. Moon came to Portland in the spring of 1974. Ray went to hear him at the Hilton Hotel. Well-dressed young followers were everywhere, some of them as bodyguards. After a time of listening to that excited karate chop (even given the fact that the Korean language is explosive, Moon's style is fanatic), my understated husband with his quiet, self-contained way, went out into the park blocks to walk in the dark for an hour.

That Sunday he wrote to Barb:

Dear Barby,

It's been a long time since we've seen you—since last February. We miss you very much. Telephone calls are no substitute for seeing you in person—although they help.

I often think of the good times we had when you, Doug, and Jeff were living at home with us and, later, when you came home from Santa Cruz. You were always so lively, sensitive, so tender, so vital, so talented. I'm afraid that you're now having all these capacities thwarted, stunted, and sacrificed. It doesn't seem right that an individual's capabilities shouldn't be encouraged to develop and flourish.

I remember your many searching questions about our society and about your relation to it. Your conceptions were often perceptive. Many of them stemmed from an assumption of the rights of individuals to freely question, discuss, and criticize, and to fully exercise the individual right of choice of social and political leadership and to hold that leadership fully accountable for carrying out the responsibilities of leadership. It doesn't seem right to me that your views in these matters should now be sacrificed to an unquestioning loyalty to, an unquestioning acceptance of mandates from self-designated leaders.

You could reply to my feelings of the unrightness of your present allegiance by saying that it's necessary to accomplish the great objectives of remaking our society so that it will be a better one. But, honey, I can't help but question whether the ends, the purposes, or the objectives, however worthy, ever, ever justify means, devices, or procedures which are not *wholly* consistent with the ends sought.

One further thought. Loneliness is a terrible trial, and the last two years you had more than your share at Santa Cruz. But fear of loneliness or separateness from others shouldn't be a basis, even an unconscious basis, for accepting a warmly comfortable in-group if such acceptance threatens the integrity of your character and personality.

I implore you to use your intelligence to confront courageously those realities to which I've referred and I'm confident that, if you do, the you we knew and we all love so much will survive the present testing. I'm confident because of my faith in you and because what I've said is motivated only by my love for you and for the truth.

As ever, Dad.

On a hot afternoon that summer of 1974 I went out to Marysville Rest Home to see Aunt Edna. She'd been the kids' beloved adopted aunt when we'd lived in the old neighborhood. There she sat in her wheel-chair, erect, pink-cheeked, bright blue eyes, those little black braids still coiled over each ear. Her face lit up in the same old Irish way.

On her bedstead was a snapshot of our kids. Instantly she wanted to know all about them.

"And what did you say Barbie was doing?"

"She's in a . . . she's in a religious community, Edna."

"Well, what does she do there?" the bewildered old voice asked.

"She ... well, mostly she sells flowers to raise money for the church."

"Sells flowers? What does that have to do with a church?"

"I don't know. Not much."

"Oh, Betty, she was such a dear little girl; I loved her so. I can still see her tagging along with Doug and Jeff."

Heavy with memories of better times, I went away. Underneath all Ray's and my busyness, the fact of Barb never left us.

I was beginning to be afraid of the changes in Barb. I felt like we hadn't seen her in an eon of time. True, we had these occasional bright telephone calls from around the country and the occasional cards that expressed closeness. But the behavior belied the messages. Was she rebelling against us? Doug had not seemed rebellious. When Jeff had gone through rebellion, he'd come out swinging and we'd known what was happening to him. Why couldn't we have a chance to be with Barb, really talk with her, see if we couldn't get to her inner feelings? Why did we have to be left with these Hallmark cards that expressed religious fervor but told us virtually nothing about what she was doing, and successfully prevented true relating?

I didn't know then that one of the tormenting things cult parents deal with is exactly these expressions of mixed feelings. Love and loyalty, on the one hand, walking along with a never-come-home, hands-off behavior.

About then, a good friend asked me, "Do you still love her?"

"Of course," I flashed fiercely. Then reality overwhelmed me. "I know I love her as she used to be."

Nothing is more tragic than a familiar stranger.

There seemed no way to recover from a bitter sense of shock and grief. And all of us were growing increasingly bitter, too, at the organization that had wrought so much change in Barb.

Christmas of 1974, we persuaded Barb to let us fly her up to Portland. It wasn't a good Christmas. She was uptight, something harsh, defensive, hard coiled in her. So were we. She couldn't leave alone the subject of what she was doing, even when we pleaded with her, even when Jeff, in rage, rushed out of the room saying he didn't want to talk about it ever again. "Please," I pleaded, "let's just *accept* our different points of view, try to enjoy just being together." Ray, driven by Barb's insistence, finally told her how repelled he was by what he was seeing on TV and in the newspapers of the methods and views of her leader.

We went to the Kah-Nee-Tah Indian reservation to escape the travesty of a merry Christmas. One afternoon in the lodge lobby she began to read to me the biography of Mr. Moon. Her voice took on a loud, unnatural sing-song which made me shrink and caused me to wonder what *was* her true psychology.

After the evening of harshest exchange—she was trying her best to be patient but underneath I could tell there burned a hard fury—I woke in the night, head in hands.

"I can't handle this," I whispered to Ray.

He rubbed my back, replied, "While we're in this perpetual tizzy about her we should be worrying about Doug making himself stick it out in Columbus and Jeff without a job in that lonely, TB-incubating apartment."

At the end of the vacation, the four of us went to a basketball game and Barb held my arm, saying, "I want so much for you and Dad to understand and it hurts so much when you don't, I can hardly bear it." She seemed more human then, she seemed close.

Yet at the same game, when Ray leaned around Jeff and asked if she'd got her teeth fixed, she coolly said, no, would Ray pay if she did?

"Well, you bring them in a lot of money, why can't *they* pay?" Ray countered.

She struggled briefly, then replied matter-of-factly, "Because I don't want to ask them."

Next day she made phone calls down to Family people; her voice was eager talking to them. I knew then, and with finality, she was arranging to go home. After she'd called, she wrote Christmas cards at the kitchen table as I moved around the utility room. For the first time in our two lives together, I felt she and I had nothing to say to each other.

One early morning the following spring I was on a car repair errand in a downtown Portland shiny-damp with new day's beginning. I pulled up at an intersection. A confused and very mad-looking seagull stood in the middle of the asphalt. He couldn't seem to fly—his body heaved with effort. No luck. Comically he waddled from this side to that side, dodging cars. Finally a huge truck pulled around the corner and, terror giving impetus, the gull ran pellmell for the sidewalk. But he "stubbed" his "toe" getting up on the curb.

If Barb were here, she'd probably have jumped right out and gone to the rescue, I laughed to myself.

Suddenly I had an overwhelming memory of the little girl Barb standing over a blob of gristle and flesh that was a baby wren just fallen out of the carport rafters. "Don't take it in, Barb," I'd tried to head her off, not wanting her to see it die. But stubbornly she had, had fixed it a box, got up at all hours to feed it bread soaked in milk. Soon it had waked us in the morning with its triumphant chirping; she'd taught it to fly.

Near the art museum two college girls in tight jeans romped along with stretched canvases on top of their heads on the way to the museum school to paint. They looked exuberant, happy. They reminded me of the old Barb.

What, I wondered, driving home, would I *do* with memories like that if things didn't clear up? How could I bear to carry them around with me the rest of my days?

The summer of 1975 I went to the International Women's Year conference in Mexico City as a representative of the Oregon Governor's Commission for Women. We were going to take our vacation in Mexico afterward, so Ray came with me to part of the conference too. The evening before we left, Ray went to the grocery store. In the parking lot an earnest, fresh-faced, appealing young woman was selling candles for Mr. Moon.

"Would you want one?" she asked Ray.

"No, thank you."

"Would you care to donate, then?"

"No," Ray said to her, so stricken he could hardly get the words out, "I've already donated a daughter."

On the way back from Mexico City, we stopped off in Berkeley to see my father, my brother, his wife, and Barb.

Ray and I had especially hoped for time alone with Barb, but by now her priorities were clear and I, for one, was no longer willing to make her guilty about them. "If you have a Family conflict and can't spend the night, say so," I told her on the phone at the airport. "We're not here to make you hassles."

We spent a lunch and a beautiful afternoon alone with her, though. We drove up on the heights above Berkeley and looked with her at the land and the water she loved. We talked of what she was doing, which was riding the new Bay Area Rapid Transit trying to win converts "because right now we need people more than money." When she'd get home in the later afternoon, she was cook for the house and had to make supper for thirty or forty people. She was helping manage the Dana Street house.

She showed us a photograph of herself wearing an historic Korean blouse given her by her beloved Onni for being a top fundraiser. But she showed it quietly, with no braggadacio, always her way.

She was sun-tanned, rose-skinned, strong and happy-looking with her soft long brown hair cascading down her back from the crown of her head.

And, close to the personal resources we couldn't threaten, she seemed marvelously serene with us, didn't argue, didn't insistently return to the tormenting issues which divided us.

But she did have a quiet talk with Ray. "If you reject what I'm doing, then you reject me, don't you?" She listened carefully as Ray explained that no, we could never reject her, that there was a difference between the two.

She drove with my family to the airport. The family conversation was casual. She and I sat close, listening. I had little to say. At the airport we said good-bye to my brother and his wife, then Barb and I hugged each other and for a long, long time I cried and she simply held me and let me do it.

A strange healing about her filled me; I longed for it to be permanent.

For weeks after we got back, I kept thinking of my daughter Barb, of her eyes looking out over that golden bay land, of her laughing when I said someday we'd like a grandchild, and her "Never fear. I'm going to get married, you'll see."

She sent a letter to us early that August. It came from Boonville.

Dearest mom and dad,
Hello from the sprouts—spiritual and vegetable—in Boonville.
I had such a special two days with you. I really felt like we reached a purer level of trust and sharing.

The past two weeks I've been here on the farm. Haven't seen the city since you left.

The days are so rich and cleansing and sincere up with Micah and Janet. We run a week-long seminar and then, of course, weekend programs. So many people—over 250 last weekend. I'm now leading a group and have so much to learn. I really love the new Family members, searching, willing, grateful people.

My own life's been an explosion of amazing discoveries; God has really grown close and personal. Whether I'm praying under the night clouds on the mountain top or helping the younger Family manage to wake up in the early morning or maybe just leapfrogging in the squash patch, I feel that I'm beginning to see the reality and magnitude and perfect love of God and the way He shows it through brothers and sisters.

I have such a longing to throw away the complications a false life creates. Life is joy in God and the relationships He gives us here.

If you could just experience these days your whole world would be transformed into hope, relief and thanksgiving. Please come some day.

Love, Lael.

I believed I would never go up to Boonville with her. But reading that letter, it hurt less that she was there.

My last visit to Barb turned out to be a nonvisit.

She didn't come home the Christmas of 1975. She phoned from the Washington Street center one evening in late spring 1976 nearly a year after we'd seen her in San Francisco to say they were having a parents' weekend and would we make every effort to come. No way was Ray going to go, and he said so. For almost the first time, Barb got openly mad and said he didn't have the courage. Ray calmly replied, "Barb, you're simply going to have to accept that we don't agree with the movement and make the best out of our love for yourself."

When she pressed me, I was briefly torn because she'd made no real overtures to us for months and because I sensed she was somehow under heavy personal pressure. But conscience and reason took over; I, too, didn't want to go back into the midst of a group many of whose beliefs and ways I now had such disrespect and repugnance for. So I told her I couldn't see what coming down now would add to the weekend I'd spent at the seminar three years ago. But I did say that I hoped to see her in early summer and was planning a trip just for the purpose of visiting her, my dad, and Scott and Lauriel.

When, very crisp, she hung up, Ray and I shared the same tormented instinct: she was about to give up on us. (Our instinct was right, as the end of chapter one indicates.)

The parents' weekend was subsequently called off.

Yet when I called her a little later about my coming down she seemed pleased. We had several long-distance conversations making the arrangements.

I phoned her from my brother's Berkeley house Friday night at eleven; we agreed Lauriel and I would meet her at ten the next morning at the Washington Street house and we'd spend the day in Berkeley together.

I indicated I hoped to see her alone in San Francisco on Sunday.

A combination of longing and fear propelling me, I rang the bell of the Washington Street center Saturday morning. Pleasantly greeted, I was invited into the hall. Saying only that Barb was not there, a young woman handed me a note.

It still didn't dawn on me that Barb wasn't just delayed until I stepped back out on the porch to read the note. Her message indicated that after she'd talked to me the night before, she'd been called out of the state on behalf of a Church friend. In shock, I held the note thinking over and over, *I could never have done this to MY mother.*

It was a crazy thing to just stand there with a simple-minded refrain like that racing through me, but crisis brings out funny reactions in people. I realized the deep bond between mothers and daughters. I was part of my mother, Barb was somehow a part of me; without her I felt lost and finished.

I was crying when Lauriel came up and joined me; her tears joined mine.

"What would you like to do?" she asked understandingly.

"Let's drive to the coast, get away from here."

Instead, we spent the day wandering the city. That day I didn't deal with anger so much—fury at the group which was consciously, I was sure, keeping us apart, resentment at Barb for letting or wanting it to happen. Instead I dealt with indescribable feelings of separation, of wonder at a once-deep bond, strangely failed, of failure in myself that it had strangely happened.

But next morning when I got up, a very clear vision had emerged out of mystification, separation, loss. Whoever's fault it was, mine, ours, hers, theirs, by not being on that porch Barb was telling me she did not want to be with me. She was telling me there was no place in that world for me, for us. She was telling me that's where she intended to stay.

Face it. Face it and finally make yourself get used to it, was the grim resolve forming in me.

I heard nothing from her the rest of the week I was in California. I returned home. The days, the weeks wore on, and no call came from her. Ray got upset and started to phone the northern California centers to ascertain where they'd "put her" and try to find out if she were all right. As he got the usual runaround, his tone grew more and more insistent.

Finally Barb telephoned and confirmed that she had been back in Ohio with Amos trying to get Michele away from the deprogrammers. She told us something about deprogramming, as it had been described to her, so of course it sounded wretched to us. She didn't indicate why she and Amos had returned empty-handed. She sounded friendly and regretful; I laid no guilt on her. My hunch was that she'd been told to call by some leader concerned over Ray's determined efforts to reach her.

After three and a half years, done with charade, I finally took her clothes out of her closet, packed or gave them away, cleared her room. At the time I felt it was a numb and mechanical act in simple acknowledgment of reality.

I wasn't aware then how stubborn I could be.

These visits, these nonvisits, were just the tip of our iceberg.

It's strange how cult membership can devastate families more than the traditional rebellions and distances. It's partly, I believe, because the tragic fragmentation is often so sudden and so cloaked in mystery, one side knowing *both* questions and answers, one side only the questions.

From 1973 to 1977, we saw Barb seven times, four at home (once overnight and two of these visits made with her flower team) and three in California. Although Barb was in our lives like a permanent presence, we grew aware that we were in her life only in the most marginal way. Our knowledge of her was gleaned from irregular phone calls from far-flung states (we could seldom ever reach her by phone) or from cards which spoke of love and concern in cultish clichés and, as they grew more infrequent, came to have an inauthentic tone.

We knew that after she gave up her typing job at the Berkeley

Forest Service in the summer of 1973, she became a full-time fund-raiser until August 1974. The last months of 1974 she appeared to be on Bay Area streets witnessing. From January to June, 1975, she was fund-raising in sweeping guerrilla van expeditions around the country, but when we saw her in July she was cooking at Dana Street and witnessing on Bay Area subways. Shortly after that visit, Barb was sent to Boonville as a staff member for six months, and by then we were aware that Boonville was an isolated indoctrination farm camp for new inductees. She left Boonville in early 1976 and spent the rest of the year selling roses around the country, largely, it seemed to us, in the upper midwest and Canada. From time to time she seemed to be on brief "detached service." She apparently worked with Daniel on planning an energy conference for prestigious scientists (with no indication to the public at first of who was sponsoring it). At one point we thought she might be used in the cult's New York City newspaper because she told us she'd gone to the airport to pick up the Tokyo editor who was visiting Onni. We wondered if they might not train her as a paralegal after sending her east with Amos in that role. But eventually we realized our ideas were grandiose: no one apparently got training that cost the cult money, least of all the women (though Dr. Durst did encourage Barb's poetry).

If she stayed transfixed by her illusions, she was going to end up a forty-year-old flower seller, we concluded in despair. And apparently loving it. (Her phone calls from around the country indicated occasional fatigue, even cloaked exhaustion, but everything was customarily "wonderful." "I had to get my fighting spirit from somewhere," she once laughed: "I got it from you.")

Out of our continuous unclarity about her life, the flower selling became the one constant. Except for the big question, why would she do it?

Obviously sacrificing all forms of comfort, reputation, health, and safety, she and her teams endured such hardships as a mute testimony to absolute, dedicated belief, we had to conclude. Later we were to know that Barb had experienced on the road with her Oakland teams close, loyal, and unselfish companionship, an urgent sense of purpose, the high excitement of escapades and problems solved, astonishing money success. Her own moneymaking ability was reflected in a 1975 award given her as top fund-raiser on the West Coast. In our early days of shock at the commercial street-and-bar-run game that her religious "vocation" was turning out to be, we'd figured she was bringing in thousands. But it wasn't till later we knew her daily average had grown to be about $400. Nor did we have any idea how much her total earnings were in that four-year phase. (As she later said matter-of-factly in an interview, "I was earning substantially more than my father, who's a lawyer.")

We had less than a clear picture of the national fund-raising setup of the aggressive Bay Area group, and didn't realize that Barb was on a special kind of national team that won both the admiration and opprobrium of its own brother and sister cultists. Only later were we to know that under Oakland's Onni Durst, cult fund-raising had reached a new height of profit. While Barb had said the West Coast was "different," we'd intuited that to mean less pseudomilitary, more comfortable with men and women working together, than the austere eastern infrastructure. We didn't know that Onni, in recognition of her great productiveness, was permitted a kind of covert autonomy. Unaware of this "cult within a cult" phenomenon, we also didn't know that Onni had developed a special brand of "guerrilla" fund-raising in which she boldly sent out her hard-driving teams to invade the territories of other Moon centers and lieutenants. It was on one of these sweeping Oakland-based teams—going under the name of New Education Development, or N.E.D., but more commonly called by other Moonies the "Oakland Raiders"—that Barb was put. Rising to assistant team leader after the kidnapping of Yacov, she was made a team leader.

When she was at the centers we noticed that her handwriting was crabbed, small, as though it reflected a hemmed-in life and spirit; out on the road, it was large, flowing, expansive. "Going back to the center after a flower trip" was "like a dark curtain coming down," she later admitted.

Life on the road was a melange of hairwashes in café rest rooms; laundry that could only be done on infrequent days; begged or donated meals, munching whatever came to hand; chanting before morning selling "runs"; prayer conditions faithfully said at six in the morning, never forgetting Moon and the Dursts; sprinting alone miles, flower-burdened, through factories, office buildings, and dangerous midnight taverns on tough city streets, no matter the weather; flower pickups at airports or bus stations; horrifying close-call van accidents; police encounters; brief hours sleeping huddled in freezing vans or shivering on street corners—all a mad journey filled with hope and ecstasy and hurry because apparently Father Moon had revealed precise timetables when, event by event, month by month, she must win the world for him.

Both her brothers had suffered from Barb's startling exit from our family. Doug earned a graduate degree in public affairs journalism and began his first newspaper job in Michigan. Jeff graduated from the University of Washington, went to Kentucky with Vista, and returned to work in its legal services program in Seattle. Time moved along for them as, in their different ways, they tried to reconcile their sister.

Doug wrote in 1976, "Well, she got out in this world, got slapped around, experienced so much alienation and cruelty, a person like her had to find a refuge. And sometimes who can blame her?" With Barb's defection from our family, Jeff had lost a good friend: "There are a lot of kids into cults and with some I expect it's permanent. I was depressed for three months after I got back from being with Barb at Christmas, but I'm over it. I figure somehow she's all right."

Ray's and my lives moved on without Barb, too. Ray continued to battle for the Oregon environment: the salmon of the great blue Columbia river, the preservation of the coastal estuary, the quality of air. My second book, *The Forge and the Forest*, came out in 1975.

For me there were many sleepless nights. Repeatedly I told myself if there's a rite of passage for adolescents, there's a rite of passage for parents too. Children close up the inevitable wounds of their rearing; parents close up the unexpected wounds of their children's departing. Stunned and grieved as I was by what a short interlude family life had been, I'd lecture myself that life had to go on, that perhaps it was more realistic to face it as the individuals we were.

With the help of such self-addressed sermons, I tried to accept that our own daughter had elected in an especially wounding way to exchange her natural family for one she apparently preferred. (Mercifully, we weren't yet aware we were "Satanic.")

But considerations over and above simple rejection haunted us. If she didn't want us, she *ought* to be allowed to have herself, she *ought* to be her own person.

What of her ability to protect herself when ordered into strange streets, into strange factories and taverns? Small and vulnerable, how safe could she be in the city after midnight moving among tough and often dissolute people? What of her sensitivity and the talents that flowed from it, the paintings, photographs, the poems and journalism articles, even the inscriptions in books? Shouldn't she be able, if she chose, to exercise these? What of her former curiosity, her aliveness to everything; what of the intellectual blinders she seemed to be wearing? What of her right to choose where she'd live? We dreaded the day we might get a call: "I'm off to join those long lines at Barrytown," or "I'm off to Sri Lanka or Zaire." Or, worst of all, "I'm ordered to Seoul to be married to someone I've never seen before."

What of her inability to take care of her health? We feared that if her life continued on a similar course, she'd be a physical wreck in a matter of years. In this area we maintained a dogged sense of responsibility for Barb, especially when we realized the cult took little. Precult, she'd had a possible endocrine problem, which in the cult went untreated but resolved itself. Hoping at first that if we didn't pay for dentists and glasses, she'd have a more realistic understanding of what the cult was all about, eventually we capitulated, unable to see our own flesh and blood in that kind of want. Sometimes we heard after the fact about strep throats, blood infections from rose thorns, concussions from van accidents, seven-day fasts while working eighteen hours a day. From what Barb said it was clear her treatments were always far too short-term and sketchy. When she got a hairline fracture below her right knee—"from sprinting on pavements too much"—she did share its current status with us, since that was about the time she was calling us often to find Yacov and Evey. So far as we could determine, she had had an X ray at an osteopath's who pointed out the break and told her to stay off it, but, as leader of her team, Barb had taken no time off at all. "It hurt for a couple of weeks, then it went away."

We finally came to experience a whole second dimension of sorrow, too. More and more information was beginning to come to us from the national media about Moon and his cult. Not only was Barb herself caught, she was dragging in others, too.

Yet even with increased information, we didn't hear of the concept of coercive persuasion. That she'd been pressured and changed was apparent. (Ray always pondered hypnosis, but I'd been unable to accept that theory.) But that she'd been subjected to certain clearly defined and self-conscious processes that had made her incapable of extricating herself, hadn't occurred to us. As to parental intervention, all we knew of was kidnapping, something that in conscience we opposed as against the law.

So much was unknown to us, until a phone call in late summer 1976.

Betty:
Deciding to Take Action

"An act of love that fails is just as much a part of the divine life as an act of love that succeeds, for love is measured by its fullness, not by its reception."
—Unknown source

SEPTEMBER, 1976.
    A stranger's voice on the phone asked Ray if he could come to a meeting of parents of cult people being held at the University of Portland. Ray sparred briefly with Anne Greek to make sure she wasn't some spokesperson for cult indoctrination; no, she let him know, she and her husband, Adrian, had two fine young people caught in Unification they fervently wished weren't there.

    Anne told Ray she and Adrian had just got back from a visit to their daughter, Sheryl, at the San Francisco Washington street center and Barb had spent so much time with them one night as hometown denizens that, Anne told Ray quietly, "I couldn't help but feel she was in need of genuine love."

The Greeks' other young person in the cult was Phil, who had been a Stanford honors student before Evey Eden, aided by Barb, had talked Phil into the group.

Ray couldn't go to the University of Portland meeting, but I went and heard Father Kent Burtner, an engaging and knowledgeable young Catholic priest from Eugene, speak on cults and on Unification in particular. I met the Greeks and very much liked them; there is an unspoken strong bond which quickly develops among parents of young people in cults.

A second parents' meeting was held later that month, where we heard young Chris Rudie of Salem describe his experiences coming out of the Unification cult. He'd gotten a frostbitten foot selling flowers in Michigan the same weekend he'd heard that Moon had ostensibly spent $4,000 on fish bait for a sport-fishing weekend. After he was sent back to the big eastern cult center at Barrytown, Chris had developed other health problems, which kept getting worse because he was not able to obtain proper medical treatment. He planned to get out, go home until he recovered, then come right back to the cult. His own trinity head gone, Chris tricked a training center nurse into faking him a pass out of Barrytown and after a series of moneyless adventures ended up stranded overnight in New York City. He finally got word to his family, who sent him plane fare to Salem. A few days later, into Chris's life walked Ted Patrick, one of the country's first deprogrammers. A few days after that, with friends and family present, Chris "came out" of the cult.

When I asked Chris Rudie how someone who had been in for three and a half years might be feeling right then, he answered flatly, "On some level of her being she wants out." It was the first ray of hope I'd had about Barb in nearly two years.

At this meeting we first heard of the theory of mind control as applied to cults, and had several good books recommended to us, including Robert Jay Lifton's classic on coercive persuasion in China, *Thought Reform and the Psychology of Totalism.* We also got our first clear explanation of deprogramming and a sketchy mention of *ex parte* conservatorships (Chris had not been a conservatee). We heard names which were to become household words to us: Wayne Howard, Mike

Trauscht, Gary Scharff, Joe Alexander, Freedom of Thought Foundation, and others.

We went out into the hot sun of a late summer afternoon.

"What did you think?" I asked Ray cautiously.

"I thought it was very interesting," he cautiously replied.

We talked about it for a while; I wasn't yet able to describe to him the sudden spark, lit by that comment of Chris's, that now began to live in me: *I want to do something.*

As we read Lifton's book together, especially chapter 22, Barb kept leaping out of those words over and over. Ray and I kept looking at each other, repeating in the grip of discovery, "That's *exactly* what she was like," "That's what *she* said," "That's what happened to *her.* . . ." Someone had put into words the very essence of our daughter, her experience, our experiences with her.

In October, at the parents' meeting, as we listened to a horrifying description by a young ex-member of a sick and violent small cult in a Portland suburb, our sense grew that something new and strange and inimical to American values and practices was selectively being introduced into our society. The trouble was, who would believe it? And who would do anything about it? The parents' meeting in November brought us more names to add to our growing list of western people working with ex-cultists. In December a young Quaker came to talk to us about American political ties to South Korea's Park Chung-Hee regime and possible Moon ties to Park.

But Ray and I were stalled. *Ex parte* conservatorships (where only the petitioners are present in court) had to lodge a long time in Ray's scrupulous legal conscience before a decision could surface, and I remained concerned, if we did anything drastic, for Barb's psychology, by now a very unknown quantity to me.

Saturday afternoon, December 18, 1976, we were working in the den when the phone rang.

"Mrs. Underwood, this is Evey."

Evey . . . Evey. I pulled myself in a hurry out of my absentminded fog. Evey Eden! Hadn't we just heard the electrifying news at the last anticult parents' meeting that Evey and another big Oakland leader, Yacov (Jeff Scales) had left the cult in some startling way? Evey who'd had pneumonia at our house, the young woman I'd come to love . . . Jeff Scales, whom I'd guessed a year ago was someone Barb had a special feeling for, even if such emotions were *verboten* in the cult. (Why was there always that lift in her voice when she mentioned her team leader?)

"Evey!" I yelled. "Where are you? Are you all right?"

"Yes," she laughed reassuringly. "I'm fine. I'm here with Jeff Scales. We're at the Freedom of Thought Foundation rehab center in Tucson, Arizona. Our folks just brought both of us out of the church a week ago."

"Well, how *are* you?"

"Don't worry!" Evey had answered. Then she explained that she and Jeff had been deprogrammed, felt "liberated," "relieved," "wonderful."

Evey said softly, "Mrs. Underwood, I can read a book, *any* book; I can read a poem, I can go to a movie. But best of all, I can love *everybody*."

In that downstairs den on that peaceful Saturday afternoon, I shook apart, hearing that.

I turned the phone over to Ray while I went—in a state of total upheaval—to pull myself together from the waves of joyous hope and relief flooding me. Evey and Jeff were all right. It could happen to Barb too. She could be saying, "I feel relieved, liberated, wonderful...."

Ray hung up and, with agreement barely needing to be spoken between us, put in a call to Morton Eden, Evey's lawyer father in Detroit. Her dad, Evey had said, had gone all through it and could give Ray a first-hand account of what conservatorships entailed.

The instinct of anticult parents is to drop *everything* when another anticult parent calls; Morton Eden shoved back an evening engagement to take a lot of time with Ray on that phone call. They talked over the temporary guardianships granted in some states not only for the disabled and senile but for those thought to have been coercively handled, like certain cultists. Eden told Ray he had also had strong civil libertarian concerns but had been persuaded that if there were, indeed, a legal avenue available, those concerns were second to the advice that he'd been given in Washington, D.C.: "If you want your daughter let out, Mr. Eden, you're going to have to go get her."

Ray hung up. As far as I was concerned, I'd decided. But Ray's good judgment reminded me that all points had to be checked out and no final decisions could be made without them.

(That phone call had its wryly amusing elements, too. Morton Eden told Ray that Onni Durst, with Teresa, flew to Tucson to try to see Evey and Jeff when they were at the rehab center. At 11:00 P.M. on a December night, with several other Unification cultists, Onni and Teresa came out to the first rehab house—which the gutsy and devoted Alexanders finally had to vacate because of cult harassment—and Onni took her stand by the front door intercom to scream repeatedly, "Evey, Yacov, my children, come out, come out." . . . Morton Eden, rehab personnel, and ex-cultists finally came out on the steps while Jeff and Evey took refuge upstairs under the bed. Eden then had an altercation with the agitated Moonie leader, who announced that she was chosen by God. With Onni refusing to leave and the uproar continuing into the night, rehab personnel and Eden sent for the police. When the car arrived, like magic Onni stopped shouting and said sweetly, "Why, sir, wasn't I *invited?*" Before the cultists were finally taken away in handcuffs by the police, squad cars and a police helicopter had arrived, the helicopter keeping its beam on Onni at all times. Onni, and Teresa, and the others were held several hours in jail, and released on bond. A local judge later fined them for trespassing and disorderly conduct. As Evey later told the story to Ray, she was obviously still in shock at the unseemly public behavior of her recent leader.)

The next few days both Ray and I quivered with the tentative letting go of four tight years of anguish.

Soon we had in hand Jeff Scales's letters, his brief and perceptive comments: ". . . The cult exploits and prolongs the adolescent rebellion . . ." that warned us that family relations would be bound up in anything we did to try to get Barb out. In one letter he wrote, "We want you to know, Evey and I are absolutely in love with Barb and would do anything to help get her out." And after that, there were his calls with their cheerful matter-of-factness. "Don't worry. We'll find her."

Monday, December 20, 1976, Ray got in touch with Wayne Howard of Phoenix, Arizona. Lawyers Wayne Howard and Mike Trauscht were founders of the Freedom of Thought Foundation in Tucson, where the rehab center was located. Adventurous young barristers, they'd been working hard to get people out of mind control cults. Trauscht's aversion to cults had begun when, as an officer of Pima County, he'd gone to find someone in a group called The Body and found them eating out of garbage cans. Between Mike and Wayne they'd organized a group which would (1) obtain the conservatorship from the court; (2) find and pick up the cult person; (3) deprogram them, making liberal use of ex-cult people for steps 2 and 3; (4) provide a month or more of rehabilitation at a place in Tucson managed by the reliable Alexanders and Gary Scharff. Though the fee was costly, it included repeated "tries" till Barb could be personally served with conservatorship papers at a location under the court jurisdiction, rather a touchy problem with a nomad like her.

With Ray being the main one who had to face the sober realities of money, I got on the phone to Neil Maxwell in San Francisco for a long talk. He assured me "it would be the best money we'd ever spent" because the Tucson people were highly reliable, experienced, and "had the interests of the cult person at heart." In Ray's further conversations with Wayne Howard, the young lawyer showed no inclination to take financial advantage of us. We each talked with our fathers. Loyally, both backed us up. Reassured that if we paid well, other parents who couldn't afford it might have their chance as well, we then put money considerations aside.

I had one last problem to consider. Might this be too much for Barb, despite a previously reasonably sturdy psychology? A young medical consultant, on whom I placed much faith, listened for a while, slammed down his chair legs, and said simply, "Do it."

We talked with Doug, now transferred by his newspaper chain to its Washington, D.C., news bureau where he was doing first-rate congressional reporting, and with Jeff, by now working in a Seattle drug lab and beginning nurse's training. Both sons spelled out the same apprehensions we felt, came forth with penetrating questions, and concluded in compassion that we hadn't any other options. We didn't want to make them in any way responsible, but we did want them to know; their support was of inestimable importance to us.

A choice few good friends knew what was going on in our minds. "I think you have to do it," one of them summarized quietly.

On the night of December 22, we decided. We were going to go ahead.

After three or four days' delay waiting for forms to be sent us from Arizona, we filled out a background on Barb for Wayne Howard, and Ray filled out the form of agreement.

We were in it.

Meanwhile, we'd begun to have an unusual spate of calls from Barb in Michigan, where she was leading her team in the middle of blizzards. But unlike any time in the past, she told us how to reach her, where she was and where she was headed. Notably, she asked if we had heard from Yacov (Jeff) and Evey: "We know they're calling parents all over the country." As we tried to read whether she was on the hunt for Jeff and Evey to try to bring them back into the cult, or was signalling for us to help her get out, we said no—the first and only lie we told her. By her own choice, she said she wouldn't be home that Christmas.

The last instruction we'd gotten from Phoenix was to fly to San Francisco under assumed names. ("The cults sometimes have access to airlines manifests.") "Who shall you be?" I asked Ray.

"This is a new one to me," he allowed. "I don't know."

"Ivan Popodopolis?" I asked.

"Oh God, no," he groaned, "make it somebody I can think of in a hurry if I'm asked all of a sudden."

"Your grandfather," I decided.

"Yes," he answered absently, throwing shirts in a suitcase. "That's good."

On Monday, January 3, 1977, as the "George Trumans" we flew in the late afternoon to San Francisco. At the airport we met Wayne Howard, a dark, Hispanic-looking young guy with flashing smile, and handsome Babs Baer, wife of a southwest physician, who hoped to bring her son out of Unification. Also at the airport was midwesterner Stuart Lang, a slender gray eminence, survivor of a recent heart attack and surgery but here anyway to release his son Steve. Later to join us at the Emeryville Holiday Inn was Frances Rufty, the warm, colorfully southern lawyer wife of a small-town Carolinian lawyer-squire. She had come to find her daughter, "L'il Frances," the only non-Moonie sought, a Hare Krishna.

We piled into a rented car. Coming in beside me was the very Michele that Barb had gone to Ohio to "rescue." We'd once talked by phone, so I wasn't surprised by her high-pitched, precise voice saying out of the dark beside me, "Her name isn't Lael, it's Barb," and her second rapid-fire remark, "Guess how much money she's personally brought into the cult?" When I said I didn't know, Michele supplied, "It's moving toward two hundred fifty thousand dollars—a quarter of a million dollars by now." We were to learn more of the cult story of this blue-eyed young woman who'd been very close to Onni as shopping companion and secretary and could verify extravagant living. Michele had been urged by a cult leader to charm a Bay Area tycoon in the hopes of a big donation and to "be nice" to the cultist son of a wealthy South African. It had even been "suggested" that she get herself bogus-engaged to a cult man in order to collect money-jewelry promised her on her engagement.

Next morning began one of the strangest times of our lives. For Ray it was two intense days before he flew back to work; I stayed on nearly another week.

Tuesday, January 4, after a morning's delay when Howard failed to get early consideration from another court, the five parents, Wayne, Mike Trauscht and Larry Gumbiner, attractive recent ex-Moonie, went before Chief Judge Henry Rolph of the Superior Court of the City and County of San Francisco. In his chambers, request was made for *ex parte* conservatorships for our young people. After legalities by Mike and Wayne and an eloquent description of cult life, mind control and deprogramming by Larry Gumbiner, Ray was the first and very effective spokesperson for the parents, speaking largely of personality changes in Barb. Scientist Stuart Lang spoke with emotion. Babs Baer and Frances Rufty stated the cases for their young people well. Judge Rolph listened closely throughout and at the end granted us thirty-day conservatorships.

Endless tense hours of sitting around motel rooms followed. We were driven secretly from motel to motel while the young ex-cultists, who came and went with the deprogrammers and lawyers, tried to locate our four young people by overnight stakeouts in cars, even by surveillance from the house next door to the Washington Street center.

In dining rooms and motel halls we had fleeting conversations with rushed, secretive people. I snatched a few moments with a former Unification member who told me that when his father had had a serious heart attack, he was advised by a cult leader not to go see his father: "I would be doing the best thing for my family if I stayed away because I was responsible for my ancestors and the Family." Judy, a forthright, laughing young woman, had lost a $12,000 trust fund and family jewelry to the cult by lying to her parents. "I came out of deprogramming fighting," Judy declared.

Stuart Lang and I spent two days glued to a window just six blocks away from where young Steve Lang was witnessing but couldn't be picked up because of the interests of the other three. (Not a word of complaint from Stuart.) Babs Baer was mostly not with us because her son, Laurey, manager of the cult maintenance company, had to be personally identified by her since he was a look-alike with others. Babs went on a freezing overnight stakeout of twenty-four hours, and was even accosted by a suspicious policeman.

Frances Rufty's situation was different. From the beginning our group knew where young Krishna Frances was—at the airport money-raising. Although it would have been easy to pick her up, it was nevertheless thought best not to alert others. As for Barb, she had been seen at Washington Street center, but the question arose, had she or hadn't she gone out again with her selling team? Or, over the weekend, might she surface coming and going from Boonville?

Finally, after the dashing of many high hopes for each young person, it was decided to pick up Frances Rufty on Saturday. Wearing her uproariously incongruous blond wig and big dark glasses, a nervous Frances, Sr., went along to identify. With airport security standing by and without physical objection, young Frances accepted the papers Wayne served and got in his car.

All of us were then transported across the Golden Gate bridge to a San Raphael motel, where Frances and I were lodged next door to the room young Frances was in. (By choice Frances had decided not to be in the same room with her daughter. "It's best for her," Frances said. "She's got enough things to struggle with; she can get to me later.")

Right next door to a deprogramming, I was determined to observe everything I could. It was true, young Frances was confined to the room for several days and never left by herself (two or three people always with her), but all that her confinement entailed was speaking with her and counseling with her. How the sessions were going was reported to us on the hour by those who were with her. We'd get a tap on our door; deprogrammers Howie or Judy would slip in: "She's sleeping." "She's hungry. We're going to find her some vegetarian things." "She wants some new clothes." And later, "She wants to call her old boyfriend," a request Frances, Sr., bucked, then accepted if it were imperative, which it apparently wasn't as it was never repeated. And then the best report of all: "She says she's not going back to the cult."

I helped Frances go through the heavy knapsack young Frances had worn at the airport (Krishna women are beginning to have back problems because of these loads). There was $35 in the pack. "As I stood there and listened, I heard someone scold Frances for not making more money," Frances, Sr., said soberly. "But the way those girls were all over the men, I was glad Frances wasn't doing very well."

Sunday young Frances requested a ride; I saw her briefly, looking wan and dispirited. (Barb in my heart, that glimpse troubled me.) Monday Frances, Sr., had lunch with her daughter. "She was cold," Frances said forlornly when she came back. What good friends the parents got to be as they survived mutual crises: "Do you realize I've told you things I tell practically nobody!" exclaimed Frances in the middle of a particularly anxious night.

I grew reassured by the firm but very patient and loving attitude shown by our group for young Frances. I was especially impressed with Howie, a young deprogrammer, and his understanding way with Frances, the mother; his ability to separate deprogramming processes from psychological problems and his clear statement that he was leaving the latter to those who knew psychology better. I saw Howie, in a crisis involving the whole group, clearly put his "client" first and make his decision in her interests even though the group had to bend for her. Howie had been in and out of several cults. "How better to penetrate a society than to co-opt the young?" Howie posed the question.

Tuesday I learned the hard way why there was need for secrecy. While young Frances in a fit of temper was throwing a knife through the motel window, Frances's lawyer husband was phoning her to say he'd just had an emergency call from Wayne Howard that the Krishnas had bullhorns out on the streets of San Francisco yelling that young Frances had been kidnapped. Howard had asked him, Archie Rufty, to come at once to Tucson for possible habeas corpus proceedings. Since Wayne was away from the motel on a stakeout, Frances wasn't able to reach him to confirm his phone call to her husband for several hours. When she did, Wayne flew into a rage: "I never put that call through. We've got to get your husband stopped before he gets to Tucson." There followed a wild hour till Archie was paged and successfully turned back at Chicago. That evening Mike Trauscht's secretary, Tally, flew into the Tucson airport. When she got off it was nearly empty except for a handful of young men hanging around the page calling repeatedly for "Mr. Archie Rufty." If he'd landed, not knowing what Wayne Howard looked like, he might have climbed right into the car with the young reception committee.

By Monday it had become clear that Barb wasn't going to be found. The last trace of her had been on Thursday by Howie when he'd seen her coming out of Washington Street "with that orange scarf tied at the back of her hair," a description which was so real it made me cry.

True friend Frances Rufty had flown off behind young Frances's plane to an unknown destination and heaven knows what legal complexities. Babs, Stuart, and I drove together to the airport. Though empty-handed, we were eternally comrades-at-arms; all of us kept saying those words, "Next time."

Disappointed but resolute, I flew back Tuesday afternoon, January 11, to a gray, icy Portland.

On Monday, February 28, 1977, Ray flew down to San Francisco to seek the granting of a new conservatorship based on the belief Barb was again in the Bay Area. (When we'd failed to serve the first ship papers on her in the company of a police officer, the earlier conservatorship had been immediately closed in order to seal the record, since cult people regularly checked the court dockets.)

With the Krishnas camped around his house, Judge Rolph felt his own growing "notoriety" was interfering with a reasoned consideration of the legal issue; he assigned our new conservatorship request to one of his other judges, S. Lee Vavuris.

Vavuris in the past had granted some *ex parte* conservatorship orders, but now he said he would not grant us one because he was going to follow a different procedure. The Unification lawyer, Ralph Baker, had promised he would produce any young people being sought as conservatees for an open court hearing so that they, and the cult, could make their case. Vavuris had accepted Baker's offer, and that was the condition on which he was now willing to hear applications for further conservatorships. Wayne Howard and Mike Trauscht were busy sorting out client families willing to fight the case in open court.

When Ray flew home on Tuesday night, March 1, we knew we had some long, sober deciding ahead of us once again. Only this time it was worse.

The cleanness of an open court hearing strongly appealed to our sense of civil liberties and fair legal play, but we had to face the fact that if we joined in, went public, so to speak, had the hearing and lost the decision, our intentions toward Barb would be clearly established and we might never see her again, at least in any foreseeable future. But then we considered some of the possible consequences of *not* fighting for her in court. "They could ship her to South Korea any time," Ray said soberly, "and I certainly wouldn't want to thread my way through the South Korean court system to find her." We also knew she was eligible to be "blessed"—married—and that if the cult married her off, that would really complicate our legal chances of helping her.

We decided, the evening of March 3, to go for broke.

We called Doug and Jeff. Again we didn't want to lean on them for heavy decisions but did want them always apprised of what we were doing and why. Jeff, who had gone through more years of open rebellion and was especially sensitive to parental intervention, expressed misgivings, then assent. Doug reviewed our mutual misgivings but concurred once more that if action were to be taken, this appeared the only route. He ended by saying simply, "If Moon ever had an argument that there is need to replace the American family, you two are disproving it."

On March 4, Ray called Wayne Howard and said he had decided to risk it, to go in with four other families also going for broke. We had simply despaired, Ray told Wayne, of ever being able to get the conservatorship at a time when we could also find Barb in the jurisdiction of the court.

Wayne told Ray he was surprised and pleased at his decision, that Ray's coming in (both as a public officer in the legal department of a state and as a strong personal witness) would immeasurably strengthen their case. "But then," he laughed ruefully, "Barb's coming in will strengthen the cult's case, too. I'm told by those who knew her in the cult she's strong and loving and as a witness she'll be articulate and gutsy."

After a hurried time of getting ready, and in some concern taking along Ray's ailing father who was visiting us, we left by plane Monday late afternoon, March 7, for San Francisco.

We had the bumpiest air trip I've ever had. I prayed it wasn't an omen.

Betty: Hearing

"This shift from outer to inner authority [as a more] religious position [was what] Albert Schweitzer had in mind when he wrote, 'Thinking is already religious,' that is, to ponder alternatives and then consequences, to take responsibility for oneself and one's actions is a religious act."
—LAILE E. BARTLETT, *New Work, New Life*

"Speak truth to power."
—QUAKER ADAGE

MARCH 7, 1977.
After helping us get settled at the International Travelodge near the San Francisco airport, Wayne Howard turned over the keys of a rental car to us. The three of us, Ray, his dad and I, hurtled through

the night to find Barb at the Emeryville Holiday Inn, the time and place of our meeting having been agreed on by lawyers for both sides.

Out of the parking lot she came toward us, smiling.

It was impossible, in that first minute of hugging and greeting, to remember what awful differences separated us. I wonder if mothers and fathers can ever shake off the fundamental naturalness of parenthood, not in the sense of grasping or demand, but of simple reality. There's a statement in the Bible which reads something like, " . . . and although their own, they shall be joined to thee."

When we got past that initial coming together, there *was* strain, though; it was like the love that Corinthians finds struggling in " . . . and now we see through a glass darkly . . ."

Barb looked well, taller, fully matured, her personality as before, piquant and personable, but with something firmer now, quieter and more confident.

As we went into the motel lobby, she turned and grinned to Johnny Hovard leaning on the cult van in the parking lot. One of the five young cultists sought, she had flown up with him from the southwest. His being there smacked of bodyguard; same old cult stuff, I thought wearily.

At late dinner we sparred briefly, then simply plunged in. Grandpa, in his bluff way, relieved himself of the old-fashioned conviction that she "was just in love with running around the country in that van." Barb could make what she wanted of her grandpa's words, I thought; at least they were coming from one she respected as a God-fearing religious man, a man of furious family loyalty as well.

We got right to the legal issue. Barb was adamant that she saw no need for the use of a conservatorship and bore down heavily on the civil liberties aspect with us.

"I'll come home for two weeks and talk to you," she promised us, and there was no way to make clear that, yes, if she did, we'd run around in the same old squirrel cage we'd run around in the past four years and then she'd go back to the cult. It's possible, I now know, for families to give the cultist the distance needed to step back and survey what he or she is doing but it is immensely difficult.

After dinner, Ray suggested we talk in the car. I had the eerie sensation of climbing in beside my own daughter and realizing she was nervous we'd drive off with her. Her agitation seemed to wear off shortly, thank God.

From that the need welled up in me to state my central motive in the very strange thing we were trying to do with her life. "We'd like you back," I told Barb, "but we didn't come down here just to drag you home to the family. We came down to try to give you your own life again. If I never saw you afterward, I'd feel I had to offer you this chance."

When we parted, it felt strange hugging her. I prayed for old hurts to stay submerged in me; I had need only for strengths now.

Tuesday, March 8.

On a sunny morning, we drove out to Walnut Creek to the offices of the expert-witness psychiatrist for our side. There we had an interview with Dr. Samuel Benson, a large, rather austere black man, and with his colleague, a psychologist named Dr. Margaret Singer, who was nationally known for her work with brainwashed POWs from Korea, with Jesuit priests coming out of China, and with nearly one hundred ex-cult people. (Defense had tried to use Margaret Singer as an expert witness in the Patti Hearst case. Singer reminded us that Patricia Hearst was kept fifty-seven days in two closets, transported between them in covered plastic garbage pails.) Our interview with both professionals was about Barb's pre-cult life, and we found them warm and helpful.

Coming out to the waiting room, I met Jeff Scales for the first time, although Ray had met, liked, and trusted him from the week before when he'd been seeking the second conservatorship. Tall, dark, with a straightforward, businesslike way that instantly inspired confidence, Jeff was a significant figure in all these proceedings both because of his importance to Barb during their cult years together and because both Evey and Jeff had helped make what we were now trying to do possible. I knew there was no underestimating how crucial Jeff and Evey might be to Barb in the days ahead.

By now I had learned something of Jeff's story.

Like Barb, Jeff had loved most of all the nomadic flower selling; as a team leader he had been the "most sacrificial, the most righteous," Barb had told us. But the amazing young Jeff had also been founder and first manager of Aladdin's, the cult's large and successful Jewish delicatessen in Oakland. (Jeff: "If someone asked if Aladdin's was connected to Moon, I'd say, 'You're kidding. Isn't he that Chinese guy?'") According to Jeff, paychecks from Aladdin's cult workers were routinely signed over to "Onni's personal fund; she spent freely on clothing and jewelry."

At one time Jeff had also helped run the cult's maintenance company with its lucrative contracts with several California restaurant and office chains. "With no labor costs and people willing to work fourteen, fifteen hours a day, you could undercut anybody."

It was from Aladdin's and the maintenance company's profits and paychecks that Jeff took $21,000 to buy Onni a blue Mercedes. When she saw it, her only response was, "Why that color?"

Jeff had lived for a time with Mose Durst when Durst was just coming into the cult. As do many of the cultists, Jeff really loved the fatherly, kindly seeming man who sometimes appeared unaware of what was going on around him. ("When you're on the street, witness for Dr. Durst; when you're at the center, witness for Onni," Onni had once advised, recognizing Durst's drawing power with the young.) Jeff was helping Durst "come to Principle" but often Durst would get stuck and turn to Onni. "She wanted to marry him," Jeff recalled.

After Jeff was deprogrammed, he was so anathema to the cult that a refrigerator he'd bought for the Gardens was returned. Shortly after Jeff got out, he saw the Moons, Dursts, and Salonens enjoying themselves at a Las Vegas casino.

Now the Jeff before me in the doctor's anteroom was still struggling to shed the weight which he'd gained on his sleepless years with the flower teams. To keep him awake while driving, his teams had fed him.

In that waiting room we also met Skip Guarini, a personable young writer following the adventures of Mike and Wayne.

We drove Ray's dad to Rossmoor and had an absurdly hurried lunch with my father, also standing by with great and practical loyalty.

In the Travelodge dining room that night we found the whole "team" assembled: Joe Alexander, Sr., the hub of the wheel in any deprogramming, the dean of deprogrammers, a firm, fatherly, likable man who'd done his first counseling on behalf of his nephew; Gary Scharff, the stocky, awesomely brilliant but personally comfortable young Princeton theology major, whose writings had earlier made more sense to us than any others' and who had, in the cult, been a chief lecturer at the Unification workshop in Barrytown, New York (headquarters for the cult nationally). Michele Tunis was there with Mitch

Mack; also Larry Gumbiner of January fame. We had a better chance to get acquainted with the elusive blond Mike Trauscht, whose Robin Hood reputation didn't seem to fit with his brisk matter-of-factness. From January also was the quiet young deprogrammer, Howie; he seemed an old friend. I was interested in Joe Alexander, Jr.—Joey—a slender, black mustachioed man who, before I had occasion to see his beautiful simplicity and firmness of character, appeared almost sinister to me. A Vietnam vet who'd had a rough time, he'd brought a number of people out of cults, most recently several Children of God members living in Paris. He had briefly used a Paris sewer pipe for his reconaissance site. Also sitting around those dining room tables were recent ex-cultists Jerry Feldman and Bob Stewart and, best of all, Steve Lang, whose father's loyal patience had finally been rewarded several weeks before.

Important to us in the extreme was the meeting with Louise and Attorney Carl Katz of Wolcott, New York, parents of Jackie; Burt Kaplan, mother of Jan, from Toledo, Ohio; and Tom Brown of Berkley Heights, New Jersey, father of Leslie. These were the parents of the three other women who, along with Barb, were being sought. Not until next day in the courtroom would we meet Gail and John Hovard of Danville, California, parents of John, the only male cultist of the five.

But the meeting that evening which held most joy for me was with Evey Eden. Hugging Evey wordlessly, I knew there are brief times in our lives when it's less complex to be parents to someone else's child, just as someone else's parent can on occasion seem easier than one's own. Bright, casual, green-eyed Evey had a blithe-spirit charisma hard to define but powerfully present. (She had the same worrisome, tender quality Barb had, however. "What is it?" I once asked Ray. He thought, then answered, "Oh, she seems so vulnerable, so hurtable.")

Evey's story was a much less dramatic one than Jeff's. Five years before, she had got in the cult through a boyfriend who had three sisters in Unification. The pair of them had dropped in to Oakland center, which was putting on "Madame Butterfly" and "needed a clarinetist. So I played for the weekend and never went home. I didn't know about Moon for three months." For the next five years, Evey now feels, she was not only under mind control herself, but was taught to use it on others. As team leader and staff member, she brought many members to Unification—over forty. "I was good at something called 'heavenly wisdom': 'I know best,' or psychological 'bribery,' as it would be consid-

ered outside the cult. You use people's emotions to change their minds.
You use their love and trust to affect their thinking by first winning
them over on a very personal level.

"Over and over I told people to 'trust me'; I never let them alone. I
enticed them to the centers or at Boonville. And after they were in, I
used the pleasure then pain—first reinforcement, then guilt treatment."

In early December 1976, Evey had been paged in the San Francisco
hotel where she was in the rest room reading "Master Speaks." She
walked out the door, to be served conservatorship papers by Wayne
Howard. After having merely pretended that the deprogrammers were
getting through to her, on the fifth day Evey suddenly realized that
Onni was not perfect and that she didn't want to go back to the kind of
group she now understood Unification to be. Taken first to Las Vegas,
then to Tucson, she met up once again with Jeff Scales, who was also
there after his deprogramming. It had been Evey's father who had had
the Tucson ruckus with the hurt and angry Onni.

Wednesday, March 9.

We entered a room of the Superior Court of the City and County
of San Francisco in the great federal-domed city hall. Judge S. Lee
Vavuris, a white-haired man with a pleasant, intense face, would pre-
side. The room held about one hundred people, and it was soon
crowded. I saw some cult faces I recognized from four years ago: Daniel,
looking now not like an energetic stripling but inflexible and somehow
middle-aged; Esther, still slight and anxious; Shelly, big and still-faced;
the lean, intense Mark; matronly Becky; Micah, somber as ever; Mose
Durst, grown puffy, thin-haired. No Teresa. No Onni, of course. At first
I wanted to at least speak in a human way with them, but a few days
later I didn't even want to look back in their direction. (Daniel,
kneading my hand: "Mrs. Underwood, *what* are you doing to Lael?")

We sat down beside Barb who greeted us with apparent affection.
What was my feeling? I loved her; I wanted to help her if I could.
Would the day come when we could be natural again? (And days into
the hearing, I asked in terror, will we ever heal this polarization?) I felt
very protective of her self-dignity, her personality.

Up at the bar our lawyers, Mike, Wayne, and the Shapiros (our
local counsel) sat to the right. The Shapiros were Carl, with long gray
hair, rumpled pants, and the courtly manner of a reflective intellectual,

and his daughter, Sylvia, who had just graduated from law school and entered her father's firm.

To the left were the cult lawyers, Ralph Baker, a lean sharp-profiled Armenian of disarmingly simple stripe. Associated with him was Paul Goorjian, shorter, shrewder; he would use the constant sharp histrionics of the criminal lawyer, having apparently overlooked the fact that there was no jury in this room.

To the right, the small brown press box was filling up.

Outside it was sunny.

A little after ten o'clock, all the lawyers conferred. A motion to consolidate the five cases was denied. Mike Trauscht made the opening statement. "Our goal is to obtain temporary conservatorships of five young adult people for a period of thirty days. . . . Our contention, allegation, our proof will demonstrate that these young adults . . . are the victims of artful and designing persons, specifically the New Education Development, a front organization for the Unification church. . . . It is our position that proof will demonstrate these people are victims of artful and designing persons due to coercive conversion, oftentimes referred to as thought control, thought reform, brainwashing." Mike enumerated methods by which this was achieved: sleep and food deprivation, isolation, overwork, withholding of information, force of authority, "the same tactics used on our prisoners of war during the Korean War crisis." Coercive persuasion is, said Mike—"and will be so explained by our medical witnesses"—behavior determined not by internal decision but rather coercion from outside forces, "specifically in this case, fear and guilt tactics." Mike said the solution was reality-inducing therapy consisting of a number of elements, including adequate sleep, books on coercive persuasion, opportunities to speak with "former cult members." These young people, said the young lawyer, are victims of psychological kidnapping, to which they were susceptible as young, naïve, idealistic people. He also pointed out that the initial recruitment was through deceit.

Cult lawyer Baker responded that the question was whether all five young people were competent, was their right to choose their own religion being violated, was there a clear emergency? The real villains, said Baker, were the Freedom of Thought Foundation deprogrammers.

At 11:30 Ray went on the stand and was there an hour and fifteen minutes, before and after lunch. Wayne Howard examined and Baker cross-examined until Goorjian stepped in. After being asked by Wayne Howard for his educational and work background, Ray was asked to explain what he knew of mind control, what changes he had observed in Barb after her joining the cult, why he wanted a conservatorship.

Ray indicated what he'd read and learned of the theory of coercive persuasion as applied to cults, stated from his own observation of his daughter that he believed it exists, that "while it may be extreme to say it, these young people are put in a form of slavery, mental enslavement, and once in it, the pattern is to keep them so busy, so preoccupied, that there's never an opportunity to stand back free of the influence of the cult." On getting in, Ray said, "Unification is legally different from other faiths because at least on the West Coast it recruits members without telling them what they're getting into. Barbara didn't hear Moon's name until she had been swept up in the movement. I know of no legitimate church that brings in its members on the basis of lies."

Ray said he believed the difference between a cult and a church was that a cult was "a self-interested imposition between God and the individual."

He stated the personality changes we had observed in Barb: (1) loss of her independent attitude and a maturity level commensurate with her peers: "She became somewhat childlike in her acceptance of this unitary system of beliefs. . . . Her demeanor was, I would say, childlike"; (2) loss of the ability to consider questions with reason; (3) voice and handwriting changes: "Her voice was always hoarse"; (4) lack of interest in all former concerns and goals: "Whereas before she was open and curious and very interested in all kinds of ideas, political and social, she no longer was after she joined the movement"; (5) total unconcern for social action as commonly understood; (6) withdrawal from our family, though there had not previously been serious problems; (7) control rather than humor or spontaneity.

When Ray was asked about the civil liberties issue, he reiterated that the first denial of rights came when the individual stepped into the cult; that he "respectfully dissents from the national and local ACLU position and, though a longtime member, is aware the ACLU doesn't require its members all to agree." He also said he didn't see how there was any great threat to civil liberties so long as the deprogramming was conducted under court supervision. "It's a special situation that ordinary principles of free choice don't apply to, because these people aren't free."

He made the point of the existence of two principles, freedom of thought and freedom of religion, and said you can't have the second without the first.

Ray stated that he felt Barb was being imposed upon because she was spending "all her time raising funds for a movement without receiving any compensation personally other than minimal food and a place to put down a sleeping bag."

On cross-examination Ray acknowledged that his daughter looked healthy, had appeared healthy on all visits.

Goorjian couldn't shake Ray's insistence that he wanted the conservatorship, not in order to change his daughter's religion, but to "give her a chance for an untrammeled opportunity, free of the influence of the movement, to reassess her beliefs."

Goorjian: "Isn't it true, you intend to put your daughter in the hands of certain individuals who call themselves deprogrammers?"

Ray answered steadily, "I don't know what they call themselves, but I think it's a very apt word because I think she's programmed and needs deprogramming." He went on: "I think she has her own mind, but I think it is controlled like someone under hypnosis; and in certain areas, she cannot function as an independent human being."

Ray's testimony was summed up by part of a sentence he later used: "We want our daughter to regain exclusive control of her own mind and to begin to experience the challenges and joys of using the God-given gift of a free and inquiring intelligence."

We heard later from Barb that the cult was very worried when Ray stepped down.

I hadn't expected to be called to testify, but Wayne Howard now wanted to put me on the stand to complete the range of parental expression, Ray's testimony being considered firm and wise but his emotions very controlled. Privately I didn't intend to go on that stand and have hysterics, either, but I recognized I had my feelings less under control than Ray had. I was painfully aware of Barb sitting at the counsel table facing me.

Wayne asked me what were Barb's personality changes. "Forgive me," I said, really to her, not the courtroom, "this is very difficult for a family that was a loving unit." I then described how, when she first went into the cult, it seemed like the life and warmth drained out of her, that I'd known she was frightened because she'd told me so personally and because she'd written in her journal she was afraid that, like Michelangelo's *Captives,* she'd "be stuck in the marble."

I described how she seemed to us to become docile almost overnight, unquestioning as a parroting child. "She'd been a bright, challenging, show-me kind of person before. She didn't take things on faith. It was really like she parked her brains at the door of the church."

I described her brother Jeff's and my going to Dana Street for a weekend and how they almost wouldn't let Jeff out the first night. "I began to realize this was a threat, a cage."

I told about the episode at the airport when we were having dinner with Barb and she asked us if we thought her personality had changed; "Doug does. And I don't want my personality to change." I explained how, when we'd told Barb we agreed with Doug, her old personality with all its fire, the essential nonprogrammed Barb, came leaping out again with its original verve and spirit.

I said that she showed a strange feelinglessness toward her own family, an example being that when the flower team came to stay after I'd broken my arm, she scarcely asked me about it and made no concessions to things I could't do. I finished by saying she'd taken very uncharacteristic advantage of us by asking us to pay her clothes and medical expenses since she wouldn't ask the cult to pay.

On cross-examination Baker asked if I knew she'd taken drugs. I answered yes, and told what the limited experimentation was; I had her story of her taking psilocybin.

Did I know about the "feminist house," he asked, and did I know it was a house for lesbians?

"It was called the Radical House," I countered, "and she was advised into it by a professor at UC Santa Cruz. It had men and women living in it—the owners were that kind of pair—and it had one lesbian pair and one other lesbian, I think. There appeared to be no sexual pressures on Barb at first; if there were any later, she handled the problem well." I indicated that I'd been concerned, however, and that she and I had had frank talks about it and why I didn't feel lesbianism was a major part of the women's movement, was a civil liberties issue instead.

When Baker questioned whether I approved her "being involved in this feminism stuff" I'm afraid I fired up and said I wouldn't see her life as having gone to perdition if she were concerned with equal pay for work of equal value, and women's equality. (Later I suspected the uninformed Baker had the words *feminism* and *lesbianism* confused.)

Baker tried to force me to answer if Barb "went back to the Radical House, would you deprogram her?" I had a hard time squeezing into the proper legal framework my protest to the implied assertion that if she weren't in the cult, that meant automatically she'd have to be in some radical house.

I left the chair, went to my seat, and cried quietly. I'd been on the stand half an hour.

But in that time the grand scheme of the cult had been made clear to me. They were going to take these kids, put them on the stand, and get them to crucify their own characters. In other words, everything that had happened or ostensibly had happened to them precult had been terrible. Would Barb fall into that trap? I knew she'd led a more wholesome personal life than many people her age; just before she went on the stand, whether she could hear me or not, I determined to make an appeal to her: "Think of yourself. Remember you'll have a life after you come out of this hearing room."

It had been agreed that the other parents would submit written affidavits rather than personally taking the witness stand.

At 3:30 Jeff Scales testified. He seemed unexpectedly subdued; we found out later he'd been outside in the hall with that great layer-on-of-guilt, Daniel, Jeff's former friend. Jeff stated his cult background: joined, without knowing it had anything to do with religion, International Ideal City Project from the Berkeley campus; managed Aladdin's; led selling teams; was a Bay Area staff member. He said he "came out" under a temporary conservatorship and counseling that enabled him to realistically assess the church with the range of information necessary for this process. "Without deprogramming I couldn't have come out. In the group we were taught that doubts sprang from our own evil or inadequate natures." He spoke of leadership pressure to negate individuality, tremendous polarization between the group and the world, the use of guilt to get cultists to behave in certain ways, and the fear of spiritual (which to the cultist means actual) death to keep the cultist in the group. Jeff described fund-raising and the luxuries the money sometimes went for. He also indicated he was taught in the cult that his natural parents were his "Satanic" parents. Goorjian objected to some of Jeff's testimony on the basis that he, Jeff, had now been brainwashed by the deprogrammers. Because of the feeling I knew Jeff and Barb had for each other, I realized this confrontation, almost eye-to-eye across the court-room, had to be extremely unsettling. My heart reached out to the ex-cult people called to testify before their former dear friends and cobelievers.

Gary Scharff was called up but had scarcely started his testimony before we were adjourned.

We went out into halls crowded with TV lights and mikes. That first day Ray gave several interviews; thereafter he wouldn't, saying he had to keep his mind clear for the courtroom and Barb. But the cult kids, Barb as spokesperson, were indefatigable in responding to media requests. It was clear the natural sympathies of the public lay with the young people; I wished with all my being the whole thing didn't have to be taking place in the context of parent-child relationships. The issue of mind control was being blurred, obscured.

The first day was over. How many more to go? Two, possibly three?

Thursday, March 10.
Lauriel came to the hearing and it was fortifying to see her. Ray and I couldn't say enough for the feeling of concern and family soli-darity, the selfless help with solutions to our problems, that my brother Scott and his wife Lauriel gave us.

Dr. Benson, our expert-witness psychiatrist, was called first. Trained at Stanford medical school, he had impressive credentials. In each interview with the cult person, he said he was checking for symptoms such as orientation, affects, speech patterns, ability to answer questions when confronted, manner toward others. He said he didn't expect to find classic psychiatric symptoms.

Regarding Barb, he said she was aware of self, place, and setting. He said, however, that penetrating questions asked to cause anxiety brought very little response except a childlike smile; her affective be-havior (how she came across to others) showed. blunted affect, or limited emotionality; she had a narrowed range of responses, showed no anger when it would have been appropriate to do so; had little knowl-edge of what was happening in the world; her language and choice of words were constricted; she had difficulty with abstractions (which was inconsistent with what he knew of her background); she gave predict-able answers; she had faulty memory, especially of childhood; she was paranoid about former life and friends; she confabulated (a process of covering up when memory fails—the confabulator never says "I don't know" or "I can't remember"); in talking with her it was as though she couldn't make her own decisions; at first she seemed sincere and well-meaning so long as the right questions were asked, but soon it became important to manipulate the questions and answers to show that the cult was absolutely blameless throughout.

Benson gave certain examples. For instance, Barb thought Ford had run against McGovern. When Benson asked her a hypothetical question about what if Moon were indicted, she didn't know the meaning of the word "indicted," though she'd had a course in constitutional law at UC Santa Cruz. Benson also noted that Barb had no interest in previous goals, had no new personal goals. He said she had little interest in self and noted the "childlike manner of touching in the group as they sat in his waiting room—total denial of normal signs of adult sexual relating." Barb's personality was described as having had longer time to overcome earlier cult pressures and to have stabilized at a somewhat more normal-appearing state. He said she was not psychotic, that she did not have any symptoms of a standard medical diagnosis, that she was not hypnotized, but that she was living in an abnormal situation and the sooner out of it the better. He couldn't tell from his examination whether there would be change in her mental state in the next thirty days, but there was no indication of imminent mental deterioration. (Of Hovard he spoke differently as to this.) Benson said Barb's symptoms were consistent with the results of techniques of coercive persuasion.

On submitted written testimony Benson said all five persons had symptoms *not* present in the average individual of their ages. In addition to those characteristics he found in Barb, he mentioned several others: their answers were preset: there was effort made to answer all questions out of a preset of answers; there was a "childlike inappropriate smile to all input, hostile or not"; attention spans seemed short and ability to concentrate impaired; all were defensive about "id" urges. "It was," wrote Benson, "as though their inner sense of authority was lost. In general they did not respond as one would expect from their background and personality types."

When Benson had finished answers about Barb, I was worried to death. Luckily I came to feel, in reference to all medical testimony at the hearing, that the language used was very rough, imprecise, could not convey subtle qualities, that each side overstated its case, that there needed to be developed more accurate vocabulary and imagery to define a person who has experienced coercive persuasion. Also, as each young person took the stand and seemed to refute Benson's very words, I reminded myself every court day was one more away from their self-denying, high-tension, mind-dulling routine.

Benson held up well under cross-examination though he took a long time to reply. He showed good awareness of the literature of coercive persuasion, gave the classic description of its processes—isolation, sensory deprivation, hypnosis, captivity, anxiety, fear, no privacy, overwork, lack of sleep and food—and summarized that it "induced a pattern of thinking by systematic, ritualistic procedure until the individual takes on the identity of those around him."

On cross-examination Goorjian asked questions like: Is it unusual for a person deeply involved in a religious movement to be limited in information? Not to the extent of Barbara Underwood, said Benson. Does such a void in current knowledge mean she is susceptible to artful and designing persons? Yes, said Benson emphatically. Would it be unusual for her to try not to get mad if she knew you had some part in a conservatorship being taken for her? Possibly, said Benson, but the quality of control seemed different to him: "I'd see brief moments of loss of control but each time she regained control which became a frozen emotionality." Goorjian asked: Doesn't someone take on the nomenclature of their particular group? Yes, said Benson, but Barbara Underwood's was too limited, too constricted; she pleaded simplistically, as though she had regressed intellectually. Did Barbara have a major emotional crisis before joining the group? Did she say she was living in a feminist community? Benson replied he understood the crisis had to do with a male relationship but she had indicated to him an alternate lifestyle had been presented as an opportunity. He added that he had found a strong denial of any interest in sexual relationships with individuals.

Goorjian: "Aren't most patients guarded about sexual questions with a doctor?"

Benson (big grin):"It is unusual for a patient to be reluctant to talk about sex life in an interview with a doctor."

Goorjian: "Did Wayne Howard ask you to determine if these people were brainwashed?"

Benson: "Shapiro told me the purpose of the interviews was to establish if these young people for any reason were especially susceptible to artful and designing persons" (a requirement of the California conservatorship).

We had lunch in the basement of the courthouse with Jan, Barb's good friend from Santa Cruz. Her old friends were coming forward. Jan, a warm, sweet young guy, was obviously concerned.

When we got back from lunch a young ACLU lawyer, as friend of the court, was trying to introduce a brief on the constitutional issue: "It will only take a month to prepare." Judge Vavuris said dryly he wouldn't stop the proceedings for oral argument on the constitutional issue but would be glad to receive written arguments when they were completed. We were startled to have the ACLU take a hostile position before our evidence was even in.

That night I was totally beat, so Ray joined Barb for dinner. I knew it meant a lot to Ray to share that time together; I thought it might to Barb. Ray picked her up at Goorjian's office; Barb picked out the seafood place down on Fisherman's Wharf and did the driving. Ray came back full of food, happiness, and hope.

Friday, March 11.
Benson finished his testimony. He said of Jackie Katz that in his interview with Jackie's parents she had been described as active, bright, happy, a leader, valedictorian of her high school class, but in the forty-five minutes Benson spent with Jackie, she was preoccupied, had a gloomy global sense of responsibility, abstracted poorly, had a narrow range of interests and responses, markedly used the defense mechanism of denial, answered, when asked the indictment question about Moon: "I would have to ask a church leader; I would have to ask Micah about that." He said Jackie's answers were preset, her judgment inconsistent in getting solutions, and that she couldn't recall events of her childhood. Of Hovard, Benson said his physical health seemed to indicate he should see an internist at once, that he showed some signs of actual malnutrition. Benson thought Hovard was the only one of the five who was disturbed in the conventional mental health sense and that he needed psychiatric counseling: "His responses gave some indication that his sense of reality is fragmenting."

When Goorjian asked Benson if the Marine Corps weren't coercive, Benson flashed a knowing grin and answered, "Yes, but you can get out." He stayed the rest of the morning listening attentively in the courtroom, an elegant figure in his black velvet suit.

Late morning Dr. Margaret Singer, our clinical psychologist, was put on. Her testimony was an expansion, in greater and more consistent detail, of Benson's. The newspapers picked up a lot about the Draw-a-Person test which Dr. Singer administered to the five young people. (There are no good tests for coercive persuasion, either.) She said these sexless cartoon drawings displayed characteristics of pictures drawn by prisoners of war who had been subjected to coercive persuasion. After lengthy questioning, she made an important point, one which seemed obvious but had not yet been flatly stated, that on the basis of her data she felt the Unification cult was practicing coercive persuasion. To previous definitions of coercive persuasion, Margaret added several elements: the individual is reduced by being made to feel a neophyte, a newcomer to a strong in-group; the deception of not telling the new recruit what the organization really is becomes an additional powerful mechanism of control. Once in, Singer concluded, the individual ends up with a feeling of guilt so strong the controllers can stop the social isolation and send him or her into the world with safety. Margaret also strongly dissented from a cult lawyer's assertion that he believed anyone could have his faith shaken if he were bombarded with negative talk about a church. Not so, replied Margaret, who said she had interviewed Catholic priests who were beaten, starved, and harassed in Korean War camps but had kept their faith. The implication was that if it is a genuinely arrived at religious commitment, or conversion, it will stick.

We had lunch with Susan, a sweet young woman who had been a good friend of Barb's at Santa Cruz and had also gone into the cult. After three months she had had an acute psychotic breakdown from which, several years later, she was still recovering. She was very helpful about some of the feelings Barb was undoubtedly having and very helpful about Barb's past life. "Of course they'll get on the stand and say they were awful. But if Barb does, she's lying. I didn't know anyone at Santa Cruz who led a more responsible and moral life."

At the end of Friday the judge gave the parents the right to be with their young people over the weekend. There was no jumping for joy among the "Faithful Five," as they were now being called in the newspapers. We made plans to be with Barb.

Saturday, March 12.

We picked up Barb at the Ashby Street center, a pleasant old house on a pleasant Berkeley street, and with family drove to Boundary Oak country club near Walnut Creek for lunch. Barb was nervous in the car for a while and during lunch excused herself to call in and tell the cult her whereabouts. I tried not to think how strange it all was.

We then had a fine drive up Mount Diablo, at the summit watched someone hang gliding right overhead, enjoyed the soft, bare, pale green hills. Sometimes Barb seemed pretty relaxed, though after the hearing was over she said when she was with the family it had been either "nicey-nicey" or "argumentative."

Sunday, March 13.

After standing uncomfortably on the porch of Ashby Street center waiting for Barb to come out, I watched her emerge with the inevitable bodyguard, this time Len Foster, a cult person studying at the Barry-town Seminary who had been taken out by his parents, gone partway through rehab, and been released early to return to school, whereupon he had slipped back to the cult. Len accompanied Barb over Ray's strenuous protest. Ray pointed out that the constant calling in, the constant bodyguard stuff was just more sharp evidence of childlike submission to control.

We drove to the Emeryville Holiday Inn and there Jeff Scales met Barb and us. Barb and Jeff went off to have breakfast together in another part of the dining room, while Ray, Len, and I had a somewhat uncomfortable breakfast. Len, like many cult kids, was a bright, attractive young man, and he filled me with sorrow for the human severance that cult life causes and the kind of limiting life he was caught in. Barb later told us he had gone into the movement right after a bruising divorce and when he was being deprogrammed perhaps came out just long enough to realize he wanted and needed the cult as a substitute for his lost relationship. "In deprogramming," he advised the Faithful Five, "just close up like an acorn, don't listen to anything, make yourselves deaf."

Len went off to study and we to read. Barb and Jeff took a walk outside and when they came back—miracle of miracles—Barb told Len we would take him back to Ashby Street so he could study but she would spend the afternoon with us and Jeff. No phone consultation, no getting agreement from Len. In quiet awe we wondered if we weren't witnessing the first independent decison Barb had made in four years.

Amazed but relieved, we drove north and had lunch in one of my January haunts, Frogmorton's Folly in San Rafael. It was fascinating to watch Barb with Jeff; she used the cult practice of waiting on him—the first bite was extended to him, the napkin was offered, she even carefully turned back his cuff. I couldn't help but wonder how this struck Jeff in his new liberation. Would the modern man chafe under that after a while? Perhaps not.

Jeff was magnificent with Barb, treating her with obvious care and concern but with brotherly cult correctness. I knew he was trying also to prove something to Barb: part of the fiction cultists are taught is that those who leave become instantly "fallen": grow long hair and beards, smoke dope and cigarettes, drink booze, and exploit people sexually.

It was equally fascinating to overhear the conversations between them. Barb was doing her level best to win Jeff back to the cult; the "remember this and remember that" flew thick and fast. Of course Jeff was trying to puncture Barb's cult-induced opacity by a rapier question now and then. (Though Jeff and Evey had consistently emphasized that they wanted to meet with Barb during the hearing, Jeff had told us that when—he didn't say "if"—she came out of the cult, he would take no part in her deprogramming unless she asked him to. In their walk together through Muir Woods, we knew Jeff told Barb about his own deprogramming, though she made no comment about it to us.)

It wasn't the easiest way to be together, riding around in a car driven by parents, but both young people survived with dignity, and we slept off our nervous strain later. In Muir Woods they walked with arms around each other, and quiet relief welled up in me that Barb could trust enough, could let herself feel human enough, for that.

We drove home by the coast, let Jeff off at the Holiday Inn, Barb at Ashby center, and had supper with Scott, Lauriel, and Ray's dad, who would fly out to Boston the next day.

Monday, March 14.
This was Margaret Singer's day in court, and great she was. Through a long and grueling cross-examination, she sparred magnificently with Goorjian and he won no points. She concluded by saying she felt the cult members were all victims of artful and designing people employing coercive persuasion, that it was an emergency situation, that conventional forms of therapy did not apply, and that the only appropriate therapy she knew of was available from the staff at the Freedom Ranch. She was so knowledgeable and so well organized that at the end of the day Ray told her she had just become his all-time favorite witness. Margaret described Goorjian's rolling eyes and looks of an-

noyance as very distracting but, she said, Goorjian was facing not only her but the judge, and this judge watched everyone, witnesses and audience alike, like a hawk.

Gary Scharff, the director of the Freedom Ranch rehab center, was called next. After giving his background as a four-year ex-cultist who had been director of the cult for the state of Pennsylvania, lecturer at Barrytown, national director of C.A.R.P. (Collegiate Association for the Research into Principles), and assistant director of planning and development for the Unification Church Seminary, where he was responsible for recruiting and teaching faculty, Gary gave a low-key but graphic description of programming as practiced at Barrytown. "We could induce such a state of mind in a person that he would practically come to ask us which water faucet to turn on." How do you do this, Gary was asked. Keep a person, Gary answered, from his home and friends, isolate him from his own mind by a structured program of no free time that goes from seven in the morning till one at night, that allows no activity to be conducted alone—including washing, exercising, and eating—and add to these factors a deluge of religious concepts that leaves the participant so confused and fatigued he can't figure out what's been said, except that if he doubts any of it or fails absolutely to follow the teachings, he is bad. Lack of sleep and low-protein food reinforce the process by reducing the physical person to low ebb.

Gary then got behind these separate methods to the underlying psychological process. "The newcomer to the cult learns in a series of carefully managed revelations that there is a new messiah who understands God's will and that the greatest thing he personally can do is follow and obey, just as those more spiritually aware around him are doing. He's told that if he has any doubts, that's to be expected because he can't fully understand a revolutionary new awareness all at once; he should expect conflict within him or herself, but the more he serves and obeys, the more God will clarify all and the better he will feel. In St. Paul's phrase," said Gary, "the entering person 'is subjugated in hope,' or 'strangled in his own idealism.' The trusting idealist is the one the cult's tools fit," said Gary, "out of an awareness that nothing is free, the skeptic won't even come to a 'free' dinner."

If the newcomer becomes a "solid" member of the cult—"solid" meaning someone whose mental energies are directed toward willing his own obedience, even to the point of blocking out rational opposition—he can't leave of his own free will, Gary said. Less "solid" members, unable to deny their rational misgivings, sometimes leave on their own, explained Gary, while others who are less talented or less useful to the cult are pushed out. And some few have personalities exceptionally resistant to severe peer and leadership pressures. Those who are pushed out generally leave feeling it was somehow their fault, that God has rejected them, with attendant heavy psychological complications, occasionally including hospitalization.

Of deprogramming Gary said, "What actually goes on is simple and straightforward. We show how mind control works. We *study* and *discuss* the doctrines of the group. We give cult information withheld from the cultist. I feel," Gary finished, "a very great concern and respect for anyone who has joined a group like this. They're deep-hearted people who really want to do something right with their lives. I don't consider it fair to go in there and start telling them how to think. What I do is give them the opportunity to open their minds, to release themselves from the control they've unknowingly been subjected to. Then they can make their own decisions."

We heard in the early afternoon that Babs' and Richard Baer's son Laurey had been picked up over in Sausalito causing a lot of commotion and attracting a lot of attention, including newspaper headlines. Mike Trauscht had been in charge; he had just withdrawn from our case. Ray was upset about the effect this might have on our hearing, but, remembering the fine Babs Baer I'd spent a sunny January afternoon with in Sausalito, and knowing the pressures both parents must be suffering under, I could understand how it hadn't been possible to wait.

Tuesday, March 15.
Four and a half days into the hearing, after Dr. Singer had been called back for a few final words of testimony, petitioners rested their case. We thought we had come down for two days. Many more days still loomed before us as the cult prepared to put its people on the stand.

Composed and attractive, Barb was called to testify in the early afternoon. My heart stood still.

Baker did the questioning of the cult people.

We had sat side by side with her in the courtroom; now Ray and I went up to the counsel table facing her, as did all the parents during the questioning of their young people.

As expected, she was very articulate.

She indicated she had left home at eighteen to finish her last year in Lake Oswego high school, trying to give the impression, I suppose, that she had been prematurely disconnected from us. She said she had lived two and a half years in Lake Oswego, thus lopping off half her years there. She said when she was growing up she had had "no concept of Jesus, God, or religion," thus wiping out eight years of Quaker First Day school and several years reading the Bible at home; she said "A few times I asked to go to Quaker meeting with my father." She testified inaccurately about her part in my first book.

She spoke of her trip to Europe and her life at the Radical House, said there had been sexual pressures in the House but did not lie about her sex life there. She said Europe had taught her she wanted roots, she was searching for a community, wanted to change her environment, was searching for love. She said she had felt trapped by loneliness: "At Santa Cruz everybody just sort of flits through your life."

She told about the college courses she had taken and the books she had read on mysticism: *Don Juan* and *Doors of Perception*. She said she had had an overwhelming feeling many people were oppressed and cited books like Slater's *Pursuit of Loneliness* and Friere's *Pedagogy of the Oppressed*.

She told how a good friend, Joanna, with whom she'd shared a rented house for a few months at Santa Cruz, had joined the church and had written her of it while she, Barb, was traveling in Europe. She said in October 1972, because of pressure from Joanna, she had gone up to Boonville for the first time, with a girl friend. She said she had "decided to be open to the group experience, which consisted of a discussion of religion, group prayer meetings, songs, hikes," had lasted thirty-six hours and had been attended by about forty people.

She testified that her second exposure to the cult had been in February 1973, again at Boonville.

On the second visit Barb had again taken a friend; that friend had not "wished to respond," but Barb had "wanted to understand"; "there was great unity among the people," and "the lectures were dynamic and seemed to cover a lot." (She later told us that she had been visiting the Dana Street center one Saturday morning and had asked for a ride to the bus station so she could return to college. Instead, without explanation, she'd been driven to Boonville for the weekend. Protesting once, she'd then shrugged, deciding to just let it happen.)

After that weekend, Barb stated she had "felt a challenge" and had decided to move in with the Family. When asked by Baker if she sensed Boonville was behind "lock and key," she simply answered, "I don't remember."

She said she had felt no coercion to join and was "not fooled or deceived."

She testified she had thought she might possibly get college credit for studying the cult, and would write her senior thesis on it. (Our understanding also.)

She said she had come home before moving into the Family and discussed it with "my parents in depth." She indicated there had been no opposition from us; she slipped over the fact that she couldn't possibly have discussed the cult "in depth" with anybody, knowing virtually nothing about it herself.

She testified she moved into 6502 Dana Street, Oakland, on April 10, 1973, the day before her somewhat chaotic journal of that period indicates.

She spoke of the cult's meals, said they got casseroles, cheese sandwiches, juice, rice, fruit, salads, "the kind of food I had at home." (What happened to all that protein she'd been brought up on? She said they went to bed at eleven, got up at seven.

At this point, Barb's journal was entered as evidence.

She testified she had had a good relationship with her parents, "now more than ever."

She said she had come home on vacations from college, that, since joining the cult four years ago, she had come home seven times. (Truth: four visits home, two with the flower team and one of these overnight. We had visited her in the Bay Area three times.) She admitted that in the last year and a half she had been in touch with us less frequently because "parents were getting conservatorships on people and church members were afraid of being kidnapped." (This statement rather belied the previous one that her recent relations with us were better than ever.)

When asked about our petitioning for a conservatorship for her, she said she had been shocked: "I thought my parents had greater respect for my living my own life."

She said she now had real happiness, a sense of deep fulfillment and growth, and that her highest allegiance was to God. She said she liked being in a community that shared her goals.

She explained she had spent most of her time in the cult flower selling in the Bay Area and around the country. From July 1975 to

January 1976 she had been in Boonville serving as a junior staff person, after which she had gone back to fund-raising.

When asked if she had feelings, the essential candid Barb suddenly popped through the total control: "Oh, sure," she said, then looked uncomfortable and came up with these as her feelings: "I feel grief, joy, fear. . . ." She said she was frightened of her family, but it was unclear which family she meant, though I assumed we were the heavy ones.

Adjournment. Barb stepped down quietly. Even if we hadn't loved her and she hadn't been in our own family, we'd have felt that there went a remarkable person.

But that day our hugs and good-byes with her were truly painful because Ray and I were both experiencing anger and depression, and for the same reason. Barb hadn't perjured herself about a heinous life pre-cult, she had just coolly obliterated us as though nothing meaningful, pleasurable, or nourishing had happened to her in all the years she had been with us.

That evening our presence was requested at a conference at the Fairmont Hotel with the cult's expert psychiatric witness, Dr. Ash. Ray was very annoyed, because he knew it was not legal protocol for us to see such a person after we had testified. But we knew that if we refused we'd look evasive, so, in high dudgeon, we drove through a cold, sloppy evening rain and found our way to the Fairmont lobby.

There, while other parents were being interviewed, Ray and I went through Barb's journal, which the cult lawyers had just entered in evidence. There was so much in it which was "incriminating" that Ray began to shake his head in disbelief. "Apparently they didn't read it. It looks like the cult lawyers didn't read it before they had it entered." And if Barb had reread it, she had misjudged its potential for damage to her case.

When our turn came, we went upstairs with Dr. Tom Brown to be interviewed by what had been described to us as a "hot-shot doctor from Washington." Ray was in no mood to cooperate, not even a little.

We walked into a large, expensive suite where a lean, bushy-haired fortyish man rose to greet us. A woman was sitting on one of the beds. When she was introduced as his wife, Ray asked, "Is she a psychiatrist?"

"No."

"Then I don't think she should be here."

"But we work together."

"I don't care," said Ray.

So the psychiatrist took us down the hall to what looked like a laundry room.

"I've agreed to tell you exactly what we told our expert witnesses, and no more," Ray said, never sterner. "After that, I agree to answer questions."

"Will you let me say something first?" And before Ray could stop him, Ash threw fuel on Ray's fires by announcing that our young people were perfectly all right, there was no evidence of any sort of psychological problem whatever and he "just wanted to reassure us by telling us that."

I've never seen Ray so upset as when he answered, "Dr. Ash, coming from you, that has got to be an intimidating comment."

Ray recounted what he'd told Benson and Singer; I added my examples. Then ensued a heated civil liberties statement by Ray, after a question by Dr. Ash.

We made our exit.

We waited in the hotel's back hall for Tom Brown to finish his interview with Ash. Tom's handsome face was beet red when he came out; a Scottish burr sounded in his infuriated words. Dr. Ash had scoffed at Tom, said he "was absolutely unconvinced by our parental point of view."

We made our way back to the motel and had a ten o'clock dinner at a nearby restaurant, trying to calm down by huddling before its fireplace until late. We enjoyed the chance to get better acquainted with Tom Brown, the affable Scots-Canadian just leaving as head of research for a large national drug company to go to Vancouver and set up a medical practice. Tom was looking forward to the arrival next day of his young Dutch second wife. By and large, we hadn't yet become as acquainted with the parent families as we had in January. To our regret, our paths didn't ever cross with Burt Kaplan's very much, nor the Hovards', an attractive pair who came and went from court every day from Danville.

Wednesday, March 16.

When we entered the courtroom, the Laurey Baer case was on everyone's lips. Barb had all the details of the "pickup" except that the woman cultist with Laurey had socked Babs Baer, a fact we learned later. At this point we could honestly tell Barb we knew nothing about it except what was in the newspapers.

With Baker still doing the examining, Barb was put back on the stand. She read three of her poems, to show that her creativity had not diminished. Baker than asked her to estimate how many people stayed on in the cult after a weekend at Boonville. She said she was guessing as follows: twenty out of fifty stay after the first visit; eight to ten of those stay after the second visit. After that, only one or two drop out.

Wayne Howard took Barb's cross-examination. Tough and tender young Wayne, after he'd cross-examined Barb and Leslie, said they almost made him cry, they were so easy to trip up.

Wayne asked how Barb had spent her hours precult. She gave these approximations: when she was really working at it, sometimes as much as eighteen hours a day on photography; five hours a week on writing; eight to ten hours a week reading; when she was involved, sometimes five hours a day painting and similar amounts of time in hiking, caving, swimming, riding.

"Were you not from December of seventy-six to now captain of a fund-raising team?"

"Yes."

"How many hours did you work?"

"Early morning till late at night."

"What hours exactly?"

"From about seven in the morning till one at night."

"How many days a week?"

"Seven."

"And isn't it true that most of your years in the church you've been flower selling?"

"Yes. I also spent some time witnessing and some time up at Boonville."

"How many months?"

"Six, maybe seven."

"Have you read the *Divine Principle?*"

"Yes."

"All of it?"

"Some of it."

"Didn't you tell your father you'd only read a third of it?"

"Yes." By now her composure seemed a little shaken; the answers began to come slower. I sensed in Barb mental considerations: *How do I answer that?*

"Isn't *Divine Principle* supposedly written by Moon, and isn't it your church bible?"

"Yes."

Wayne next elicited the facts that she'd had a concussion in a van accident and suffered a leg fracture from continuous running on pavements while selling, but that neither injury had received proper medical treatment.

"Does," he next asked, after a glance at her journal before him, "the church believe in the Blood of the Lamb?"

"What?"

Wayne repeated.

Barb, slowly: "I don't think so."

"Didn't you write in your journal that an old lady asked you if the church believed in the 'Blood of the Lamb' when you were selling flowers to her and you told her yes, and then wrote, 'We must learn to accommodate'?"

"Yes."

"Isn't it true when you fund-raise you represent yourself as a Christian or as part of the New Education Development?"

"Yes, sometimes."

"Barbara, does the church teach the doctrine of 'heavenly deception'?"

A very reluctant: "Yes."

"Who has the highest authority in this area?"

She replied, "Onni Durst."

"Do you chant to her during the day when you're fund-raising?"

Reluctantly: "Sometimes."

"Were you ever kicked by Teresa?"

A *very* long pause. Wayne then read from her journal about Teresa's kicking her. "Well, it was just a little tap," she explained, obviously shaken. (Later truth: it was a real bash and happened more than once. "Smashing out Satan" was the rationale for such occasional personal violence directed at cultists who can't quite conform to all the demands of the cult.)

Again Wayne quoted from her journal: " 'Always find out before anything is done what Onni wants. STAY AWAKE. Onni says she will glue hot peppers on our eyelids.' Did you write those things?"

Barb said "yes," but "the peppers were a joke."

Wayne asked her if she hadn't been idealistic in college, hadn't been interested in minority rights, social justice, rights of women, the elderly. She said yes. He then asked Barb to describe any cult community assistance projects she knew of in the Bay Area, and she stumbled around, citing a clinic just opened for the aged, the occasional giveaway of some of the Boonville garden produce, and their dinner program (designed to catch converts, of course) which was put on at "small cost to the attenders."

Wayne asked Barb if she and all cultists didn't have the assurance they'd marry and have children someday. Did she want to? She responded that she did.

"Isn't it true," he asked, "that of the three hundred full-time people in Oakland's Family, only twelve are married?"

She said she guessed that was right.

"How many have had children?"

"None," she said.

She stepped down. We broke for lunch, Ray and I to go with Scott and Lauriel, Barb, ashen and bothered, with the cult. Picking up silent signals of disapproving freeze from the courtroom rows of cultists, I was afraid Barb would get harsh treatment for some of her reluctant but revealing answers, and despite the fact that such treatment might have given her needed perspective, I prayed that they wouldn't be rough on her. Barb later told us that Daniel had taken her severely to task for the admission about "heavenly deception." Daniel claimed it was not an actual church doctrine. The local media, however, did not buy Daniel's fine distinctions and quoted Barb extensively that night, both her court testimony and a later interview in which she tried to explain it away by saying "heavenly deception" was based on a biblical acceptance of the "minor trickery" that had occurred between Jacob and Esau. It was just a "white lie," she said, and by way of example cited my occasional failure to answer the telephone when I was home.

By now, we had become very aware all the Faithful Five were being provided with fancy lunches and unheard-of new outfits of clothing. The first day of the hearing I'd watched Barb open up a tissue package that contained a good-looking but not valuable lavender and gold locket and bracelet supposedly sent her by Mrs. Moon. John Hovard was proud of the sports jacket given him by Durst and a tie ostensibly sent him by Moon.

When we came back after lunch, Margaret Singer had told the bailiff that Barb was getting signals from Daniel through Amos, who always sat up near the cult counsel table to the left against the wall. Judge Vavuris literally exploded. He said there would be no such behavior tolerated in his courtroom. Barb later told us that a signaling system had been set up but that she'd pretty much tried to ignore it in order to think straight.

One-thirty P.M. Dr. Ash took the stand. A teacher of forensic psychiatry, Ash testified he first saw the Faithful Five on March 10, 1977. He said that in interviewing them he did not use notes but a tape recorder.

He indicated he didn't really believe in coercive persuasion but if it existed, he felt it would have to involve physical captivity, drugs, or hypnosis. Therefore, most of his testimony would concern whether the young persons were competent to "stand trial." He said anyone over twenty-one was to some extent artful and designing. He said he had a strong interest in civil liberties and that he had testified before a legislative committee on the issue of cults and civil liberties so effectively as to have influenced that legislature to drop any plans for conservatorships in that state. Dr. Ash was excused about 3:00 P.M.

Leslie Brown took the stand, a wholesome-looking, fresh-faced woman with high color and lovely features. Leslie's quick moving slenderness was incongruous with the muscled legs of the pavement-pounding woman flower seller's flat, utilitarian gunboat shoes that had become necessary in order to preserve what was left of her feet. She said she had been reared a Presbyterian, wanted to be a public health nurse or go into the Peace Corps, had had two and one half years of college, was twenty-three. She said she had joined the cult a week after her first contact with it, that she had then spent three weeks at Boonville and had spent most of her time since then as a fund-raiser.

She seemed a direct, candid person in her admission that two months before the hearing she had briefly left the cult for a few days while in Vancouver "to study, pray, and visit Bible study fellowships." Contacting no cult members, living under an assumed name so she couldn't be reached, Leslie had begun to feel guilty about her "desertion of God," and had called Oakland Unification center to ask if she might on her own sell flowers for the cult to expiate her guilt. On the stand she gave the impression she had been reassured she had no need to feel guilty or work alone and thence had been flown to Oakland center. What she *didn't* say was that her center man had flatly refused her flower-selling offer, demanded that she accept that God worked only through Onni, and ordered her back to the Bay Area. Fear-ridden and without resources (her own family was still far away in New Jersey), Leslie had suppressed her concerns about cult fund-raising practices and returned to the cult.

Cross-examination got only so far as to have Leslie deny she kept a journal. (Her father stated afterwards that she had shown him a journal before it had been demonstrated that unedited journals were a courtroom hazard to the cult.) Then court was adjourned for the day.

A week had now passed. It seemed a month.

Thursday, March 17.

Dr. Ash was put back on the stand for direct examination. Goorjian opened by saying his client wanted to use his tape recorder in the courtroom "to refresh his memory." With the prospect of verbal testimony spilling out over entranced courtroom listeners, Judge Vavuris looked briefly dismayed. Not only humane and gutsy, he now proved inventive. Yes, he could use it, the judge said, with earphones. Apparently *solitary* refreshing was not quite what counsel and witness had had in mind; with egg on his face, Goorjian dropped the matter.

Dr. Ash then began his testimony by referring to written notes; he kept reading them aloud and being admonished by the judge and our counsel not to do so, but persisted, apparently unable to recall the lines he had just consulted. He said Barb was no more subject to artful and designing people than anybody else; he saw no problems in her. She was able, he said, to concentrate, there was no evidence of blocking, loss of thought train, no blunted affect; her functional vocabulary was superior, the evaluation of the church she gave showed ability to abstract. He dodged her ignorance of the current world by naming her precult social interests; he said she had pleasant childhood recall.

Dr Ash described Hovard as able to handle himself well, and cited an example of Hovard's taking a telephone call from CBS when in Ash's room. His responses, testified the psychiatrist, showed no impairment. He said Hovard showed no signs of needing psychological treatment. As to Jan Kaplan, he cited her adequate emotionality and creativity by stating that "she belted out a very good rendition of 'Summertime' " for Ash's recorder. Jackie Katz he described as shy, less sure of her answers, less outgoing, less sure what she was doing in the church, obviously under more stress. But as with the others, he said Jackie was well groomed and dressed, responded directly, was able to be critical, had a good attention span when he, Ash, deliberately attempted to interrupt her train of thought. He also said she showed no sign of long-term memory deficiency, had an adequate vocabulary, could abstract well, but was having a hard time handling the conflict between her parents and herself. Dr. Ash indicated that Jackie was the only one who admitted she might not have joined the cult if she had known it was a religion.

Of Leslie Brown, Ash said she could concentrate, that while she was more outgoing than Jackie, her affect seemed more inhibited than the others. Her appearance, he said, was good, she was basically unconfused, even got irritated at his own interruptions, had no long-term memory loss, could make negative evaluations, had no loss of IQ, and felt her father had been brainwashed by Mike Trauscht and Wayne Howard.

Cross-examination was to be masterfully handled by that remarkable, gentle-spoken, razor-thinking carpenter-turned-attorney, Carl Shapiro. He rose now, hands bulging from his coat pockets, thin gray hair flying.

Under Shapiro's questioning, Dr. Ash admitted he was no expert in coercive persuasion, said instead he was looking for irrationality of ideas, inflexibility, inability to form opinions or to control selves. Though he claimed competency was his basis for judgment, he said he hadn't recently been involved in any competency evaluations. With great authority, Ash said the concept of unfreezing, as used by the national authority Edgar Schein to describe coming out of coercive persuasion, was a speculative theory. But when Carl pressed, Ash couldn't even give the basic components of Schein's theory. It next turned out he had not read Lifton's classic on coercive persuasion, *Thought Reform and the Psychology of Totalism.* More and more caught, the doctor took to rambling.

"How much time did you spend with each person?" Carl asked. The answer being unclear, Carl offered to help out. He said that at noontime he and others had reviewed the doctor's tapes and they had shown that Ash had spent ten minutes with Leslie Brown and nine minutes with Jackie Katz. (Later we learned the first thing he had had Barb do was straighten up his room.) In each of the five brief interviews, Carl stated that Ash had himself talked approximately 60 percent of the time. (By next day Carl had developed a game plan to see if Ash would take nine minutes for any of his increasingly digressive responses. Carl never quite made it but finally, one response lasting six minutes, Carl looked pointedly up at the clock and said it had been just three minutes short of the time he, Dr. Ash, had spent with Jackie Katz. "And yet in that amount of time you expected to make a determination?" "Yes.")

Late afternoon produced a shocker when Carl elicited from Ash that he couldn't remember if Durst and several other cult people had also, for a brief interval, been in the room with the young people during Ash's interviews with some of them. At that point Paul Goorjian put his forehead in his hands and just sat there for a while.

"How," asked the "gentle" Carl, "if you judged John Hovard's responses by a telephone call, was this possible when all you could hear was one side of the call?"

"Well done, Clarence Darrow," Ray laughed admiringly after that cross-exam. And it turned out that the scholarly Carl had, indeed, spent the evening before reading *Inherit the Wind*, the play which shows the brilliant Darrow pitted against the fundamentalist William Jennings Bryant.

Friday, March 18, 9:00 A.M.

Dr. Ash was put back on the stand and Carl continued with his disingenuous mayhem ("Your honor, I'm a simple man..."). Under questioning, Ash stated that he had been in the courtroom part of the day before his own testimony, making him privy to some of Leslie Brown's testimony; that he had *asked* the Faithful Five if they were under mind control (!); and that he saw nothing wrong with the practice of heavenly deception, saying it was no different from telling a white lie.

The morning's last shocker was Ash's admission that he had been hired by the Unification Church to testify on bills pending before a state legislature to allow conservatorships in cases involving cult members. "And isn't it true," Carl asked, "that those bills were not, as you claimed, stopped by your testimony but are moving through committee with some chance of passage?" Ash admitted this might be a possibility.

On redirect by Baker, however, we paid for Ray's intransigence in the hotel interview as Ash tried to nail us in particular. He said we were the first parents he'd ever met not interested in his, Ash's, evaluation of their daughter, that we were intent on deprogramming our daughter's religious beliefs, and that maybe what we were really interested in was having her "learn about socialism and communism." Both of us were incandescent with rage by that time and having a hard time restraining ourselves. Although the notion of pacifist Quaker communists seemed impossible to me, I was beginning to be numb to any wild charge, having just had a brief and unpleasant encounter in the hallway with an abusive lady rabbi wearing a swastika. Shapiro, of course, brought out that "Ash's reassuring the parents the young people were absolutely all right had to be regarded by the parents not as an objective judgment but an adversary position."

Paul Goorjian, who at one point had wearily admonished his talkative witness, "Just answer the question," didn't redirect at all.

Dr. Ash disappeared.

11:00 A.M. Great stir. Neil Salonen, president of the Unification Church, came into the courtroom. Daphne Green, the noted San Francisco woman who has been fighting a running battle with Unification but at that time was keeping her bridges open to the cult because her daughter was still a member, rose to tell the bailiff that, since Salonen is regarded by cult people "as a god," he should get special seating. The poker-faced bailiff placed Salonen up against the front-left wall where he, with a deserving expression, looked on.

Leslie Brown went back on the stand. She said in fund-raising she averaged $300 a day; one single day in Alaska she earned $1,300. Wayne Howard, his low-key, casual manner softening the sharp point of his cross-examining, got Leslie to admit that up at Boonville Micah had a key to the phones to shut them off for outgoing calls.

Leslie ended with the somehow pathetic claim that she knew she should get her teeth fixed and see her parents more often. I felt sick hearing that. Is that all the Faithful Five think we're about?

Leslie's true cult story we learned later. She had spent a lot of time fund-raising for the cult in Canada and Alaska. It was the duplicity in their selling activity in Canada that had finally driven her from the cult during those four days in Vancouver, for buried in Leslie was her father's Scots sense of rectitude. It was also this selling deceit which had so enraged certain Alaskan individuals against the cult that Leslie was several times attacked in bars and alleys when trying to sell flowers. Her center man had been stoned by a mob when it was discovered that he and Leslie were selling for New Education Development without telling people of their connection with the Unification Church.

Despite these hazards, the warmhearted Leslie grew to love the far north and its people, the Indians and Eskimo, as her flower selling took her as far north as Kotzebue. Peddling in bars or from shack door to shack door, she was even allowed into the public schools. She described once taking her bundles of red roses into a schoolroom of little Eskimos; none had ever seen such flowers before and they rushed forward with soft exclamations to smell the rose toilet water she'd sprayed on them. But, despite her love of the children, her flowers and an occasional gift made when guilt didn't overwhelm her, had to be sold for Moon for two dollars each, so she went away having made no sales. Late that afternoon, as she was walking down a rutted path, she heard a voice shouting, "Leslie, Leslie!" Flying toward her was a little Eskimo boy waving two dollars. "Somebody sent me a coconut but I sold it," he confided, "because I wanted a rose for my mother."

In interviews after the hearing, Leslie said one day a far north bank had mistakenly credited her center man with a thousand dollars more than had been deposited. He said nothing, then asked Oakland headquarters what he should do. The word came down that several years before a bank in the Bay Area had shorted the cult a thousand dollars so, yes, in God's eyes it was all right to keep the extra money.

Later Leslie was to say of the authoritarian pressures of cult life: "Whatever your center person tells you is the truth, that's the truth. There can be no questioning. They're always saying, 'Trust what you don't understand.' You're always just trying to respond automatically; the more automatically you respond, the more trusted you are."

Of the hearing Leslie also said: "They put incredible pressure on us during the trial. They glorified us, calling us the Faithful Five, and told us we had an enormous responsibility. They put it like this: out of all history, out of the past two thousand years since Jesus died, we were the first ones to stand up in court before all America and declare our love for God and our dedication to the Messiah.

Mercifully escaping the confines of the courtroom, we ate Lauriel's lunch out by the reflecting pool in front of the courthouse. Barb came with us, and raised the panic level in me by saying that if conservatorship papers were served on her she'd fight physically. Ray seemed not to take this seriously; he and Barb—those two Irishers—sparred in fun back in the courtroom as everyone took their seats. But if there is physical resistance at the service of papers or deprogramming, the problem is very much compounded, as Laurey Baer's case was soon to show.

On the stand, John Hovard did what I'd been afraid Barb would try to do, paint a totally bleak picture of his life precult. John said he'd taken a lot of drugs in college, spent a month in jail in Oregon on a stolen gun charge that was later dismissed. He conceded that when he was in jail his parents came to see him to help out, while the cult "sent some cards." He claimed he had been expelled from a Latin American country on drug-smuggling charges. (His parents said he was not directly involved in this.) He said he had learned about Moon a week after he'd gone into the cult. When asked what his life goals were, he said to travel, get married, have children, sail on a sailboat.

John's impassive manner seemed deceptive to me—I got a clear sense he was really doing some inner suffering as the cult lawyer bored into and brought out some of the alleged details of his past. I felt very badly for his parents, Gail and John, and for his pretty and anxious-looking sister, who had left college to be with her parents during the hearing.

Margaret Singer told us that out in the chaotic halls—crowded with TV cameras and media people, cultists and onlookers—she had been followed to the elevator by three Moonies chanting "Out Satan!" When Wayne Howard requested that Salonen be seated in a special place for fear he might signal witnesses, the cult lawyers had responded that Margaret Singer might do the same thing for our side. So the judge—whose patience in this pandemonium was as Job's—ordered Salonen and Margaret to sit together near him. "There goes the odd couple," Barb quipped (at which I breathed a sigh of relief for a flash of her old humor).

Saturday, March 19.

Not waiting to hear from Barb who said that she would phone us as her schedule allowed, Lauriel, Scott, Ray, and I took a beautiful hike in Point Reyes state park. What a long time we've known each other. We laid plans to take a trip and "just talk about things fifty-year-olds think about."

Sunday, March 20.

Ray and I met Barb for brunch at the Claremont Hotel. She was so unyielding and adamant that I had five steamy minutes when I was ready to give up, and came close to saying so. Ray's five minutes had luckily not coincided with mine. When we took Barb back to Ashby Street, Burt Kaplan was pacing on the sidewalk, so we picked Burt up and drove her to Scott's and Lauriel's, where we shared our Point Reyes crabs. Ray hurriedly packed and, with a sinking sensation, I watched him drive off in the rental car for the airport. He couldn't be away from the office any longer.

That evening Laurey Baer escaped from the deprogrammer's motel in Fresno.

Monday, March 21.

John Hovard was put back on the stand, and Sylvia Shapiro established that John knew very little about the belief system of his faith. The one concept John explained with great clarity, however, was that of the center man.

At midmorning, Jackie Katz went on. There was a reserve about her, a sensitivity that I found attractive. She spoke of her schooling at Tufts and Oberlin, remembered her grade school teachers and named them, said she'd been a Presbyterian but had studied Zen in college. Her effort to paint herself as a black sheep came when she said she'd first taken marijuana at a junior high school Girl Scout jamboree; even she joined in the courtroom laughter. In June 1976, she had gone out to California to visit her brother, was approached in Golden Gate Park by cultists, went to dinner, was on a bus to Boonville shortly after. She had left Boonville the next night to drive an eastern friend to the airport, but returned to stay at Boonville for four weeks. Two weeks after she went in, she had learned of the Unification Church and Moon. Accompanying herself on the guitar, she sang a folk song, "Rock Me on the Water." She said she wanted to marry and wanted to be an urban planner.

For reasons unexplained, Jackie's testimony was interrupted to put on Dr. Lee, a Southern California psychologist hired by the cult. He appeared a pleasant, competent guy, who stated openly that he had made an inside study of the Krishnas and, in lieu of the payment he'd expected, "was going to get a couple of articles and a book out of it."

He had administered some standardized psychological tests to the Faithful Five—the Minnesota Multiphasic Personality Inventory, the Rorschach test, the Draw-a-Person test. It was very hard to hear a detailed personal analysis of Barb's psyche made public, but I thought I should listen because of the bearing it might have on her capacity to withstand stress. I may be in error in some of the specifics, but in the main I believe my notes about both test and interpretations are accurate as they relate to the findings on Barb.

MMPI
Lie scale: elevated but normal.
Candidness (honesty with herself): normal.
Candidness outward: elevated but normal range.
Hypochondriasis: elevated but normal range.
Depression scale: right on normal.
Hysterical: elevated but in the normal range.
Anger scale (pd): elevated but within normal range.
Sexuality and sex role: normal.
Paranoid: suspicion and guardedness tested above the normal
     range.
Schizophrenia (sensitivity to others and possession of feelings):
     normal.
Manic (agitation, excitement): elevated but within normal range.
Social introversion scale (withdrawal): extroverted.
Truthfulness: not elevated.
Intellectualizing (also used as a test of evasiveness): normal,
     although she might use intellectualizing to defend herself.
Psychostenia (emotional instability): normal.
Rorschach
Introversion/extroversion: highly extrovertic.
IQ: high.
Relationship to parents: anxious about father, somewhat afraid of
     him (all the girls showed this).
Dependency: fond of mother; might still be a little dependent on
     her.
Creative
Perfectionist
Sensitive, to hypersensitive, to criticism
Mature
This test showed an overriding problem was present.
Draw-a-Person Test
Showed persistence, ambition, a reasonable security, a certain
     amount of unconventionality, some impulsiveness, some
     humor, some anxiety
Showed high energy, tension

This type of report was made on all five young people; all showed equally high or higher levels of agitation. Hovard was, Dr. Lee admitted, in somewhat dubious shape: "If he walked in my office I'd suggest he come regularly to see me."

Lee said Barb was not susceptible to artful and designing persons, had a good memory, a superior vocabulary ("She talked about sea life by names I didn't even recognize"); had good feelings toward people; in novel situations her feelings came to the surface but she could recover; showed good sexual adaptation, firm cultural interests.

Dr. Lee testified he had talked to Edgar Schein on the phone and Schein had said that if the person were physically free to leave a situation, coercive persuasion was not present; he claimed young people stayed in the cult only because of peer pressure and proselytizing. In cross-exam Shapiro questioned the validity of Schein's opinion, which had been formed on the basis of brief telephone conversation. In general, Shapiro's cross-examination was directed toward establishing that the tests administered by Lee were not relevant to the matter of coercive persuasion; nobody was claiming the young people were crazy.

We had lunch with Barb at the reflecting pool, joined by Father Kent Burtner from Eugene, a grand Oregon presence, a vast teddy bear of a young cleric, equal parts intelligence and compassion. He laughed when he told her he had been studying Unification before a lot of the current leaders had ever heard of it. Trying not to cry, I told Barb I couldn't understand how someone I respected as much as herself could believe in some of the morally outrageous views from "Master Speaks," writings based on Moon's talks to cult members. Sylvia Shapiro had given me some sections of that set of speeches; Barb now skimmed through the one on Moon's views of family life, made no comment, said she wanted a copy.

News of Laurey Baer's "escape" from the deprogrammers greeted us in the headlines that afternoon. How dreadful. What had happened?

Tuesday, March 22.
Nearly two weeks had passed. Dr. Lee finished up. The judge ruled at eleven that a third cult psychiatrist couldn't testify. ("Each side has had two, what would we gain? I've been more than fair, given you all this time, but we've got to wind this up.") Vavuris was obviously growing angry at the persistence of cult lawyers and the way they kept trying to take advantage of his original promise of court time.

At noon there was a big cult press conference with a statement from Laurey Baer that he had been "abused" in his deprogramming. Unification president Neil Salonen made a statement; the ACLU added its point of view. I was concerned and upset, so I asked Carl Shapiro to call a parents' meeting for the next morning at nine, and we arranged to meet in a back courthouse hall.

In the afternoon, Jackie Katz went back on the stand. Wayne, on cross-examination, got her to admit that she had made a hysterical phone call to her parents the first weekend she was up at Boonville, hinting she didn't feel free to leave. It was at the end of Baker's redirect of Jackie that he made a supposed joke under his breath about Jackie's being half Jewish. Sylvia Shapiro picked up on it, and bedlam broke loose as she nailed Baker in an outraged voice and we underwent our own mini Middle East crisis.

That evening, Jeff, Evey, and I went to see the Alvin Ailey dancers. On the way back to the Alameda, Jeff told me that his attaché case had just been stolen from a friend's apartment; in it was his diary for the past three months, which he meant to use for some writing, as well as his passport and some money. Jeff said there was a clue that pointed to the cult.

Evey said she had come to court only one afternoon, that her old cult friend, Mark, had tried to embrace her in an awkward and maddening way, and thereafter she'd stayed away from the courtroom.

Wednesday, March 23.

At the parents' meeting in the hallway, Wayne stated that the Laurey Baer accusations were exaggerated. He went over the plans for the balance of the hearing. Carl Shapiro wanted to argue the constitutional issue in his summation, but all the parents vetoed this as taking more time than was possible.

When I got to the courtroom, I told Barb about Jeff's attaché case being stolen. I could tell she was bothered. After the hearing she told me she had asked Amos whether he knew anything about it, but Amos had just replied crossly that taking it might have been necessary, and that concern for it wasn't relevant to this hearing. Barb said she had been very upset that Amos didn't deny knowing about the theft, very shocked that he simply scolded her for being concerned.

Jan Kaplan was put on the stand. Jan, a handsome, freckled brunette, struck me as the toughest-minded of the five, good-natured, confident, fun loving, realistic, hard to visualize as a selfless missionary.

Her story was pretty typical, except that she testified that after her classic pilgrimage west to San Francisco, she'd worked in a massage parlor for three months on the Tenderloin, then lived on unemployment for a year.

Scott, Barb, and I had lunch at the San Franciscan hotel. Barb seemed to remember with fondness the weeks she had worked in Scott's law office right after she had joined the cult; I remember she had commented on what a nice, warm office it was and that he was the reason.

1:45 P.M. Shrouded in long black robes and wearing a black skull cap, the strangest-looking young man, black-bearded and grim, was in the courtroom when we got back. He was surprise witness "Father" Randy, who belonged to the cultish "Old" Catholic church and who had apparently had a deprogramming experience with Wayne Howard. Put on the stand over Wayne's protest against a surprise witness, Randy claimed that his clothing had been torn off and he had been roughed up in his deprogramming. He had been quoted in print as saying Howard had tried to get him to forsake his vows of chastity. But on cross-examination by Wayne, Randy admitted that all Wayne had done, when they were about to go to dinner with his parents, was to ask him if he wanted a date.

3:25 P.M. Norma, star cult witness for those who had undergone deprogramming and then come back to the cult, was put on the stand. According to Norma, her deprogramming had been a horror. She had been taken to a motel in Marin County; her parents had not been allowed to be present. She was then flown to Phoenix; on that flight Wayne Howard (one of the world's best straight-faced jokesters) had told her she could try out any court in Arizona she wanted: "I own them all." Norma declared she had been humiliated at the Freedom of Thought Foundation and made to feel guilty.

She said she had seen the rehab psychologist eight times.

I had already heard the deprogramming rehab side of Norma's story and tended to believe it, how the cult had actually tried to have Norma committed to a hospital rather than go through deprogramming, how the judge had finally ordered that she could go either direction she preferred, how, of her own free will, she had then returned to the rehab center. (I had been told that Esther Alexander, Joe's warmhearted and hard-working wife, had several grateful letters from Norma in her possession.) But after a month at the rehab center and after promises by the cult of being put on staff and being married to an old boyfriend, Norma had gone back to the cult, which duly delivered on its promises. I watched the young woman and inwardly shook my head: here was a kid who felt she didn't have a place to lay her head, and was unable to imagine that she could take care of herself.

Vavuris would not allow Len Foster to testify—"repetition of what we've already heard"—and thus the cult lost what I'm sure would have been a real star. He was an impressive kid. Also not allowed to testify was Dr. Stillson Judah from Pacific Theological Seminary; we understood his remarks would be friendly to the cults.

At four o'clock the judge announced he was clearing the courtroom because the prime minister of Japan was visiting the city and would come to the courthouse. "What, is he going to testify, too?" Carl Shapiro quipped, and with that everybody cracked up, cultists and noncultists alike.

After the laughter subsided, the judge announced he would render his decision the next day.

That evening I took Lauriel, Scott, and Logan to.see a noisy movie about which I remember nothing.

I didn't sleep at all that night.

Thursday, March 24.
The courthouse halls were a madhouse. Long lines were waiting at the courtroom door as we came up. How, my weary mind asked, had a family like ours, people like us, ever gotten into something like this? Through this mob scene the bailiff pushed the Faithful Five and their families into the courtroom. I'd arranged with Lauriel that if I were in circumstances where I couldn't get to a phone, she would call Ray the minute we had the decision. In a numb condition, I settled back to wait the verdict. At that point I thought our chances were fifty-fifty, though our counsel seemed cheerfully confident. But so did the cult's.

Barb sat in deep silence beside me; I was getting absolutely no emotional signals from her.

Because of Lauriel I have a record of some of the remarks in the hour-and-a-half Shapiro summation, which opened the morning. It was presented in the civil manner and tones of the gray-haired wise man and in exactly the dignified way, with the right emphasis, I longed for. The way he spoke of Barb made me realize he had seen in her what we had always seen in her. It brought tears to my eyes.

"This is the most difficult case I have ever had to summarize. It is not the law upon which my summation will be based, but what I have observed in court.

"I will treat the five cases as a unit; I don't want to cite specific evidence since Your Honor has judicious notes and it would be both redundant and presumptuous to say what *I* think the witnesses said.

"There are things in this case which give me great concern, both as a parent and as a lawyer. This concern springs from a chain of events as well as from witnessing the deep care of five loving parents who have testified to personality changes in their much loved offspring. (I reluctantly use the word "offspring"—I know no better way to call them.)

"These parents have seen changes in their young people of intellectual functioning, social concern, health, ability to challenge and judge for themselves, and, finally, rejection of the family structure which has nourished them.

"It would be unfair to attribute any motive to the parents other than love and a desire to restore a free life to their children and, with those, reestablish the family ties which have been so important in the past. Parents have a right and a duty to continue their concern for their offspring even after their eighteenth birthday.

"The most significant part of this case is that in a period of one week or two, five young people made a complete turnabout of their social, religious, moral, and personal attitudes. This dramatic change took place after they became involved in the Unification Church.

"They each went up to Boonville not because they had primarily a religious goal but because they wanted to find a new communal existence. After participating, the change in every case occurred within weeks.

"These young people are from middle-class, educated families; each has had college, each has had a higher social consciousness, and each was concerned with helping the oppressed, the disadvantaged, the handicapped. Each was the sort to challenge what he or she heard. Each was gifted in other ways additionally: music, poetry, sports. But the turnaround in every case was completed in two weeks. In that brief time they had ceased to be questioning individuals, they had ceased to be active in social concerns, they had withdrawn from their families, they had relinquished their cultural environment, they had adopted a totally new philosophy and way of life for themselves. It is astonishing to find such a complete reversal; no experience I have had or read about comes close to this fast, dramatic transformation.

"Not one young person attributed the change to divine revelation. If they had, I could have understood that. But the testimony describes the communal experience as the chief reason for change. I would therefore have to assume that what happened in Boonville was some kind of powerful coercive persuasion; if you will, mind control.

"Each of the five had some need, was drifting physically and emotionally. Each had problems, some sort of identity crisis or relationship crisis. Each was seeking an acceptable and accepting place to live.

"Yet we are aware that in eighty-eight to ninety recent cases, persons who have had a similar experience have gone to a facility in Tucson, Arizona, and there have experienced a complete reversal and restoration of their old values.

"I don't understand such overnight change and overnight return, except that I have to assume change was originally programmed by someone within the cult institution.

"I do not understand the deprogramming process, but whatever it is, it indicates that the individuals were capable of being controlled. This phenomenon violates every rational concept I have ever heard about the ability of the human mind to challenge, assert, accept, reject.

"I haven't talked about the testimony of experts" [and he went on to expand on the fact that honest experts can disagree].

"To my way of thinking, the most significant evidence in this case is the journal of Barbara Underwood. Without in any way criticizing any of the other four, Barbara Underwood represents the most developed intellectually, socially, and culturally. I can also relate most closely to her parents, because of their background and position.

"We have entered in evidence a journal Barbara prepared, showing every aspect of her life right before and right after she joined the Church. Six months after she joined, the journal abruptly stops. Yet in its earlier pages she expresses concepts and challenges, questions philosophy, demonstrates a wide range of interests unexceeded in any adult with whom I am acquainted. She shows many concerns for the socially disadvantaged, including the importance of women participating fully in every aspect of life. She seeks answers in a probing way I have never seen a young adult seek. I see her, as a matter of fact, as a young, potential intellectual giant.

"That impressive questioning abruptly ceases. From July to September 1973, only two words are entered: flower selling.

"Then Barbara goes home in late August or early September. After that visit with her parents, she again writes in her journal, she again raises questions, wonders about Satan, wonders about men-women relations, wonders about the fall of man, wonders whether she is doing things contrary to her true values. Once more her private thoughts flare up in her journal. She even *says* she can question because she had stepped outside the cult briefly, albeit without the full break which provides the neutral environment necessary for freely made decisions.

"After that visit, she returns to the church. And now she begins simply to mouth the words of others. From then on her own personality disappears; there is nothing of Barbara.

"I submit you cannot explain this in any way except by some process which has turned this young woman—these young people—around overnight. Their defenses were down and they were susceptible. Conditions within themselves were matched with processes used on them in Boonville.

"I personally have never seen this situation before; I personally have difficulty understanding it. All I know is, it did happen.

"As a long-time member of the American Civil Liberties Union, I have problems as to whether this hearing represents an invasion of religious rights. I must, however, rely on the conscience of this court and repeat that I feel it is an exercise of judicial function to restore to people their free wills and minds by order of such an instrument as a conservatorship.

[Carl Shapiro then cited cases involving conflict between the state's police powers and individual religious rights. In some of these cases—matters of blood transfusions, fluoridation, compulsory education, polygamy, the use of drugs, snake use in religious worship—the courts found for the church or parents, in some against.]

"Temporary conservatorship is necessary for these five young people because they need protection from something which represents a threat to their mental health, their physical health, and their long-term relationships.

"If conservatorships are granted, at the end of thirty days these proceedings will be terminated and from that point the court can then decide where the matter should best be handled."

In his courtly way, Carl Shapiro thanked the judge for his generous allowance of court time, his patience, humor and fairness. He then paid his respects to opposing counsel and sat down.

When it comes to summations, I don't pretend to objectivity; I have no record of Ralph Baker's closing statement. I remember he said no urgent need for guardianship had been established, there was no evidence of incompetence, medical judgment had indicated this as well as the manner and behavior of the five young people in the courtroom for eleven days. I remember he was very forceful when he said there was such a thing as religious conversion; he'd undergone that experience himself and he told us something about it. I remember that he made a great issue of the fact that the young people no longer used drugs, engaged in promiscuity, drank, or smoked cigarettes, and that he thought that such change was absolutely for the better and distinctly a part of the American way. He said he couldn't believe this "trial" was happening in America.

I'm sure that to many minds Baker's statement seemed more dramatic than Carl Shapiro's quiet comments with their very sensitive uncertainties as well as their very clearly stated certainties.

All the while I listened, my mind refused the imminent possibility that after this day I might never see Barb again.

We didn't go to lunch together; by now I was aware how hard these get-togethers were for her, and sometimes for us, and I knew that today of all days she would want to be with her friends and supporters from the cult. The two sisters, Laile Bartlett and Lauriel, my nephew Logan, and I, joined the crush at the courtroom basement lunch counter.

The bailiff got us into the courtroom through the judge's chambers. By now the hallways were hellish.

1:30. Judge Vavuris came in and quietly sat down. The silence that fell on the room was thick with unspoken apprehensions and expectations as he spoke.

"This has been a very emotional case. I have been deeply involved in it, as have all of us, since March 9.

"I want to thank the attorneys, petitioners, and objectors for handling themselves well and responsibly.

"I also want to explain the presence of the bailiffs and police officers here. We expect order after the decision is made, and acceptance of this decision in a peaceful manner. This is the American system of justice; there is no better judicial system in the world. It is easy to criticize, but there is no finer system.

"We are fallible human beings and subject to error. Justice is also slow.

"One side will like my decision, the other will not. But my decision is made. If attorneys on either side oppose that decision, they can appeal. That is their right and I encourage them to use it.

"There is no precedent for the case before us, and I feel that this field needs the opinion of higher judicial authorities because of its many complicated aspects.

"I, too, am fallible. But I have done what I think to be right.

"This has not been the run-of-the-mill case that involves some money, some damages. . . . "We're talking about the very essence of life here, mother, father, and children. . . . There's nothing closer in our civilization. This is the essence of civilization. The family unit is a micro-civilization. . . . A great civilization is made of many, many great families, and that's what's before this court. . . . One of the reasons I made this decision, [is that] I could see the love here of a parent for his child and I don't have to see beyond that. Even our laws of this state, the probate laws, have all been set up—the laws of succession—so that children succeed to the estate of their parents if the parents die intestate. . . . The law looks at that binding thing between a parent and a child. It is never ending. No matter how old we are, it's there. And that was one of the things that influenced this court.

"I have researched the law, attended the case, listened carefully to the witnesses and the arguments.

"It is hereby ordered that the petition of Mr. and Mrs. Raymond Underwood for appointment as temporary conservators of the person of Barbara Lael Underwood is hereby granted."

Vavuris then granted the other four conservatorships in identical language.

He further ordered that a hearing on the permanent conservatorship, or such other proceedings as might take place, would take place on

April 27, 1977, at 10:30 A.M. and that all parties had to appear at that time without further notice. During the temporary conservatorship, he said that the conservator, or the conservatee's other parent, had to be present with the conservatee at all times.

If either side, concluded the judge, wished to make a statement, it might do so now.

Beside me, Barb sat unmoving, unspeaking. The whole room was quiet as a church at midnight.

Goorjian rose to request that the following restrictions be placed on the conservatorships: the parents not be allowed to turn the "children" over to the deprogrammers; the "children" be allowed at any time to contact their attorneys, that "I be allowed to contact them at any time to check to see if they are being mistreated in any way"; that the "children" have access to their religious materials, be allowed the practices of their religion, and have access to their Church elders during the thirty-day period. He concluded with the sincerely impassioned plea, "I'm asking Your Honor not to turn these five people over to the wolves."

The judge's response to this request for restrictions to his order consisted of an acceptance of some limitations, but a denial of any attempt to forestall deprogramming. He said that in putting the young people into the custody of their parents, he assumed those parents loved them fully and would see no harm came to them. There would therefore, he declared, be no restrictions placed on the manner in which the custody was to be exercised, whether with deprogrammers or not.

He agreed that conservatees could be contacted by their counsel at "all reasonable times" and "should have access to reading material of their choice."

He then stated that the conservatorships would begin immediately, but that until 5 P.M. the following Monday, March 28, "in order to give Church attorneys time to appeal," the conservatees had to stay in California within parental custody and under the jurisdiction of the court.

All the while these legal details were being worked out, we sat without saying a word. But while I sat, I realized that deep inside me there had always been the conviction that the judge would decide for us. If he were in any way reasonable or humane (and these things he had seemed to be), he would have the mercy to liberate the exceptional young woman beside me from the stone that held her.

As I write, I can't think of those moments except in tears, but at the time I had been through so much, and it had been so hard, that I could only sit there and endure, missing Ray's presence and the steadfast spirit he'd shone throughout.

And then, all I could care about was my seemingly stunned and wordless daughter.

They cleared the court, and with this my friend Lauriel and I parted. The young people were taken immediately back to the judge's chambers to await further instructions from him.

Wayne Howard said later he couldn't understand why there wasn't jubilation from the parents; I learned he was crestfallen and felt his efforts had gone unappreciated. But somehow it wasn't a time for hurrahs; there had been too much polarizing and there was too much uncertainty ahead. And after that, so much mending, if mending there would be. . . .

We waited around, chatting quietly, then each of us was welcomed into the judge's chambers. I thought Vavuris had the kindest face on record. All I could say, as I shook his hand, was that, for my husband and myself, we thanked him. He seemed to understand I wasn't capable of eloquence at that moment. In later remarks he was to prove himself consistently sympathetic to what we were trying to point out. Though the decision, as spoken, was limited to the issue of family relationship, in post-hearing public statements Judge Vavuris said he had become convinced that coercive persuasion existed and had been used.

We had before us the awful exit from the courthouse, as the growing uproar we could hear outside in the courthouse halls kept reminding us.

With Vavuris's kindly bailiff, other bailiffs, and police officers going ahead, the doors were pushed open against the mob and we were shoved out into the maelstrom. All of us feared violence from the crowd. I tried to keep track of Barb beside me, but she was instantly stopped by T.V people shoving microphones at her. I'm indebted to the bailiff, who, with impatient, sweeping gestures cleared a pathway for Barb and we went down the hall to the freight elevators, the mob pressing and streaming along beside us.

At the elevator I was suddenly parted from Barb; as the glass doors closed against me I shouted to Wayne Howard to stay with her. As I left the corridor on the next elevator trip, what swam before me as I glanced back was the concerned face of Father Kent Burtner; he was tall enough to stand out in the crowd.

Downstairs and outside, the five cars of the deprogrammers, as the media said, were waiting in an "ominous" row. I grabbed Barb and we climbed into the first one. In the front seat sat Gary Scharff beside Skip Guarini, who was driving. In a few moments, under police motorcycle escort, our procession took off through the streets of San Francisco, headed for the freeway.

I couldn't imagine what Barb must be thinking in the car beside me. It flashed through me that if my mother had taken me away like that when I was twenty-five, I might now have turned and socked her. But if nothing else, I suspected Barb was as relieved as I to have pushed her way through the mob that had made our exit seem an outrage; Hovard shouting his defiant TV statements, parents looking grimly anxious, sensation-hunting media pushing mikes at people. Barb's single white-faced comment had been: "I'm shocked."

At first it was utterly quiet in the car.

Then, with his great sense of the rightness of things and his deep sensitivity to Barb's fear (the cult having instilled such terror about deprogramming), Gary Scharff turned in his seat and started to talk to Barb. He began by saying that he wouldn't talk to her unless she wanted him to. She greeted this with silence, so he went on to explain in the briefest and clearest way possible what he, as an ex-cult deprogrammer, had on his mind. That was absolutely not to force his views or convictions on anyone. (And as I watched him in the days to come, that's exactly the policy he firmly adhered to.)

She was listening. We all knew that. Suddenly a tight coil of worry eased in me; Len Foster had advised, huddle up in a ball, don't listen to *anything*. So far, at least, she showed no signs of that. Just as, contrary to the remarks she had made before, she had showed no inclination to resist physically.

Skip Guarini then asked Barb some questions about what she was feeling right then. I don't think she was very explicit about her inner psychology, but she did say that she was absolutely shocked the conservatorships had been granted; neither cult nor Faithful Five had apparently thought there was any possibility of that.

She answered. She talked.

Again silence. By now we were tearing along the freeway toward the airport, the other big cars of the group flashing in and out, keeping together.

The personable Skip next told a funny story. He'd sat in the press box for a week until he'd gone down to the beach to try to start the book he was going to write on the Faithful Five. One day he was sitting next to a newspaperman when the term "blunted affect"—meaning limited emotionality—was first mentioned. He said the reporter had nudged him with a worried look and asked, "Is that terminal?"

Skip then went on to say he'd been with Laurey Baer some of the days of his programming and that if he, Skip, had had any doubt that there was such a thing as mind control, his experience with Laurey Baer had dispelled it. He described how Laurey was "coming out of it," how he, Skip, had left him in a reasonable frame of mind, how he had come back at the point when cult members had discovered the motel room where Laurey was and when he heard them it was like "turning a knob." Laurey went back into a continuous chant, a continuous pacing, and wasn't "reachable anymore."

Gary Scharff picked up where Skip left off and told how, "when Jerry Feldman was 'picked up' he yelled he was being kidnapped. 'Of course you're not,' Wayne Howard had said, 'we have an order from the court to serve you.' So Jerry had got this hang-dog, apologetic look and answered, 'But I can't yell I'm being conservatorshipped.' "

We were almost to our destination. Just before we arrived, Barb said she would talk because she couldn't imagine anything short of abuse that would get her to give up what she'd believed in and worked so hard for during the last four years.

We pulled into the airport Travelodge.

In retrospect, I believe the last thing on Barb's mind—faced as she felt she was with a personal battle between championing God or succumbing to Satan—was her relationship to her own natural family. But I had been experiencing a silent and terrible empathy for her, and so I said, "I want you to know I love you. But you don't have to respond in any way; it mixes people up when someone loves them and they can't love back." She didn't say anything; I didn't know if she heard.

We all got out of the car.

Evey Eden was the first one to walk up to Barb.

"I'd like to hit you," Barb said. Evey eased away. I wasn't around when Barb greeted Jeff Scales.

The ex-cult people seem to take these threats of violence and escape in stride. When Daniel told Jeff Scales that if he, Jeff, ever got him in a room with deprogrammers, he'd "punch every nose in the place," "Go right ahead," Jeff had answered cheerfully, "start with me. I'll stand there and be your punching bag." When I'd worried to Evey that Barb was flower selling on a broken leg, she'd answered instantly, "Good." "Good!" I'd groaned, "what's good about it?" "Well, Barb runs real fast; this way she won't be so hard to catch," Evey had chuckled.

We went to our room, and with the late afternoon sun streaming in the open door, made small talk. Pretty soon Evey slipped in. Hers and Barb's first words together were of practicalities: where were Barb's toothbrush, books, knapsack?

Evey slipped away, reappeared soon. Each time the talk seemed to get easier; I even heard a laugh as I lay resting.

Ray had grabbed a plane out of Portland at four o'clock, managing to clear his desk in a scattershot of papers right after he'd gotten Lauriel's call from the courthouse that the conservatorships had been granted. Lauriel and Scott brought him to the Travelodge a little before eight, and Ray went right past us to hug Barb.

With Evey in the room, Barb lay down to rest. She had been fasting all day and refused the food we suggested; her fast wouldn't be over till midnight. After a bit she got up and went into the shower. She stayed an eternity. "She's taking a cold shower and praying," Evey whispered matter-of-factly. I tried not to shudder, remembering the heavy head cold Barb had.

When Barb came out of the shower she crawled, fully dressed, into bed. Without words, Evey lay down beside her. Pretty soon she was talking softly to Barb, stroking her hair. There was brief laughing and murmuring before Barb fell asleep. I thought care for each other in the cult could not possibly have been this beautiful. As Evey made plain to us, setting her alarm clock, *she* would get the food at midnight so that Barb could eat.

I slept right through that, but I did waken several times later in the night to look over at the neighboring bed and let myself at last feel the overwhelming joy of having gotten our daughter out. Whatever lay ahead, whatever its uncertainties, its possible failures, tonight I would never forget.

Barb: Hearing

"But I, being poor, have only my dreams;
I have spread my dreams under your feet;
Tread softly, because you tread on my dream.
—w. b. yeats, "He Wishes for the Cloths of Heaven"

"It is love that I am seeking for,
But of a beautiful, unheard-of kind,
That is not in the world."
—w. b. yeats, "The Shadowy Waters"

MARCH 31, 1977.
Based on tapes made at Big Sur.
The last two weeks have been the most crucial, momentous, and
agonizing of my life, an amazing process of unraveling, sorting out

what's been internal feeling and external motivation, what's been internal desire and what's been external pressure.

I've been involved in a hearing called the trial of the "Oakland Faithful Five" at which my parents sought a conservatorship order to remove me at least temporarily from the Unification Church, in which I've been a member for four years. This hearing has been unique in the country: the first time parents and church have met in open court, the first time issues of mind control have been debated, the first time the question has been raised of whether the constitutional right to freedom of worship is nullified by a previous denial of freedom of thought.

I was in Santa Fe, New Mexico, with my close-knit flower team—Dale, Will, Lynn, Dick, Johnny Hovard, and Jan Kaplan—when by telephone I was told that Johnny, Jan, and I were to take a plane immediately to the Bay Area, that a court hearing was to start March 9 about our Church membership. The three of us, as well as the team, were in total shock that our parents would take such a course of action.

I personally could respond only with a depth of anxiety and fear hard to describe. If the California conservatorship were granted, I knew I could expect attempted deprogramming.

The deprogramming I'd heard about was a brutalizing process where one was totally humiliated. Physical force might be part of it, people were stripped of their religious beliefs, their ideals, their faith in God, their devotion to a supposedly freely chosen way of life. Faced with this enormity, faced also with the responsibility of being the oldest member of the group of young people at the hearing, I'd never felt such pressure as I did when I got on that plane to fly home to California. But I was determined to be faithful to the past four years of my life, to those years devoted unconditionally to loving and serving God, which is all I really cared about and all I still really care about.

When we arrived on the five o'clock plane from Albuquerque, we were picked up by Amos, who drove us immediately to The Gardens where Dr. Durst and Onni waited. Johnny, Jan, and I met with Leslie Brown and Jackie Katz, who'd been conferring that afternoon with our attorney, Mr. Ralph Baker, to find out our personal histories. When I got there I felt impelled to learn as fast as I could what the rest knew, what the legalities of the case were, and what was expected of us. So we met with Teresa, Onni, and several others to talk about the upcoming trial.

That same Saturday night at The Gardens I showed Leslie, Jackie,

John, and Jan my small red diary, my comfort for the past three months, ever since Yacov and Evey had been kidnapped and deprogrammed. In this diary I had pictures of the whole Family, of Reverend Moon and his wife, of Onni and Dr. Durst, pictures of beloved brothers and sisters. But the pictures I cherished most were of Yacov and Evey, the two people in the movement who'd inspired me the most, given me the greatest faith and confidence in my own goodness and ability to be a loving person. I'd been in such total shock when they vanished; I'd not gotten over it, had been obsessed with where I could reach them, how I could understand what they had gone through. For three months I'd looked in every single magazine on every flower trip to see if there were any news of them. When Teresa saw Jackie and Leslie looking through my diary, she leafed through it and then drew me aside to speak to me in private. It was absolutely wrong and destructive, she said, to have the diary, and more so to let younger members look at it because there were pictures of Yacov and Evey in it. She said I had to rip those snapshots out, that I couldn't think about either of them for the rest of my life, that they were working against God now, they were working for Satan. In effect, Teresa warned, it was blasphemous even to remember them. All I could say was that I accepted what she said, repented, and apologized for my insensitivity. I took the book away and hid it, as if it were a totem. I promised myself I wouldn't show it to anybody, but I couldn't remove the pictures. I knew at the very center of myself, Yacov and Evey had been, and were, a moving force in my life and I could neither invalidate nor dismiss them.

The next day the five of us drove with Teresa up to Boonville after a visit to the Holy Ground and breakfast at a Lake Merrit coffee shop. When we got to the farm we went right into the advanced *Divine Principle* lecture with Teresa; all five of us were in a discussion group with her, a first for me since my early months in the Church. We talked about further revelations of Moon yet to come. We also talked about the "marriage blessing," that ritual in the Church in which matings are determined by Reverend Moon who can "see" by spiritual vision each person's ancestry. After individuals prepare for the blessing by confessing to Moon all previous sexual experience, he lines couples up in mass ceremonies as in past marriages of 777 and 1800 couples in Seoul, Korea. By blending racial and physical features, and considering ancestry, he guarantees harmonious marriages. For four years my own secret feelings about the blessing had been a mix of fear and outright desperation. But I felt my fear was because I didn't have enough faith to trust someone else arbitrarily choosing a mate for me. Now Teresa tried to alleviate our anxieties about not having choice, and mentioned one example of a couple who had recently been given the chance to marry as they chose.

We drove from Boonville back to The Gardens. On our way we discussed deprogramming. The first thing I'd ever read about it was a manual called "The Constructive Destruction of Religious Beliefs" put out by APRL (Alliance for the Preservation of Religious Liberty), a group ostensibly supporting religious freedom, funded in part by Scientology. Purporting to advise people on methods of deprogramming, it planted seeds of terror in me about the process. Though I didn't know whether its methods were used by Wayne Howard's and Mike Trauscht's Freedom of Thought Foundation, which had "snatched" Evey and Yacov, I was convinced the physical abuse it described did occur—the total humiliation, included forced nudity, sleeplessness, lack of food, even the forced defecation on pictures of cult leaders, and the possible use of rape and seduction. Teresa's confidences were certainly not reassuring. She said that during Evey's deprogramming there had been a point where Evey had considered cutting her wrists, committing suicide or committing herself to a mental hospital, in order to get away from her deprogrammers. "But," said Teresa scornfully, "she didn't have the guts for any of it. God could have saved her spiritual life if she had." Teresa ended our talk by reminding us that Micah had said many times he'd die before he'd be deprogrammed. By the time I got to The Gardens I was more aware than ever that I might be faced with a life and death matter, both physical and spiritual. My extreme fear of the deprogramming process grew. I worried about suicide.

By Monday morning we had started to have a group identity, to be called "The Faithful Five." We were put on the prayer condition list that the Family chanted every morning; we were on the daily fasting list. We were growing acutely aware of our position as representatives of the whole Unification Church, not only in the Oakland area but for the whole nation. At breakfast we were warned that what we did would determine the whole future of mankind. We were being placed in a historical, chosen position to represent God; the blueprint of history would be affected by our degree of faithfulness and adherence to Reverend and Mrs. Moon, to Divine Principle, to Oakland Family. What we did, it was said to us, would influence the whole future blessings and accomplishments of the Church. An overwhelmingly burdened position to be in, it nonetheless kept us pumped up.

On Monday we were scheduled to see our parents. My parents not being due to arrive from Portland until later that day, I sat with Amos in the Holiday Inn lobby while the other four saw their families. Amos had made it very clear that if at any point anyone wanted to leave the discussion with their parents and come back to join him, they were free to do so. Already a tremendous wall was being erected against the parents, who were put either in the Satanic position themselves or severely misguided by Wayne Howard, Mike Trauscht, and ex-cultists like Yacov and Evey, now instruments of the devil. Meeting with parents proved tense; each person came out frustrated. During the time the other four were with their families, I shared with Amos my relationship to Yacov and Evey, entrusting many private things to him not previously entrusted to anyone before. I admitted to Amos how close they were to me, how difficult it was to believe they had become evil people.

After lunch Onni and Micah came by to take us to a movie called *Silver Streak* that Onni said Reverend Moon liked because he thought it was symbolic of the collision course America was on without God to keep it on the track. Onni seemed to show genuine love and concern for our mental states, our faithfulness, our physical well-being.

After the movie, while Jan and Leslie went to be interviewed by the "enemy" expert witnesses, Dr. Benson and Dr. Singer, I was brought back to spend the evening at the Holiday Inn with my mother, father, and grandpa. They'd just gotten in from Portland. Uncomfortably, I found myself trying to defend my viewpoint. I tried to show them that however much they thought my faith in God was inauthentic, it *was* the main dynamic of my life. Yet it was here that I first experienced a brief, puzzling glimmer: they didn't seem to be trying to test my faith in God but rather my ability to use autonomous judgment and act for myself. Still I felt myself judging them, dismissing my grandfather as old and emotional, my parents as insensitive people who didn't understand what I believed in, had never really tried to understand or apply themselves to my beliefs, and weren't spiritual anyway. I felt they didn't know God as I did, that I was the only one of the four at dinner who did know God's will, heart, and desire. I felt pity for my parents, thought somehow Yacov and Evey had smooth-talked them, Freedom of Thought Foundation people had pulled the wool over their eyes. I suspected they were being taken for a tremendous amount of money, though they wouldn't tell me how much. I just felt that it was a deep shame they were involved in this at all. But that night when I came back to Ashby Street after being with them, I recognized that it had been wonderful to see them. I hadn't often allowed myself to miss them the last four years, but when I could be with them, I knew how much they meant to me.

On Tuesday it was my turn to have an interview with Dr. Benson and Dr. Singer. Based on what Jan and Leslie had said the night before, I went in convinced they were a threat to me. What I experienced was a pair of clinicians who seemed emotionless and unresponsive. I imagined them as Auschwitz-like characters. The point of some of their questions grew clear: they were trying to show that I'd lost my interest in many things like writing, reading, sports, hiking, backpacking, photography, politics. They were trying to show that I had no knowledge of the current world—which was, of course, true. Because they didn't ask any questions about my spiritual life, about higher purpose or value, they seemed to me completely in the dark about who my God was and what my motivations were for being in the Unification Church. I came away judging them. Whatever their opinion of me was, I felt it was in no way a true evaluation of my inner character.

Later in the day I went to Napa to be interviewed by our expert witness, Dr. Thompson, who, I'd been assured, was more sympathetic to the Unification Church. I felt warmth emanating from him. He asked me more spiritual questions, appeared to be attuned to my inner motivations, and was concerned less with my "affect," how I appeared to be on the surface. He didn't test me for memory or recall, didn't test me for my potential to be manipulated or confused, seemed just to be trying to get at my feelings. I'd been told by the Church that I could trust him, so I did.

That night a group of us met with Mr. Baker, who reviewed many of the questions he would be asking us on direct examination in the courtroom. We discussed the various questions anticipated on cross examination. Daniel as chief Church public relations person, freely gave his opinions on how to be diplomatic about our lives of faith, lives we assumed no one in the secular world would understand. Daniel warned us to phrase our answers in a way that wouldn't sound too fervent, zealous, or extreme. Ralph Baker, however, said over and over "just be honest." *Just be honest.* Even then I discerned the difference between the

Church itself, which wanted first of all the best representation, and Ralph Baker, who wanted truthfulness.

On Wednesday, March 9, the hearing began. As I sat waiting I wrote in my journal, "I keep hearing the song 'Oh Healing River' and in my imagination waves seem to crash through the windows of the court. I want the Red Sea to part. . . . I want an escape route."

My own father was the first witness called to the stand, my mother the second. It was an emotional trauma to see my parents on the witness stand. I was angry at their unwelcome intrusion into my four-year life of faith of choosing God over parents. But when my mother cried on the witness stand and I saw the depth of her concern for me, I was very upset.

When Yacov, now Jeff Scales, got on the stand, I was extremely affected. I wanted him to look directly at me. But he never did. Jeff testified that the cult made it impossible to leave it without feelings of individual destruction, threatened fears of losing one's life, being completely ostracized, forsaking God. Jeff seemed to me to speak with dispassion about the Kingdom of Heaven. It struck me that he'd lost all his ideals.

Next morning, Thursday, I saw Evey in court. Evey's hair was down; in the Church women who wear their hair down are regarded as fallen. I felt immediate pity and sorrow because I knew the disdain her appearance would evoke in members like Becky, Shelly, and Amos. Even to me Evey wore a kind of wild look, the look of a loose woman of the world without innocence or purity. But my heart went out to her.

Dr. Benson was called to the stand and gave testimony about ways in which he believed all five of us were brainwashed. I felt he was fabricating the whole story. He talked about our being controlled, said our affect was blunted, our vocabulary limited, said we responded, each one of us, in like manner, said we had an abstract global view, but knew few specifics about the current world. I sat there seething, denying his points.

That afternoon I'd talked with Jeff Scales in the hallway of the courthouse. I was less frightened to talk to him than I'd been the first day, though I still felt he was betraying the Church and trying to bring about Satanic destruction. At first it was difficult to look at him, but growing compassion and longing to know what he was experiencing helped me. Wearing a leather necklace around his neck, he seemed to me reduced to worldly influences. But when I commented on his ornament, I instantly realized he was hurt by my laughing judgment. That was the *first* time I actually *felt* that I was harshly—maybe erroneously—judgmental. After we shook hands, after I told him I'd been waiting to speak to him, I asked Jeff if he'd gotten my notes, those guilty clandestine Church notes I'd sent to him after he left. I couldn't help myself, but felt, standing in God's position as I did, it was sinful for me to be in communication with someone in Satan's position. The Church teaches that God and Satan can't exist in the same place simultaneously; you choose either one or the other; one, the person, one the nonperson; one who is worthy to live, one who is not. Jeff said he was grateful to get my messages, especially the photograph of us in November at Children's Day celebration. All the time we spoke, I felt extremely guilty and apprehensive talking to him. I knew I shouldn't spend the time, but I was overcome with wanting him to know that I still cared. I was struggling to reconcile his startling behavior with the person I remembered.

That night, although my request met resistance from Becky (Dr. Durst and Paul Goorjian thought I should comply), I went alone to dinner with my dad. My dad picked me up in downtown San Francisco, and asked me where I wanted to go. When I suggested the top deck of a Fisherman's Wharf restaurant, he accepted the idea quickly and asked me to drive. We had the most natural sharing I'd ever had with him in my life. He told me how much Grandpa loved me and it was the first time I allowed myself to feel the devotion to the grandpa I'd loved very much four years before. I cried and I knew my dad felt my heart, at least, was responsive for the first time in years and years. But I concluded, once back with the other members of the Church, that because my dad had allowed me to drive and find the restaurant, he'd humbled himself to me, accepted that he was object to my subject position. If he could trust me in that way, I reasoned, it was still possible he could be humbled before God. I felt God *must* work through me, that I *must* be responsible for my dad's spiritual life. I also interpreted my dad's behavior as the first sign of his seeing *my* life as *I* saw it.

By Friday the question in all of our minds was what the court would order us to do with the weekend days. When I came back from Friday lunch, I told Amos I wanted to spend the weekend with my mom and dad. Amos looked so disappointed, his hang-dog eyes punishing me: "Onni will be *so* unhappy because she really wants you to be a group leader up in Boonville." Suddenly I felt completely violated, in a raging straitjacket. I wanted to lash out at Amos, demand some freedom of choice with what I did in my life. I wanted to yell that I hadn't seen my parents in years, that, besides, this get-together could be potentially beneficial for the Church. Concluding that we'd talk later, Amos repeated that it was his *suggestion* I go to Boonville. One of the manipulations in the Church is to *suggest*, to *appear* to leave free choice. But you've been intimidated with so much fear and guilt, and the pressure not to be considered faithless is so heavy, that of course you do what is "suggested."

On Saturday, however, I went with my parents, Aunt Lauriel, Uncle Scott, and my grandfather out to lunch at Boundary Oak Country Club. We had a tense time. I was nervous because I felt I had to be God's representative and maintain His position, surrounded as I was by a force of evil influences. I excused myself from the table and called Becky to check in. Then we drove up Mount Diablo. There were hang gliders in the sky; the wind was blowing. I felt very close to my mom and dad; I felt like I wanted to reach out to my grandpa, even if he wasn't in a prime position to influence my life or benefit the Church. Through four years my mind had operated that way: I'd sought out only people who could benefit our great purpose. If somebody was too old or too young, or not capable, or lacking the necessary attributes, I cancelled them out just as I found myself doing with my grandpa.

That night I joined the Faithful Five and Onni at a Japanese restaurant. We talked of a letter one of the sisters had written to Onni, a confession about a sexual "non-Principled" relationship she'd had with one of the brothers, a person who'd left the community. The talk made me dare to bring up with Onni something my mother had shared with me about Evey Eden. Apparently one of our staff members, Mark—who had been very much in love with Evey before they joined the Family—tried to kiss her Friday afternoon in a courtroom waiting room. *Principle* demands that before marriage you remain chaste and pure in every gesture and thought. Mark's behavior had completely shocked Evey. Knowing a sexual advance to be a violation of Mark's own nature, "Who put him up to it?" was Evey's stormy question to my mother at dinner. Now I wanted to know if Onni had instructed Mark to pressure Eve. (A few days before I'd overheard a Church leader mention that Daniel had been encouraged to "love up" Michele in order to get her back to the Church.) Onni's response to me was that she didn't know exactly, but she imagined Mark had just hugged Evey as a brother would do. The answer didn't satisfy me. But I put my doubts aside, as it had become habitual for me to do.

Sunday I asked Onni if I could go out to breakfast with my parents and Jeff Scales. I told Onni I thought that it might be productive to see Jeff, learn about his psychology, then share with Onni, who was very concerned about Jeff's work against the church, what I'd found out. She said I could see Jeff only if Len Foster, a brother from the Barrytown seminary, were with us. So I told my mother and dad that if Len came, I had permission to see Jeff. Mid Sunday morning, mom, dad, Len, and I went to the East Bay Holiday Inn to have breakfast. Jeff walked up half an hour after we arrived. Even though I knew it was a violation of Onni's order, I longed to see Jeff in private, so we went to a separate table and talked, while Len sat with my family. During the course of our conversation I felt real sincerity on Jeff's part about his own experience in deprogramming and his past three months away from the Church. I was completely shocked. I had expected him to be literally under the control of the devil, to have given up his relationship to God, to be consumed by a selfish life of alcohol, cigarettes, relationships with women. Above everything else, I'd been led to believe in the Church that the reasons he left were not based on rational choice. He told me he hadn't been humiliated or debased in deprogramming, hadn't even been stripped of free will. "I haven't lost my ideal of a Heavenly Kingdom, I just oppose the manipulations, the coercively inhumane methods Unification uses to reach that ideal." It utterly surprised me when everything Jeff had to say came out in his usual sincere, thoughtful, humorous, well-intentioned way.

Len Foster had to study for his seminary exams and I, too, was supposed to go back to Ashby. But instead, I invited Jeff to go with me and my parents to Muir Woods. That was the first time in four years I hadn't phoned the Church to say where I was going and with whom; my first independent decision.

We spent a beautiful afternoon together in Muir Woods and driving along the Pacific coast. But when I arrived back at the Church, my defenses were up instantly. Becky and Amos wanted to know *exactly* what had happened to me and declared I'd acted "off-center" in using my own free will, something absolutely and always forbidden. I tried to talk with Becky, but we weren't making too much progress when a call came through from Onni, who wanted the Faithful Five to come to dinner at The Gardens. Before we left, Becky gave each of us twenty dollars "escape" money in case we were in a situation where we had to get away from parents, ex-brothers and sisters, or in any other way felt endangered.

I was hurried into dinner at The Gardens by Teresa just as everyone was sitting down, including Jonah, Lucy, the five of us, Onni, and Micah.

Onni prayed, then asked me questions about my afternoon with Jeff. As I shared about how good he seemed, how fine it was to be with him, I felt a deep anger rising up in me for the growing hostility in the atmosphere.

Onni was silent a minute, then asked me how I loved Jeff, as a brother or as a mate? Shocked, I couldn't answer.

Onni sprang up, threw her napkin across the table, and screamed, "God will *never* forgive you!" then rushed out of the room. I didn't know what to do. I felt paralyzed, caged. But I made myself jump up, follow her, catch her by the arm and say, "Onni, I have something I must tell you."

We went into the living room. Sitting on my knees at her feet, she on the sofa, I tried to explain to Onni my feelings and thoughts and actions of the past three years with Yacov. Onni actually shook with anger as I told her I felt so closely connected with him that I couldn't ignore him, that I couldn't treat him as nonexistent, that I couldn't think he was all Satanic. That afternoon, I tried to explain, I'd just *had* to find out for myself Yacov's motives for his actions.

It ended up that I must repent for my attached feelings for Yacov, deny in the face of Onni—which meant in the face of God—my care for Yacov.

So I did.

I cried and cried. Onni cried and prayed. I prayed, trying to come to some equilibrium. Still I felt tied up in knots, even after I'd repented. Something whispered in me that if it had been a true repentance I'd have felt release of tension, forgiveness from God. But since I still felt so constricted, I came to the usual conclusion: the problem was in *me*. I *still* hadn't given Yacov up completely enough to purify myself.

I went home that night feeling so sick I went straight to bed.

The next day, Monday, as we headed back to court again after the weekend break, Micah said to me, "I can't wait till we're slaves again. Being free like we are at this hearing, we can't get anything done." His words bit into the growing sore spots in me; I really thought about what Micah's words meant. Having had this brief and startling time to weigh the questions of my life, my belief system, and my faith, all of a sudden I realized: I *was* a slave! And I discovered on that short way back to court, I didn't *want* to be a slave again.

And with this awareness came another. Most of my life in the Family, I hadn't ever closely examined the *Principle,* hadn't had time to study or look into theological questions, weigh other viewpoints. Four years before, after a precult conversion experience, I had precipitously determined that my life was to be given to God and had joined the first group I'd encountered which seemed to share this great emotion. I then lived it out, pressing myself to fit in. From the first weeks I tried, as directed, to make connection with those beliefs which felt right, while suspending doubt about other matters that, I was led to believe, would become clear as I grew spiritually. But instead of actually accepting, I simply analyzed the beliefs less and less. Finally I just threw away my critical faculties on the assumption that to question and search was faithless. Most of my time, then, I'd spent all my efforts *trying* to believe, not trying to *understand* the beliefs. I followed, I was obedient, I did what was expected. . . .

But flashes of understanding, snatches of intuition alternated with other feelings in me. Back at the courtroom, when Dr. Singer took the stand and began stripping away my character, presenting severe limitations in my capacity, presenting me as having been a very different person four years ago when I'd joined the Church, I grew more and more defensive and angry. I wondered how Dr. Singer could reduce me like that. I felt so mistreated that I had an image of a courageous Jesus on the cross saying, "Forgive them, for they know not what they do." After all, I tried to reassure myself that Jeff, Evey, my parents, these people conducting the other side of the case, were in ignorance, didn't know what they were doing.

That Monday night, Church member Laurey Baer was picked up by Mike Trauscht and his buddies in Marin County under an *ex parte* conservatorship, a "legal kidnap." All of us at Ashby house were outraged as we watched the evening TV news and heard our sister, Pauline, who'd been there, describe Laurey's pickup, how he'd kicked and fought and how she, Pauline, had punched Mrs. Baer. The whole supercharged atmosphere bristled. Fear and polarization grew. Wild vibrations.

Also that night, after participating in a news interview, we five were taken to the Fairmont Hotel for two psychiatric interviews, one with a Dr. Ash and one with a Dr. Lee. The interview with Ash was quite an experience. Though he was reputable, a forensic attorney as well as a psychiatrist, right off I had doubts about him as an expert witness. I was the first to be interviewed. When I came into the room, he asked me to clean it up and said he'd step outside while I did. He asked me questions to determine my competency, my ability to deal in abstract concepts, presumably my ability to be natural in his presence, to adhere to my beliefs. The interview took only ten minutes.

I was next sent up to another part of the hotel to take some psychological tests: Rorschach, Draw-a-Person, Minnesota Multiphasic. I didn't know what Dr. Lee was looking for, but whatever he wanted, I complied as best I could.

Wednesday morning I was the first of the five to be put on the witness stand. Asked several questions on cross-examination by Carl Shapiro and Wayne Howard, I really began to worry. When I'd taken the stand I'd felt I had to protect the Church, to present an ideal, almost a blameless image. Yet within myself I knew very well how many times there had been deviation from ideal, how many times I'd personally deceived, how often I'd been dictated to, and—I was considering more and more—been exploited. One particular question on cross-examination knocked any lingering confidence out of me. I was asked whether "heavenly deception" was a doctrine of the Unification Church.

Before answering, I thought a long, panicked thought. Knowing sacred law to be supreme, knowing how important public relations was for the Church, I had also been reminded by my mother that, as I myself would once have been scrupulously aware, it was dangerous to commit perjury in an American court. Trying to work my way in between imperatives, honor and honesty, I had finally admitted that "heavenly deception" *was* a doctrine of the Church. As the testimony came out of my mouth, I felt dirty, unclean. No sooner had I stepped down from the witness stand and out into the hall than Daniel nabbed me and said I should have denied the "heavenly deception" question. I didn't answer Daniel, but rushing through my mind were the many times I'd been encouraged to deceive people about our fund-raising efforts, in witnessing to get people to dinner, in failing to tell people what they were getting into.

At lunch Paul Goorjian, Dr. Ash, Ralph Baker, Jerry Bachelor, and two ACLU leaders, came to the uncomfortable conclusion that perhaps "heavenly deception" was like a white lie where, in order to benefit or protect someone's interest, you tell a partial truth or "smallish" falsehood. Again I walked back to court filled with thought. I realized the one thing justifying my lying and deceiving the past four years had been my commitment to the ultimate ideal of the Kingdom of Heaven on earth. To move closer to that goal, had I been willing to suspend the decent practice of honesty among humans?

Ends and means. The trial was beginning to force me to examine that issue. (As I make this tape, several weeks later, it seems incredible I had had to be forced to examine it.) Part of dishonesty grew from disrespect for noncult people's rights and values, I knew. Had it been ingrained in me to invalidate people simply because they weren't useful to the Church, to dismiss them from my life, worst of all, to turn them into nonpeople because they didn't know God's heart as well as I did? And further, I didn't know God's heart as well as Onni; and Onni didn't know God's heart as well as Reverend Moon did. Had it got to the point where I'd begun to mistrust everyone's ability to decide based on free will and conscience? Later I would know that if anything could have deprogrammed me it would be the process, begun at the hearing, of realizing contradictions in my own ability to act within the Church in a truthful way. My growing consciousness of my own lost integrity was what ultimately deprogrammed me.)

Friday was a mixed-bag day. I felt that I wanted to spend some time over the weekend with my mother and dad. I'd promised them that even if the decision was in favor of the Church, I'd still try to spend some time with them going over questions about the Bible and *Divine Principle*, but in my heart I knew I'd *never* be allowed to do that, that once the Church had won, our parents would be seen as even more Satanic. That's why I wanted to spend this last weekend with them as I, along with everyone else, anticipated a successful court judgment. That afternoon in the court chambers, a decision by the lawyers and Judge Vavuris was reached that the five of us wouldn't be allowed to go to Boonville for reindoctrination. Although this was quite a blow to everyone in the Church, I'd secretly hoped I would be free from Boonville obligations that weekend.

Still, instead of being with my parents that night, I went with Becky, Leslie, and Paxe, Leslie's stepmother, to a restaurant in downtown Berkeley. Becky hadn't allowed Leslie to go alone with Paxe so we all went with Leslie together. I spent all my "escape" money on the meal!

Saturday it'd been decided by Onni that the five of us would go to the beach with Shelly. We swam and ran along the water's edge. All of us wrapped in blankets and towels, Shelly gave us a talk about laying a foundation of faith—giving up mind and body to mold our actions after center person, really being humble to him and serving him so as not to be arrogant or challenging. After returning from a swim in the ocean, we studied deprogramming material.

We then headed up to Napa to see Dr. Thompson for a final interview in order for him to prepare his testimony for the following Tuesday in court. On the way we read from Robert Lifton's book on thought reform and asked Amos a lot of questions. Amos guaranteed that methods of mind control were used only by deprogrammers and that though some manipulation and control might be used in the Church, all were excusable because they were for God. I'd been fasting and was exhausted, so I kept falling asleep in the moving car. But as I came in and out of consciousness, something about Amos's message wasn't fitting into my deeper perceptions. Wasn't he saying once again that if you were living for God, anything that was required as a means to that end was justified? Leslie must have been feeling some of the same tensions, because she suddenly began to yell that Amos was trying to mold our ideas; it took Amos a long time to calm down the shocking and irreverent quarrel.

During my interview with Dr. Thompson, he had brought out a negative newspaper article by a weekend visitor to Boonville. I couldn't, in effect, deny to the doctor that what the writer said of the Boonville program was valid. On the way back from Napa I was trying to review the negative article for the rest of them. I wasn't being very critical of the journalist's position (he had obviously felt coerced in Boonville), and suddenly I glanced up and there was Amos shooting me a steely, scornful, condemning look in the rearview mirror. Immediately, responding to cue, I changed my tone and indicated to everyone in the car that one *couldn't* have a bad experience at Boonville unless one were basically insincere. Suddenly I felt myself *totally* manipulated, just by one accusing look in a mirror.

Saturday night Onni requested that Leslie and I come see her. She was obviously concerned that we were unstable in our faith, that our emotions were interfering with our mission to be unquestioningly true. I had a talk with Onni in the study. While I shared my thoughts about my parents' position and how they were unwilling to give up their stand that I was brainwashed, I also told Onni that many aspects of the trial were upsetting to me, too. In addition, I told her I knew I should be strong and not let emotional things affect or influence me—love for my parents and Jeff and Evey, for instance—but that it was hard. Onni replied that Jeff was not to be trusted, that he was now possessed totally by Satan. It was not, she reiterated, in my interests ever to talk to him again, but I could pray that he would come back sometime in the five years of grace God would allow him. After that she had a premonition he might be in a plane crash. That was the first and only time with Onni I touched something private in her nature, sensed her clear and unswerving love of God. After that talk I felt she had once loved Jeff and Evey and longed for them to come back. Publicly she'd referred scornfully to them as "Scales and Eden." But now she spoke to me of Yacov and Evey.

Leslie and I were invited to sleep at The Gardens and have pledge service the next morning. At 5:00 A.M. the phone rang. It was a call from "Paul Blintz," the telephone name (Onni believed her lines were tapped) of Laurey Baer. Laurey indicated he'd escaped from the deprogrammers and that he'd be with Onni and Dr. Durst soon. Laurey's escape represented a great spiritual triumph; Leslie and I left a jubilant Gardens to go back to Ashby to wake everyone and get dressed.

Sunday morning I'd asked for time with my parents. If Onni had seemed human and understanding the night before, my own parents seemed of equally good intentions. The more time I'd spent with them, the more I understood their only desire was to get me out of what they saw as a limited and restricted life. Above all, to let me once more exercise my autonomous free will.

But with the Laurey Baer escape sizzling in me, my doubts about my parents were rekindled. I'd been indoctrinated to believe that my parents were ignorant of the true nature of deprogramming, and therefore couldn't be held responsible for their acts, but by the same token couldn't be trusted. Further, if they in any way guessed, why would they be willing to put me through it? I couldn't understand why no one at the hearing testified to the cruelty of deprogramming or why the psychiatrists hadn't apparently asked my parents if they were aware of the severe physical ordeal and mental stress that deprogramming involved.

In any case, Becky knew Onni didn't want me to see my parents alone, so she insisted I take a brother along to the breakfast we'd arranged. Dad got so furious he refused to have *anyone* join us for breakfast. When I called Becky to tell her this, she said, "Don't talk to your parents more than an hour. Finish breakfast and come right back. They have two on the Satanic side and if they won't let you have two on the Heavenly side, they don't deserve any more of your time; it's a waste to be with them."

During the course of our breakfast conversation, Dad and Mom asked me about certain passages attributed to Moon in "Master Speaks." Was I aware that he was quoted as saying homosexuals should be "beat upon," people should be punished in hell if they even think about sex before marriage, couples should cry if their firstborn is a girl instead of a boy—things my mother described as "moral outrages." Their arguments sank more and more deeply into my mind, and I was in painful need of honest answers. But on the outside I was obdurate. By the end of the breakfast, my mom momentarily almost gave up the idea of a conservatorship, saying that maybe I was so fixed in my beliefs about Reverend Moon's purity that it was hopeless. But my dad said of course they would go through with a conservatorship, that they'd feel very negligent as parents if they didn't give their whole effort to help me look with a clear mind and a free will at what I was doing. I left my mom and dad. I knew that night my dad would fly back to Portland because he couldn't leave his work any longer. My mom would be alone in the Bay Area the remainder of the trial. Would this give me an opportunity to weaken her will while Dad wasn't there to reinforce the negativity in both of them? I hoped that by spending more time with my mother I could dissuade her from pressing the conservatorship.

Sunday afternoon I went to The Gardens with the Faithful Five to do some studying. I promised my dad I would read the *Divine Principle*, which I'd admitted to him I'd only read a third of. At speed-reading pace, I didn't absorb very much of what I read; I was still thinking in the most generalized, simplistic ways about what it meant. We watched *The Wizard of Oz* and loved it. Neil Salonen, national Church president, was there, as were Onni, Dr. Durst, Becky, Janet, Micah. Still emotionally very tied to the Church, I found it a heartwarming evening.

Onni gave us more gifts, more clothes. Although meant to reinforce our obligation to the Church, our feelings of love and commitment, the gifts made me feel uncomfortable after my four spartan years of Church service.

Monday, Dr. Lee's main testimony was given. Our expert psychologist, he said we were all competent and capable. He also said each one of us had differing degrees of maturity, creativity . . . and paranoia. He indicated each one of us had past problems with authority figures in our lives, especially male authority. He noted we were all supersensitive to criticism. Of me personally, he noted that I was a high-energy person, an extrovert, a perfectionist with tension-filled drives, but I was no more susceptible to artful and designing persons than anyone else. As Dr. Lee finished his testimony, I wrote in my journal, "All this testing of our competence and looking for symptoms of coercive persuasion goes beyond any known measurements of psychology. I could find fault in every one of the interviews, hostile and friendly: Dr. Benson's, Singer's, Lee's, Ash's. But I thought, all of them are just psychologists, they have a small-minded viewpoint not motivated by religion. Where *is* God in this discussion? Who can challenge the divine revelation of Reverend Moon, who has deeper wisdom and spiritual experience than anyone?"

In the car on the way to the hearing Tuesday, we read from *Acts* in the Bible the story of the Sanhedrin. I knew by this we were being warned to believe in spiritual law over civil law, whatever the outcome.

A dramatic event took place that afternoon in the courthouse hallway. Shelly and Larry Grumbiner, ex-member and deprogrammer, had a confrontation. As Shelly screamed to Larry about "child abuse" by parents, and deprogramming being worse "than dipping babies in cauldrons of boiling water," I secretly admired Larry for his composure and reason. He simply stated he'd never witnessed any abuse in any deprogramming he'd taken part in, including his own.

Wednesday as I came into court, Mom said to me, "Did you know Jeff's attaché case with his journal of the last three months is missing, maybe stolen from his apartment?" A conversation I'd had with Daniel at The Gardens flashed through my mind. He'd told me they'd collected three months of valuable information on Jeff since he'd left the Church. When I asked how they'd gotten it, Daniel had said he wasn't free to reveal that. So now I sat and wondered. After Jan Kaplan's testimony on the stand, after a pleasant détente lunch with my mom and Uncle Scott, I confronted Amos and Becky in the hall about the possibility of a

Church member's having stolen Jeff's journal. Amos snapped that I shouldn't be emotionally upset over such a petty thing, that I should be praying instead for God to forgive my small mind and bring victory. "Besides," Amos demanded, "if it meant saving other lives from Satan, if Jeff had lists of future prospects for deprogramming in that journal, wouldn't taking it be justifiable?"

In the afternoon "Father" Randy and Norma—who after deprogramming had returned to their respective groups—got on the stand and declared they had had horrible experiences in their own deprogrammings. They were, however, caught on the witness stand, unable under oath to repeat the sweeping accusations they had made to the media. So many questions had built up in me by now that I asked to ride alone with Dr. Durst back to Berkeley in order to tell him my uncertainties. But because we ended up with only one car, all five of us went with him. As center person and an example to the others, I didn't feel free to ask my questions in front of the rest. So they went unanswered. . . .

At The Gardens we found dinner ready. Dr. Durst, Neil Salonen, Len, Norma, Micah, Mark, Lucy, and the five of us quickly ate and then gathered for what seemed like in Doris Lessing's words "a briefing for descent into hell." We discussed what our actions would be in case the conservatorships were ordered. Dr. Durst prepared us for critical attacks against the Church's monetary wealth and lack of social outreach. He brought out signed letters from a few people who'd received food from our Project Volunteer give-away program; all of us went over a few quotes about the fall of man; Norma told us the deprogrammers would try to make us believe Moon was sexually corrupt (which we thought was hogwash); Len admonished us simply not to have any give and take with deprogrammers but chant, pray, "pull yourselves into a shell like an acorn." We talked about escaping. One brother mentioned suicide.

By the time the session was over we had worked ourselves into a frenzy against Satan.

Thursday. Today the judge would make his decision, after both parties had presented their summations. Carl Shapiro's mild-mannered address was pretty much lost on me; Ralph Baker's torrent of inflamed righteousness for God and country spoke to me and the Church much better. Breaking for lunch at noon, we walked out of the courtroom through corridors flooded with TV lights and cameras. All of us were pumped up; we didn't feel any defeat in sight.

There was a mob scene outside the courtroom as we returned at

1:30 P.M.; San Francisco police stood by in case of violence.

As a follower of Sun Myung Moon, I was afraid for the conservatorship to be granted. As myself, I was afraid for it *not* to be granted, because by now something buried deep in me was screaming for the truth, whatever it might be.

When Judge Vavuris calmly stated that "love of family is the most binding aspect of civilization," I knew my time had come.

If I had ever sought an ultimate test of my faith, it was being given to me now: "It is hereby ordered that the petition of Mr. and Mrs. Raymond Underwood for appointment as temporary conservators of the person of Barbara Lael Underwood is hereby granted." I sat stunned, my inner being relieved, my outer self refusing the humiliating verdict.

The two people that I had become as a result of the hearing got up and entered the judge's chambers with the others of the Faithful Five. In hostile silence, arms crossed, we listened as Wayne Howard spelled out the ground rules of parental custody.

I couldn't make myself give a statement to the press about my civil rights being snatched away as I moved through the uproarious halls. Outraged as I was, somehow I also felt I was shedding a captive skin.

As I climbed into the deprogrammer's car, I was determined to find God alone in my walk through the wilderness to come.

Barb: Deprogramming

"A fate dictated from outside, from theory or from circumstance, is a false fate."
— D. H. LAWRENCE, *Women in Love*

"We shall not cease from exploration,
And the end of all our exploring
Will be to arrive where we started
And know the place for the first time."
— T. S. ELIOT, *"Little Gidding," Four Quartets*

MARCH 24, 1977.
After the judgment of the court, I was escorted through the pained outreach of my Church brothers and sisters crowding the tumultuous hallway, down an elevator and into one of the waiting deprogrammer's cars. My mother, Gary Scharff, and Skip Guarini, a

/ 233

writer, accompanied me on our drive to the San Francisco Airport Travelodge. Gary asked me some polite, nonthreatening questions. Though it was counter to Church advice, my instinct was to respond. The feeling was growing in me that there was a basic flaw in the Church's preparation for deprogramming, its admonitions to resist listening to deprogrammers on the grounds that they were subhumans intent only on "breaking faith."

I had finally convinced myself that if my faith was real, it could withstand any examination, confrontation, opposition. So in the car I turned and declared to my mother: "I have confidence that if I talk, my beliefs won't be shaken. I've spent four years believing it; I've spent twenty hours a day working for it, not to say four hours a night dreaming of it. I've sacrificed every meaningful thing in my life for it. I can't conceive of anything short of torture or brutality which would get me to change my mind."

However, as our car pulled up to the motel, all my feelings of being a defenseless captive returned. When I opened the car door and faced Evey, I wanted to punch her and strangle Jeff. In that rushing moment I literally despised my love for both of them, because they stood as antagonists to my secure construct of "total community" and "higher ideals."

I had a terrible headache and was weak from fasting and the trauma of the court decision. After awkwardly sipping water around a table in the dining room, where "cadres" of deprogrammers had gathered around each of the five of us, I retreated to the motel room my parents had been assigned. I prayed in the shower, not a prayer of petition for God to strengthen me, but rather a promise, a guarantee of my faith not to bend under pressure. I slept all evening.

Evey woke me at midnight to break my fast, as Church tradition dictated. Very sensitively, simply, without words, she offered me food. My mom and dad slept while I bowed my head in prayer.

Friday, March 25.

I woke to a vacation atmosphere: my mom and my dad in the room; sunshine pouring in; my dearest friends accessible when just a few days before they'd been as inaccessible as if they lived over the River Styx; an agenda free of the heavy Church obligations of witnessing, trinity meetings, flower selling. Curled on my knees in the bathroom, I prayed to greet the morning. With foreboding I reached out to God in desperation, not this time because I claimed to know Him perfectly, but because in naked yearning I needed Him to guide me. Then I blinked my eyes open and was seized with a sense of enormous and sad wonder. I felt as though I were waiting to enter a tournament. I dressed and went outside to boost Leslie's, Jackie's, Jan's, and Johnny's morale. Yet I caught the first strange glimmerings of a future beyond my safe predictions; I sensed our individual journeys would soon be our own.

That afternoon I went shopping with Mom and Dad for a few necessary clothes and starved-for novels. My mother suggested something light, but I ended up with *The Crucible, Crime and Punishment, St. Francis, A Death in the Family.* A heavy armor pressed me and I had to confirm the Church in my reading: persecution, sin, God, suffering.

As Mom, Dad, and I sat down together for lunch, I felt myself straining to bury my parents alive. How could I tell them that they weren't my True Parents? That they weren't close to God? That they weren't perfect as Sun Myung Moon and his wife were? Yet how could I deny the unconditional love and justice they had shown through their publicly unpopular commitment to free me of an entrapment I could barely perceive? Something hidden in my smoldering heart refused to replace their genuine, touchable love and sacrifice with my pure, crystalline, abstract image of Moon's untouchable love. My mother confided that God had pulled her through the years of my separation and rejection. As we got in the car I was forced to ask myself, if *everyone* claims God, then *who* really *has* God? I didn't know anymore.

We got back to the Travelodge just moments after Teresa, Dr. Durst, Becky, Amos, and other Church members had conferred with the captive four. They had brought us clothes, Bibles, copies of *Divine Principles.* I suspected that my dad's leisurely driving had been premeditated.

After a meeting with Leslie, Jan, and Carol Pogash, reporter for the *San Francisco Examiner,* in which we steadfastly upheld the Church but could speak of no harassment by the deprogrammers, I set out for my first dinner in the motel dining room. Walking by Gary Scharff's room, I risked a glance inside. Somehow he looked less tarantulalike, less threatening. He looked even kindly, boyish. A moment later I told my mom I'd lift the ban I'd put on talking to Gary and Joey, Jr.—my mother had promised me I wouldn't have to talk to ex-cultists I had a special aversion to because of their reputation.

After dinner I went back to my room. I was gathering my courage, suspecting that Gary and Jeff, who were close on my heels, wanted to talk. Sitting there, trying to read, I reminded myself I'd decided to listen. Weighing everything against my own "sacred" understanding, I wanted points of view from a full spectrum of experience, whatever pain I had to endure. I gripped harder onto God's Hand and in a mystical way, through this surrender, I was somehow delivered of the smug self-assurance the Church had fostered in me. Welcomed by my parents, Gary and Jeff quietly came in. Gary sat on the edge of a bed; Jeff found a place on the floor. From time to time, others drifted in, too. I waited, no longer fearful of the most dreadful questions and considerations. I would enter in, resolved to seek nothing and do nothing but what welled up within me of God's spirit and love.

In his easy, accepting, respectful way, Gary started to talk to me about ends not justifying unscrupulous means; about proclaimed absolutes and final philosophical systems coming to bad ends in history. He was a Princeton theology graduate and his style was highly intellectual; I felt challenged. After a while he asked me softly, "As a human being, one fallible person alone, do you think it's possible that you *might* have made a mistake in trusting completely that Moon is the messiah?" Suddenly I couldn't answer; the question hit me hard and made me realize that *not* to consider that possibility put me in the position of an all-knowing God myself. That smacked of idolatry. At my silence, Gary went on to suggest that perhaps my good intention to sacrifice myself for the whole no longer benefited that whole but instead had been consumed, lost inside a mechanism started by Moon.

And so began the inevitable evaluation of Reverend Moon's character that the Church had warned against. But somehow Gary's words spoke to me. I'm still not sure why I didn't react in simple outrage, but I didn't. Moon's earliest disciples, Gary said, had abandoned him, something Jesus' disciples had never done, even to martyrdom. Gary had been a chief lecturer at Barrytown, had seen something of Moon close up. Now he shared how tortured he'd been by Moon's personal arrogance and disregard for people except as pawns. Jeff agreed that he now saw Onni as incapable of a relationship of mutual respect. Gary poured out his heart about Moon's lack of forgiveness for his first wife's inability to humble herself in servitude to him. He related other instances of Moon's and about other of his punitive attitudes, incompatible with the forgiving message of "The Prodigal Son."

I listened, I didn't chant to close the words out, but every time I heard an attack on Moon, I wanted to lock myself in the bathroom to pray and cry. My emotions rushed out *blindly* to come to Reverend Moon's defense, protect him. I didn't want to hear logical arguments evaluating by worldly standards Moon's actions and words. I longed to retain my unconditional, untested faith in his purity. I can't describe the depth of pain I experienced in considering the possibility that the one I had loved absolutely might be less than what a God ought to be. I knew instinctively I was coming closer to the possibility that my love of Moon was a projection of my own mental and emotional need for someone to fill an unviolated place in my heart. All my insides fought against this like a caged animal let free and terrified of freedom. So when I began to argue for a man I didn't really know, either by experience or testing, even to myself my arguments sounded like unaimed arrows, wobbling, offtarget, irrational, irresponsible. Intuition sparked in me. It warned me my intractable love for Moon's sanctity blinded my use of reason to evaluate him with sound human standards. I wasn't measuring Moon's words and actions by my *own* idea, of what a messiah should be like morally, socially, spiritually; instead—because I'd early accepted that he was the Messiah beyond my or the world's judgment—I was surrendering my *own* ability to think, to trust my *own* instincts, conscience, judgment.

The Church so stigmatized the personal morality of deprogrammers that I wanted to test whether it was true none of them maintained their ideals or love of God. So I asked Gary about his own deprogramming, as a way to judge what might be left of his religious vision. Here, too, I was in for a rude and unsettling surprise. This once respected and powerful lecturer at Barrytown, this once devoted, probably fanatical follower of Moon, this man who spoke to me now friend to friend, held me spellbound with his description of his anguished, solitary encounter with God during his own deprogramming. "There I was," he said, "alone with God, answerable only *myself* to Him." I'd seen very few men cry in my life; I knew the tears Gary shed now were sincere.

I'd had enough for one night; I'd been too deeply touched.

At the door before Gary and Jeff left, Jeff said he, too, felt a more serious commitment to God than ever before, but that God to him had ceased to be a "possession," a "package," as the Church promoted Him. I was ready to consider Jeff's apparently honest words, but when he proposed I go away with Gary, Evey, himself, and my parents to a more secluded place to talk for the weekend, I backed off. I grew suspicious.

They wanted me away from the influence of Church visitors; they wanted me away from the other four. I still believed "deprogramming" wasn't officially sanctioned by the court and we wouldn't know what the court would actually rule until Monday afternoon, March 28, when a Church appeal would be acted on. I said I was responsible for the "Faithful Five" and I couldn't abandon that responsibility.

After midnight, Joey, Jr., came sauntering unexpectedly to the room. With Churchly scorn I'd summed up his character by his appearance: a still-faced, lean, dark, mustachioed, motorcycle type. But I'd said I'd talk to him, because I did want to know his side of the story of the Laurey Baer deprogramming, which he'd been in charge of. Earlier, I'd heard Skip give his version; I wanted to know if Joey's was as innocuous. The answer-seeker in me was desperate to pinpoint truth in the vast gap between Laurey's terrorized account and the deprogrammers' story. Obviously exhausted by constant rebuff from Jan while trying to talk to her, Joey patiently detailed every minute of Laurey's case. It was impossible not to sense Joey as sensitive, sincere, even a fanatic for honesty (one of the reasons he hated the cults so much). Joey demonstrated point for point where Laurey's written statement was either a lie or a gross exaggeration, the perception of a person panic-stricken by nonexistent perils, a person seeking hero status once back in the Church. At 3:00 A.M. Joey was still leaning against the door of my motel room spilling out his concern for Laurey. Joey simply wasn't, I had to conclude, the victimizing type. Laurey's must be a craziness induced by fear and misapprehensions. All I could do was thank Joey and say good night.

Saturday, March 26.

When I awoke I felt different, alive and restless. My enthusiasm for spending at least one uninterrupted day in my life with Jeff and Evey overruled the frustration I was supposed to be feeling for my "captivity," the infringement on my civil rights. This eagerness separated me from the disconsolate brooding of Jan, Jackie, Leslie, and Johnny, who felt my distance and didn't know how to "read" it. Unable to schedule a horseback ride (something I'd longed to do for four years), Jeff, Evey, my parents, and I ventured to Saratoga to picnic in the park. Jeff bought me an ice cream cone, teasing me about the guilt feelings he knew I was having for "overindulgence." While Mom and Dad shopped for picnic lunch, we three hit the park with the Frisbee we'd bought; it seemed appropriate to the liberation of the occasion! The joy of our freewheeling antics, the wrestling together on the soft, warm grass, the three of us arm in arm, the laughter, the tears, felt like the truest love I'd known. How could this be evil? I wondered; my loyalty to these two people felt lifelong. God *had* to be nestled in this triumvirate embrace. In the distance my mom and dad walked arm in arm, happier than I'd seen them.

At eight that night the Church sent Daniel, Becky, and Rod to visit us. By attorneys' agreement on both sides, they were allotted twelve minutes with each of us. When faced with my Church staff, my heart whispered a crack of division, a beginning self-consciousness, a touch of external masquerade. But still it was necessary to me to present myself as of indomitable spirit righteously repudiating the deprogrammers. Daniel barged in, barely knocking, assuming my parents' room to be God's property, and therefore the Church's. He brought a tape recorder and, without asking permission, set it up. My father explained that it wouldn't do.

"How was today?" Daniel turned to me, testing my answer.

"It's been a wonderful day," I enthused, not able to check myself.

"Wonderful?" Daniel's voice was scornful, reminding me. "Were you talking to Scales or Eden?" Then, rushing on, "Don't talk to them! They aren't allowed to deprogram you."

"I'm beginning to see that the position Yacov and Evey are in requires a lot of courage, Daniel," I countered softly.

"Sit down, Lael," Daniel ordered; his voice sounded like familiar thunder to me. "I had a dream from Heavenly Father today. He especially told me to warn you and Johnny, because of your former closeness to Yacov, not to be lulled into a sleep of pleasure and fun; you must take the situation seriously. Do you understand this is life and death? Six thousand years of human misery is resting on your shoulders. You mustn't give up your innocence, your allegiance, ever." Daniel was all wound up. In his emotional urgency I felt he was hardly aware whom he was talking to.

"Satan wants to trick you into thinking life outside the Church is free and marvelous. You know Yacov, Evey, and Michele have lost all standards of purity. Don't let them influence you. I've brought you a present." I leafed quickly through the book Daniel handed me; it was a cartoon book about ways in which children should be obedient to their parents. When I looked up, I suddenly realized that after the first greeting I hadn't had a chance to say a word. Furthermore, I suddenly realized Daniel hadn't asked me one question about what I might be needing. Beside Daniel on the bed, Rod and Becky sat still as statues; it was clear Daniel was center man and they had to yield to his way of dealing with me. I realized I'd never have noticed this unequal distribution of rights before the discussions of the last two days.

All at once my dad leaped up and indicated with firm authority that their time for talking to me was up. Daniel cast an imploring look my way. Becky hugged me and managed to confide, "I'm sure the appeals case will work. We'll get you out of this mess by Monday." Rod leaned over and whispered, "I've nearly finished my opera. When Evey hears it, I know she'll come back to Onni."

They swept out; the door banged shut.

I stood still a moment. Then I erupted. "They don't have the right to push me around like that, even spiritually! They haven't any idea what I've been experiencing the last few days; they didn't ask because they didn't care. Who are they to tell me who I can talk to? Daniel doesn't even know whether Jeff and Evey believe in God; he was Jeff's friend and now he doesn't even care." Outraged, I was still surprised at my outburst.

I caught an electric spark passing between my mother and dad, signaling their relief at my unexpected surge of anger.

Immediately there was another knock on the door. I opened it to a warm, brief greeting from Mr. and Mrs. Foster, Len's parents, who'd come to cheer up the deprogramming crew. Mrs. Foster, so gentle, so mothering, said to me, "Don't be afraid. You'll feel like the discussions over the next few days are sensitive and compassionate." Her remark stirred mixed feelings in me because I certainly wasn't ready to defend deprogrammers in public. But a spirit of undeniable generosity emanated from her presence; it was in such sharp contrast to her predecessors, I felt grateful for her visit.

That night Evey and I talked until 4:00 A.M., our suspended toothbrushes in hand; we'd started to bed at 1:00 and had gotten caught in a totally absorbing conversation. Evey told me she'd cried for five days during her deprogramming, that what hurt most irreparably was her final realization that Onni wasn't a perfect person, but a shrewd and calculating one.

Evey then spoke in depth about contradictions in the *Principle*, and violations of its claims to scientific logic. We explored contradictions between Moon's theology and those taught by Onni's New Education Development group. Evey stressed the incompatibility of Moons admonition, "Follow your center person beyond your own common sense" with Onni's teaching to employ your "conscientious common sense" and "unique value and ability." Other contradictory Church phrases kept boiling out of us; it was most difficult to square "self-fulfillment through unfolding potential" with "self-fulfillment through denial and sacrifice." When Evey described the mind-control techniques used in Communist China as analyzed by Yale psychiatrist Robert Lifton, to my shock I recognized these techniques as the same ones Amos had read about on the way to our Napa interview during the hearing. Whereas before I'd dozed in the car, failing to make any sense of them, now with Evey I recognized how frightening Lifton's concepts were in their applicability to the Unification Church, ironically a Church which pledges holy war against Communism.

Evey enumerated and explained *milieu control* as control of inner and outer communication by totalitarian leaders; *mystical manipulation* as that mechanism by which spiritual authorities compel you to trust with childlike naïveté; *demand for purity* as creating a world of shame and guilt; *cult of confession* as that practice wherein the leaders come to own your mind and actions; *sacred science* as an ultimate moral, scientific-sounding vision supposedly reducing other ontologies to pablum; *loading language* as the use of constricting, thought-terminating clichés to reduce the world to black and white; *doctrine over person* as subordinating individual human experience to the claims of an abstract idea; *dispensing of existence* as the practice of relegating those who don't comply to subhuman status and value.*

I stood there and shivered. It had such bleak meaning to me in relation to the Church. But also standing there, I was beautifully aware that, unlike the love in the Church that means unity of idea, like-mindedness, I could *feel* my love for Evey tested by a different litmus. I knew in the silence of that night, our two pulses in sympathetic harmony, that Evey and I were bound beyond heartbreak or difference of idea and doctrine, that we were touching the same breath and vapor of God.

---

* For a fuller explanation of mind control, see the Appendix.

Sunday, March 27.

Jeff appeared at the motel room door dressed in jogging pants, electric with his old impatience for Evey and me to emerge. He'd planned a daybreak horseback ride for us. After listening to a flood of false Church-promoted rumors about Jeff turning into a "lush," I had to laugh when our horses were parceled out: Jeff was on "Whiskey," I was on "Scotch," Evey drew "Dante." Jeff and Evey serenaded from the mountaintop a repertoire of John Denver songs and nudged me out of singing cult songs. Hardly able to walk a straight line after climbing down from our saddles, we joked about being on whiskey and scotch all the way back to the motel. I caught a brief glimpse of Johnny, Jan, and Jackie; Leslie, with her folks and ex-cultist Larry Gumbiner, was mysteriously absent.

The "brigade" which had formed around my deprogramming consisted of Jeff, Evey, Jerry Feldman (another former Church member) and my parents. This group, with my aunt, uncle, and cousin, ventured Sunday afternoon up to the Sterling winery in the Napa Valley. Caught in a dilemma of whether I'd taste the wine after four years as a teetotaler, I remembered Neil Salonen, president of Unification Church, saying, "Go ahead, indulge, if they give you alcohol during your deprogramming. Do anything external to fake them out that you've quit the Church. Then when they relax the security, race back to us." Jeff and Evey also told me the staff in Berkeley drank wine when Jeff got good vintages from the Aladdin Restaurant, a minor detail that surprised me just as I was being surprised by many other things I hadn't known as I listened to Jeff and Evey's freewheeling dialogue in the car about Church practices and personalities.

Serious doubts were entering my mind, doubts I could no longer turn away from. As we drove back from Napa Valley, I was feeling acutely apprehensive about a scheduled meeting with our Church attorneys and various Church members. Divided psychologically, I was undergoing intense separation anxiety from the Church. I could neither repress the criticism I'd heard nor face putting up a front about my presumably unquestioning faith in front of Church people. But I wasn't yet able to articulate the doubts in my mind in order to present them to staff members. I needed a refuge. I needed time and space.

I called Paul Goorjian and told him I wanted to see only him, *not* anyone from the Church. I'd wait to see him undercover at the Royal Inn across the street from the Travelodge. Paul promised to come alone and duly did, taking my hand, leading me to a table in a corner of the restaurant. I trusted Paul to be a concerned counselor and advocate for my case, but felt less sure of him, Paul; as a neutral confidant in a joust of fiercely battling oppositions. Now he wouldn't believe my so-called reversal of loyalties. He told me Onni and Dr. Durst were at the motel across the street, very upset that Leslie and I weren't there. I explained to Paul that I'd reached a decision, necessary but risky. I said that whatever the outcome tomorrow of the Church's appeal of Vavuris's opinion, I'd sign a voluntary conservatorship and allow myself thirty days to reconsider my commitment to the Church and Reverend Moon. Paul warned me against making a mistake, against letting the "bullying deprogrammers" shove me around. But I was firm. Hard as it had been, I explained it was *my* decision, no one else's.

During Paul's and my consultation, Evey had slid past all the Church members going in and out of the Travelodge rooms, gathered up the luggage of our "brigade," and loaded it into two rented cars. Anticipating pandemonium from the court decision the next day, she checked us out of the motel and rejoined the rest who were prepared, when I returned, to drive to an unknown location. Serious as the situation was, I couldn't help seeing the ludicrous aspects of our cops-and-robbers scenario. When Paul departed, Jeff, Evey, Jerry, Mom, Dad, and I escaped, will-o'-the-wisps, in two cars headed south. Under Jeff's expert management, we arrived at a motel in Santa Clara, unpacked, ate dinner, and relieved the tension by a rambunctious wrestling match, all of us young ones piled on one another.

Monday, March 28.
In the sunrise hours I jogged with Jeff, our first chance to be alone. He treated me with great respect; his own personality hadn't lost that decisive determination. I ate breakfast with Mom and Jerry, then it was time to write up the legal papers. I scribbled notes for my own conservatorship, which Dad relayed to me as he spoke by phone with Mike Trauscht in Tucson! I felt quiet, sober through most of this, but I'll never forget the exhilaration of talking by phone to Jeff's parents in New Jersey that morning. I hoped I made full reparation for the last conversation I'd had with them when I'd chewed them out royally for "kidnapping" Jeff. By phone I also talked to Gary Scharff, Joe and Esther Alexander, and even Wayne Howard in Arizona, who was becoming for me someone

quite different from the young adversary lawyer I'd wanted to snarl at in the courtroom. My darkest enemies were metamorphosing into my liberating friends; what an ironic twist, I thought.

While Dad and Evey prepared the legal papers, I sat and, largely to fix my determination and pin it down, composed a list of the ways the Church bent American law: (1) not getting solicitation permits, violating state or township codes for solicitation; (2) selling by misrepresentation; (3) forging of personal checks; (4) misrepresentation on welfare, Medi-Cal application forms; (5) avoiding payment of traffic violations, parking tickets; (6) cash donations not recorded; (7) misuse of land, health, and zoning permits; (8) no respect for private property in the selling of members' property without their knowledge or approval; (9) signing retainer agreements for attorneys without signers being allowed to meet with such attorneys; (10) evasion of truth on witness stands in courts of law; (11) renting motel facilities for one person, then sneaking many more into the room; (12) turning off odometers on rental cars to reduce fees; (13) using deceptive membership applications; (14) encouraging members to violate legal conservatorships by escape or non-compliance; (15) deceptive immigration and visa practices.

I arranged to see Paul Goorjian that afternoon to hear details of the court appeal decision and to dismiss him as my attorney. But he would remain my friend. At five o'clock that afternoon, the California Court of Appeals issued a stay order against deprogramming. This meant that although the five sets of parents still had custody over the five of us, no one, whether deprogrammers or otherwise, could attempt to alter our religious beliefs *against our will.* Paul refused to accept my dismissal of him until he knew for sure whether I was being coerced into my action. He did, however, confide in me he was glad I was "out of the Church" and that he, as well as Dr. Thompson, the Church-hired psychiatrist who never got to testify, "suspected the pressures of the hearing and discussions with ex-members would soon lead me out."

I watched the six o'clock TV news in our motel; the pictures on the screen certainly jolted me. Amos, with Dr. Durst, Onni, Bertha, Mark, and others were running around at the Travelodge screaming at Joey Alexander, Mitch, Michele, and the parents of Johnny, Jan, and Jackie, who sat in blocked cars before cameras. Dr. Durst was reading the conditions of the appeals court like they were the Gettysburg Address. Amos was yelling, pointing his fingers accusingly at the parents, shouting defiantly, "You can't deprogram them! You can't touch them!" Goaded beyond endurance, the more volatile of the parents shouted back, "They're our children. Get out!" Blocking the cars from moving, Amos hollered to the three Church members, "Refuse to talk to anyone! It's your right to refuse to see these wolves!" The unbelievable scene, drowned as it was in hate and irreconciliation, paralyzed me. Where was the "unification" in that? Where, even, the sanity? It could just as well have been Christians and Moslems, Ulster Orangemen and Catholics. All I could feel, all I could say after the news, was, "How absolutely sad. But I am glad Leslie and I weren't trapped there."

That same news program reported the tragedy of a ponderous KLM airliner crashing into another huge jet. I watched, thinking how arbitrary, undeserved death was. So many lives ended because of one moment's mistake, oversight. As shocked friends and relatives of victims were interviewed, I sat in bed, leaning against the pillow, overcome with empathetic grief. Then I cried for the unrecoverability of life, realizing at the same moment that this was the *first* time in four years I'd felt any genuine emotion or sympathy for any human being unrelated to the Church. Would they give money or join the Family? Joy in a yes, sadness in a no—that's the way I'd identified with people for four years. Exhausted by this unfreezing, by the thawing capacity of my heart, I thanked God for a stretching, a widening.

Tuesday, March 29.

Blithe yet still anxious about the unsteadiness of my disengagement from the Church, my dad was driven by Jeff to the San Jose airport to return to work in Portland. Several hours after he'd departed, an indescribable reunion occurred when Leslie—by this time "deprogrammed" by Larry Gumbiner in Big Sur—met us in Santa Clara. In the middle of the restaurant lobby, Leslie and I hugged and wept, in awe of our shared and profound liberation. Leslie's dad, her stepmother, Paxe, my mother, Jerry, Jeff, Evey, Larry joined the ever-expanding bearhug embrace. "Is it a family reunion?" the cashier asked us in wonder. We knew it would only confuse her to tell her we'd seen each other just a few days before!

Some of us stayed in Saratoga Park while arrangements were made for Leslie's voluntary conservatorship. That night we had a special celebration dinner in Saratoga in honor of our "newfound freedom." Constrained, guilty, awkward over the spontaneity of wine, Woody Allen jokes, and jubilation over our deserting what had so recently meant everything to us, Leslie and I still appreciated and took part in the comradeship. That night Larry Gumbiner departed to start school, but not before I'd heard Dr. Brown's joking account of Larry's being informed hourly of my "progress" in "coming out" and his own determination to "bring out" Leslie soon after! Unification people are a hugely competitive lot!

The rest of us drove to Big Sur under a gold moon. Jazz was playing on the car radio. Nestled close together, Leslie and I vibrated with unrepressed thoughts and long-denied hopes for the future. Our destination was two cabins at Big Sur Lodge, undisclosed roosting place until further notice. We wondered where the rest of the troops had disappeared after the fiasco of the Travelodge exit under police escort the day before.

Wednesday, March 30.

Bad morning. Buried pangs of remorse for a lost quantity, yet *what* was lost? Answers, pure and simple. A still point of pure love, detailed charts of right and wrong, power over people, over the world, over the historical future. I read Lifton on mind control three times as our fugitive party hid out from search teams of the Church. By the afternoon, Jeff encouraged both Leslie and me to call up Carol Pogash from the *San Francisco Examiner* and Julie Smith from the *San Francisco Chronicle* to give them our present status. So, we spent the rest of the day explaining our temporary evasion of the Church. In *our* minds it was a retreat, not yet a final renunciation. But the headlines next day bannered: "THEY LEFT THE MOON FOLD," "OFF THE MOONIE TREADMILL," "RESCUED FROM THE CULT." Many reporters asked questions I couldn't answer. I fought with my Church-inculcated tendency to feel I had to provide an authoritative answer to *every* one. With this I discovered I was no longer a public relations representative of Reverend Moon's truth and will. Mercifully, I had become *just me.*

Thursday, March 31.

Dr. Margaret Singer arrived. I met her this time with openness and warmth. I spent most of the day with Jackie, who'd arrived at a lodge near ours with her parents, Joey, Michele, and Bob Stewart. Jackie, Evey, Joey and I spent a relaxing afternoon playing with a grandfatherly sea otter who came lumbering pompously onto the beach where we lay and plunked down next to us! We kibbutzed through his barking, analyzing the Church and its methods: exploitative, deceptive, controlling, yes, but also joyful, fulfilling, harmonizing. We shared a magic dinner at Nepenthe, a glittering dark seascape restaurant above the cliffs of the Pacific.

Friday, April 1.

Three teams united, with Jackie now also committed to search for answers outside the Unification Church, we drove via Sacramento to Donner Pass, where the Hovards had generously lent us their cabin for "rehabilitation" until the court declared the conservatees could leave California for the Arizona rehab center.

In the car speeding toward the Sierras, I argued with Jeff. I was defending Dr. Durst as the compassionate leader in the "white hat." No way, Jeff declared of his one-time hero. Dr. Durst had to be aware of Avalon estate, Lincolns, expensive jewelry (some of which Jeff had purchased for Onni), of fur coats and clothes from I. Magnin, trips to Las Vegas casinos, New York, and Seoul. Durst, Jeff insisted, couldn't help but apprehend the luxury of his life-style and know on whose backs it was earned. I countered that I didn't think Dr. Durst could have been ungrateful when Jeff bought expensive gifts with maintenance company wages. Jeff wouldn't vouch for Dr. Durst's appreciation, but I wouldn't give up Dr. Durst's intention of goodness. "He thinks in their godliness they deserve the trappings of dignity," I defended the last of my leaders to topple. Jeff pushed me to such an angry wall it wasn't till later that I could concede that Church wealth was an impediment to people on the outside. I remember during the hearing even the Church-hired attorney, Ralph Baker, had said something like "Well, if I can drive a Volkswagen, why can't they?"

April 2 through April 7.

The Hovards' cabin on Signal Mountain, Donner Pass. Days and nights, fifteen people up in the woods, an unexpected community. Days of piercing, blue-white, snow-scattered sunshine, alternating with chiaroscuro shadows cast by towering pines on nearby slopes. Nights filled with fireplace fires, communal dinners, volatile discussions, parents wringing hands, reading, cards, journal writing, tape recordings, guitars, midnight sledding. The day Gary and Joe Alexander, Sr. ("Papa Joe") arrived from Arizona, we celebrated Passover dinner. Jeff led the Seder in a felt hat, the other men wore napkins on their heads. Kibbutzing, reclining, bitter herbs, wine. After bedding down, peace. A strange coziness. Everyone part of some larger, crazy God-initiated scheme called humankind.

Wednesday, April 6.

Gary, Bob, and I drove my mom to Reno airport to fly home to Portland. I knew her stay had been grueling. I sensed she was still very worried about my moments of sympathy with Moon or Dr. Durst, but her presence had communicated supreme endurance through the hellish moments of my rejection of her. I desperately wanted to show her my gratitude for my release from the Church. But I couldn't. Not yet. I still felt wounded by my parents' intervention in my adult life, making me face the limitations of something I had held sacrosanct. My wounds had to heal, my guilt for the pain I had caused them all these years needed to die down.

Thursday, April 7.

Everyone from the cabin drove into Marin County to meet at Carl Shapiro's homespun place and talk with Paul Goorjian and Jerry Falk, the new lawyer the Church had hired to handle the second court appeal coming up. Both attorneys wanted to determine if Leslie, Jackie, and I had come to an independent decision in dismissing them as legal counsel. Finally they were convinced, if baffled.

On our way back to Donner Pass, Gary and I stopped off at a Colfax motel where Jan Kaplan was staying. She was huddled there with Joey, Jr., Mitch, Michele, and her mother. Jan was shaky and obviously not ready to trust the word of the crowd around her. Also she was having a hard time with her mother's spiteful criticisms of the Church. Being her former flower-team commander and one-time source of trust, I was encouraged to talk to her about some of my own realizations of the past two weeks. Jan and I stayed up until four in the morning discussing the many disillusioning elements of the Family, Jan soon eager to hear what I had to say.

Friday, April 8.

Jeff had arranged for a TV interview at the Sacramento Holiday Inn. Jackie, Leslie, and I all agreed we'd like to try to tell in realistic detail, the story of our change of attitude. As we were waiting to go on,

I pulled back the curtain in the hotel studio and looked out on the rain-drenched parking lot. My mouth went dry. Like gasping in Arctic air, I managed to say, "My God! It's Daniel and Norma coming for the same interview. How'd they know we were here?"

When we entered the pressroom, Norma and Daniel offered their hands with childlike innocence, a dear wonderment. My heart flopped over with love and remorse. Still, the interview was a catharsis, totally honest, a sensitive sharing of ourselves. After final questions, we made a quick getaway around the back of the hotel and drove in a blinding rain back up to Jan in Colfax.

Jan, Gary, and I spent a soul-binding night talking together. Jan's trust in Gary's tender integrity and religious intellect allowed her to suspend those infernal questions of her "legal rights" and open up to the possibility of mind control in the Church. Through Gary, we both gained a more profound respect for the freedom to have true religious commitment as seeded first by freedom of thought.

Saturday, April 9.

Walking to the coffee shop, we saw a green Pontiac pull up, a lumber-jacketed, Brillo-bearded fellow with startling blue eyes hop out, turn around three times as though performing a jig, then run over and hug us! On his way from college to the Hovards' cabin where he'd planned to spend Easter day, Larry Gumbiner had by chance pulled off at Colfax for a coffee break. We spent the morning discussing the Church attitudes toward Communism, and he compared Communist methods to those of the Church.

Larry had never really told Jan or me about his own deprogramming the year before. Now, while we bent double at his inimitable style, Larry related how he'd convinced Yacov (Hearst Street center man at the time) to let him go to dinner with his own brother. Consenting, Yacov made it possible for Larry to borrow Daniel's new suit so that Larry could properly impress his brother. Sure enough, the "snatch" took place and there Larry was, sitting in a motel room determined to at least return Daniel's suit. Since deprogrammees are traditionally given everything they want within reason, Larry made Mike Trauscht promise he'd return the suit next day to Hearst Street. Mike dropped the suit off on the doormat, rang the bell, and moved off quickly. Yakov answered the door, stooped down to pick up the suit-without-Larry-inside-it, and proceeded to go wild over the risk he'd taken in letting

Larry go with his family to dinner. With her zany humor, Jan roared over the escapades "deprogramming" can cause.

The day before Easter, Gary, Jan, and I ventured into the sleepy little town of Colfax. Attracted by a plain Catholic church tucked in the hillside, we entered a place of flickering candles and votive incense, chose our pews, and knelt to pray. Afterward a priest padded over to Jan, offered her an Easter lily and a comforting welcome. Taking a shine to her wafty personality, he invited us to see the special vestments of the church. His simple pride in the lean riches of the rustic church transported Jan, made her see that here was one who'd given himself to God's will, yet wasn't a member of the Unification Church. Strange, what will pierce you in the incredible, wide-open vulnerability of coming out of the cult; Jan realized in that moment the limitations of Unification and Moon.

Easter Sunday, April 10.

Silence of light rising; God receives the earth. The symbol of Jesus felt pure in my heart and I was humbled. Echoing in me and rejected was Moon's telling his followers, "You must be confident that *you* are better than Jesus." We shared a breakfast while Jan tried to tone down the prickly personality of her mom. Jan was coming, in the process, to a dawning realization of her mother's true dedication to freeing her.

Hopping in cars, Jan joyfully included this time, we rushed up the mountain to Donner Pass. Our arrival brought hugs, kisses, happy thumpings and hollerings as Jan became the fourth to join our communion outside the fortress of the Church. The "Faithful Five" had now become the "Faithless Four," beating to a different drum, this time that of inner conscience.

The cabin pulsated with guitars; the aromas of a feast concocted by Esther Alexander, Joe's wife, who'd come from Arizona with her son for a few days; and news from the city. Reports from Jeff's close friends in the Sacramento hinterland said that Ralph Baker and a private investigator had come snooping around their place to hunt Jan, myself, and the deprogrammers. The only way, Jeff said, the Church could possibly have found the location of his friends was by a map that Jeff had kept in his briefcase, the one that had been taken from his apartment during the San Francisco hearing.

The rest of the day was spent skiing, gorging ourselves on our Easter feast, and preparing our luggage and our vehicles for the trip back to San Francisco, where the Court of Appeals hearing was to be held the next day. On the way back, Gary, Jan, and I again reviewed mind control, the concepts of *Divine Principle,* and the relationship between means and end.

Once we got into town, Gary and I along with Steve Lang accompanied Jan on her visit with attorney Jerry Falk in the Berkeley hills. Jan spent over two hours talking with him, but Falk refused to accept Jan's arguments about her own changing attitude toward the Church. Stubbornly, Falk told Jan that because he felt she was unsure of herself, he was going to argue as *he* saw fit for her in court tomorrow. Cavalierly, he dismissed any possible problem stemming from his representing her as a Church-paid attorney now that she considered herself out of the Church. He concluded that her "religious beliefs" must have been altered by deprogrammers against the stay order of March 28 (which didn't allow deprogramming to alter our religious beliefs against our will). That being the case, no matter what Jan told him now, Falk claimed her civil rights had been violated and that not only her mother, but Gary, myself, and others were in danger of contempt of court charges. He just shrugged when I protested, "But the Church may be filing contempt-of-court charges against my parents in my name and now I may be charged, too?"

The verbal match ended at one in the morning. Fuming, Jan, Gary, Steve, and I jumped into the car. Yet at least some relevant questions had been raised for us to think about. What *is* altering a religious belief? *Is* it possible to alter faith in God? Or only alter faith in an interloper of God? That night I once more discovered the forgotten but beautiful quality of freedom in democratic disagreement. Pluralism, diversity, even religious factionalism were the necessary substructures of democracy. The tension broke when all of us agreed that disagreement was agreeable after four years in the monotonous mental confines of the Church!

Monday, April 11.

Tension vibrated in the air. How was Jan? How would we all survive confronting the entire staff of the Church in the courtroom? What would the three appeals judges, Sims, Elkington, and Lazarus, rule? Would Johnny be released from the conservatorship and never have a chance to talk to any of us? Would our parents get contempt of court? Would I?

Before court, Carl Shapiro gathered us in a downtown office to discuss the points of his argument; he and his wife would share the plea before the justices. Walking to court, I felt I would stop, petrified, if I didn't have two strong arms to clasp me. Jeff and Evey reassured me, blew off their own tensions by criticizing Church staff. Waiting in the hall before stepping through the doors of the judges' hearing room, I felt I was in a police lineup. The quiet hall was neutral; the courtroom threatened suffocation from the opprobrium of my former brothers and sisters. I walked in between Jeff and Evey, my eyes averted from the stares of the staff. The weight of judgment pulled on me far more from behind than from the justices' seats up front. Still and self-conscious, I tried to share an easy amusement with Jeff and Evey; looking down our row, I could see Leslie, Jackie and Jan struggling with the same safeguard tactics. To my left sat Johnny, the only one of the five not to "come out"; ramrod and uncomfortable between his parents and sister, he shot me an apprehensive smile.

As Shapiro presented our case, I gathered the courage to consider looking behind me, which seemed as dangerous as leaping from a high building. But quickly I glanced back. Lined up in statuelike solidarity, as righteously formidable as graven images, were Teresa, Becky, Amos, Micah, Esther, Bertha, Norma, Daniel, and John, who seemed stapled between disbelief and judgment. Teresa's eyes bore in, shot splinters of steel. For the first time in four years I felt free of her intimidation, admitted I'd doubted there was a heart behind the mesmeric look. Micah smiled sweetly and, for a wonder, waved his arm at me. What a gift, this momentary small acceptance; it won a part of my soul evermore. Micah had caught and comforted some winged creature flying from me toward him; Teresa had aimed and shot instead. But letting out a breath, I realized her mark had missed my flight . . . forever.

Esther from the Church handed a note to me over my right shoulder. Would there be anything of forgiveness in it? "I hope we can talk sometime because we have shared so much together. Your actions confuse and disappoint me. Please return the blouse and skirt you're wearing. I merely lent them to you and it seems inappropriate for you to wear them. There is nothing and everything to say. In the heart of True Parents, your sister, Esther."

Jerry Falk argued his case against the conservatorships for Johnny and Jan on the basis of infringement of First Amendment freedom of religion. He explained Leslie, Jackie and I had already chosen to dismiss him as legal counsel. Without delay, their sharp comments appearing predetermined, the justices ordered a stay on all conservatorships until further time when the full transcript of our hearing could be studied. This meant that Johnny and Jan could return to the Church if they wanted; parents no longer had legal custody over us; any of us could go anywhere we chose, in or out of California.

A wild fracas erupted the minute the court was dismissed. Newspeople bore down upon the five of us and the two sets of parents, the Kaplans and the Hovards, who were there. Church members sought to meet with us; Jan's mother started a shoving match with Bertha ("Jan's "spiritual mother") to claim protectorate over her daughter. Paul Goorjian yelled at me for having unduly influenced Jan to leave. I said a few strained words to John and Micah, then walked alone out into the hall. My arm loaded with coats, I offered Amos my left hand in greeting. He refused contact, and I remembered the left side represented Satan in the Church. I transferred all the coats to my left arm, freeing my right to reach out. Few words were spoken between us.

After this disorganized, painfully lengthy exit from the courtroom, we gathered again and took the elevator to the silver Freedom of Thought van parked outside. When we got there, we discovered it had been broken into during the hearing! Church materials, deprogramming tapes, even a guitar were missing.

That evening all of us were invited to Mr. and Mrs. Foster's place for dinner before taking off to Tucson and the Freedom of Thought Foundation. Gary had casually asked Mrs. Foster if she'd mind having a few people in. When she inquired as to the number, he'd said, "Is thirty all right?" What a homecoming, to meet with the Fosters, Shapiros, Maxwells (a local ex-cult counseling family), Margaret Singer, other ex-members of the Church from the Bay Area.

We flew out of San Francisco that night on a wave of festive warmth and rejoicing. But even as I settled myself on the plane, I could imagine Johnny Hovard back at Hearst Street and the Family celebrating the liberation of its hero.

I joined the Unification Church because I thought I'd found the ultimate truth. I left the cult because I realized during the course of the courtroom hearing and of my deprogramming—in an environment where I was free for the first time in four years to reflect, question, and examine—that the truth wasn't black and white. I discovered it wasn't that my own faith in God was inauthentic; I'd wrongly worshipped a "God" that Moon's Principles had created in my mind, a "God" who mistrusted individual freedom of will.

Memory works best with what I loved: many magnificent Church members first of all; the mutual adventures and triumphs; the intense, sacrificial sense of collective high purpose in the deeply believed fight for our spiritual lives and for the redemption of America; becoming a person of faith through the fire of asceticism and zealotry.

But, in truth, there had begun to be, though I was scarcely aware of it, darker memories forming in me as well.

Up until the hearing, in order to carry on my work in the Church I'd suppressed and forgotten many inner rebellions against violations of conscience. The hearing and deprogramming allowed me to be an individual, not a cultist, and in the act of looking at myself apart from the movement, I didn't like what I saw. The hearing and deprogramming also allowed me to discover that in the cult I hadn't owned or had access to a private inner life of truth, free of guilt or manipulation. During the trial, I became a divided self. I became aware that my "performance self," as a Church spokesperson, contradicted the self which had a personal conscience, responding to previously taught principles of human decency and universal, rather than exclusive or polarized, consideration for all people. The values I had learned from my parents contradicted the practices of my "True Parents." Yet, how could the bringing of a universal "kingdom on earth," which was the single-minded Church mission, exclude age-old morality as the means to get there? I rediscovered the truth that means and goals had to be consistent. My parting with the Church was motivated by my desire for greater autonomy in finding and choosing goodness. It was neither resignation nor escape, but release from the womblike security of absolutes and guarantees, the perfect future universes that had blinded me.

I could see that the greatest responsibility God ever granted me, or any human being, was to act from free will, especially in evaluating right and wrong in a complex world. I had confused security with enlightenment. So I came out of the Church.

To question all I once held true; to be able to realize a limitation in what I felt was universal, omnipotent, and infallible; to accept with humility a new life; to pick up the pieces of human heartache and to find the God-force still wanting me, encouraging me; to discover God had never given up hope but has restlessly made His way into my being to stir real love in me—these are my new, hard, comforting shadows and illuminations. I realize I've come out of a prison in my mind that prevented me from trusting that love for God existed *within* me, not *out* of me.

Suddenly I'm confronted by the responsibility of relationships of my *own* making: with God and myself, my parents, friends, lover. I face a cosmorama of sudden considerations: spiritual community, morality, my own long-suppressed sexuality, pain and suffering, sensuality, individualism, political commitment, authority, eros, freedom, law, obligation, belief, fidelity, God's love and requirements, prayer, Christ's life, marriage, aging, money, honesty, my own brothers, sin, forgiveness, indemnity, career, school, mind control, trust, loyalty, children, integrity, sacrifice, understanding, joy, property, eternity, mortality, hope, judgment, messiah, confidence, choice, maturity, change, absolutism, relativism, truth.

Once more I join Everyman. Questions of purpose and existence hit me square in the face. In his homely way, Kipling said it:

If you can watch the things you gave your life to, broken . . .
And stoop and build 'em up with worn-out tools;
If you can make one heap of all your winnings
And risk it on one turn of pitch and toss
And lose, and start again at your beginnings . . .
If you can force your heart, and nerve and sinew
To serve your turn long after they are gone,
And so hold on when there is nothing in you
Except the will which says to them: "Hold on;"
Yours is the earth and everything that's in it. . . .

Betty:
Barb's Coming Out

"Not in Utopia—subterranean fields—
Or some secreted island, Heaven knows where!
But in the very world, which is the world
Of all of us,—the place where, in the end
We find our happiness, or not at all."
    —WORDSWORTH

MARCH 25, 1977.
    As parents we were about to experience at first hand that strange evolution called deprogramming, a process termed dark and monstrous by those who know nothing about it.

For the next seventeen days what deprogramming looked like to

Ray and me was a difficult and intense psychological process highlighted by painful moments when Barb appeared to ask herself, *what am I doing?* With the aid of loving ex-cult friends who understood what had happened to themselves and to her, her frozen and rigid state of mind seemed little by little to give way, releasing her to think, reason, and feel.

That progression, however, was interrupted sometimes by abrupt moments of uncertainty when she'd regress to the cult's comforting and beguiling absolutes. For parents, those were heart-in-mouth times.

But for parents to be around a "deprogramming" they must be prepared for anything. An exceedingly anxious and intense experience, sometimes it manages to be humorous, too. And sometimes it's physically rigorous. Ray had to make it possible to extricate our group—Barb, Jeff Scales, Evey Eden and Jerry Feldman—from the San Francisco airport motel and the donnybrook of Onni and Durst illegally parked in the motel parking lot, Jackie Katz locked in the bathroom crying, Tom Brown threatening to break the noses of the cult lawyers for apparently exceeding their authority, while the two cult attorneys tried to cope with their intractable clients. Dodging cult cars cruising in the dark, Ray and Goorjian drove together so that Goorjian could have a conference in a nearby restaurant with Barb before we headed south. On the way, Goorjian confided to Ray that if that were his daughter he wouldn't use "legal stuff," he'd just grab her. That remark, and Goorjian's obvious concern for Barb and the others, oddly endeared Goorjian to Ray.

As to physical endurance. After Ray left to return to Portland, our whole group hid out at Big Sur. Avoiding possible cult harassment, we then caravaned to Donner Pass in the high Sierras. The borrowed Hovard cabin was up a steep, nighttime, snow-filled mountainside. Shedding city shoes, lugging baggage, I slogged in stocking feet through the snow. Next morning I was assigned as chief cook for a dozen people and slept nearly a week in my clothes because the cabin contained three blankets.

The rare professionals sensitive to the actual dynamics of "deprogramming" call it *repersonalization*. The word fits. As time wore on, Barb became more and more someone we'd known before.

Barb's breakthroughs began to occur during the hearing, I believe. Though she said nothing at the time, I particularly sensed a silent confusion when I showed her some of Moon's less than admirable words in "Master Speaks." I couldn't figure out if she'd even read them before.

There were so many pivotal moments, including times when I wasn't at all sure which way she'd go:

—Right after Gary Scharff and Joey Alexander left our motel room, I watched Barb standing in the middle of the room saying softly to herself, "There's *got* to be something wrong if the Church says you can't listen, not even one minute, you have to shut everything out."

—Barb crying when the motel TV showed that airline crash; for us those tears seemed to be washing away almost an alien person as they flowed down her cheeks.

—At Big Sur I watched in fascination as Barb and Leslie sat at the table studying Lifton's chapter 22. They'd read a while, look up at each other, confer in low voices. Discovery was all over their faces, wonder in their voices.

—At the Donner Pass cabin Barb watched Zeffirelli's film on Jesus, quietly checking *Divine Principle Study Guide,* muttering in stupefaction at its discrepancies.

—Barb and Leslie played dress-up in Evey's black "pickup" wig. Leslie came gliding and undulating into the room, Barb burst into a jig, each dance so expressive of the two women. Something seemed to be loosening up in Barb.

—A darker moment occurred, the kind that shows why it's so difficult for parents to talk their own children out of cults, one afternoon when Barb, Jerry Feldman, and I were having a cup of coffee in the Donner Pass sun. I made a critical remark about the cult and Barb rushed off, steaming: "I just can't stand it when *you* criticize the Church."

—Most frightening of all (to me), her first setback occurred one night at Big Sur. Suddenly I looked around and discovered Barb had vanished from the fun-making. I found her outside the lodge, pacing in the dark, staring up at the sky. When I came up to her, she whispered, "I miss my flower team. I wonder if I had a right to leave them." "Come back in, Barb, where people understand better than I." She followed, grumbling. But at least the grumbling sounded more natural than the trancelike mood I'd found her in.

—And there were times of simple anguish from loss and giving up. Before leaving Donner Pass for the plane back to Portland, I went upstairs to collect the cult clothes Barb had worn at the hearing and no longer wished to wear. She crouched beside me on the floor, leafing through her red journal, studying photographs of Moon, his wife Hak Ja-Han, the Dursts, and her friends in the cult. Handing the journal over, silently she shook a little vial. "Do you know what this is?" she asked, almost shyly.

"No," I nodded, stricken by her look.

"It's holy salt; we sprinkle it on a lot of things to purify them. And this is a little piece of dried tuna caught by Reverend Moon."

"Oh," was all I could answer over the lump in my throat, watching her, realizing what the turning over of these precious things meant to her. *Four years and so much devotion and comfort—the thought ravaged me. Should we have?* "You were in love with an ideal, Barb," I managed.

"I still don't know if he's the messiah," she answered. "And I don't see only the holes in *Divine Principle*, either."

I didn't leave, I fled, though I longed to stay, to hug, to protect, to make up in some way for her loss and my part in it. To let down, cry together. I repeated to Gary what had just occurred.

"She said that?" he asked in surprise. Then, "My promise holds. If she wants to talk to me, I'm here to talk to."

Memories of the strangeness of the whole experience will never leave me, nor, deep down, an abiding sense that I will never wholly understand her going in, her staying in, or her coming out. I think it's not fully possible for those who haven't been cultists.

But while it was all happening, through moments of intense crisis, chaos—and occasional hilarity—I tried to put aside my personal responses to the way Barb had chosen to spend the past four years of her life, and to concentrate on the events of the moment.

The day I was to leave the cabin at Donner Pass to fly home alone to Portland, I borrowed some hiking boots, climbed the high slope above us, and found a square of pine needled ground where I could stretch out alone and think.

How was my relationship with my daughter coming? I asked myself. Not very well, I answered. I'd been told the range of emotions in "coming out" went from murderous to tearfully grateful. But I? I'd been treated by Barb in an absent, detached way, with what seemed to me a dutiful kindness, an avoidance of closeness. Sometimes flashes of resentment, anger.

I thought of parenthood. Had there been inadequate parenting? Mothering? Not perfect, I knew, but well intentioned and, if hugely deficient, unknowingly so.

Parenthood—not without its frustrations and its compromises of my life aims—had nevertheless given me a chance to experience an altruistic love that had made me feel human in the highest degree. I'd felt great mutual support, too; I'd been an enthusiastic partisan of my children and had felt that they reciprocated.

But this whole recent experience had been laced with humiliation. A proud, nonbegging person, I'd had to seek out and try to nurture that which didn't wish to be sought out or nurtured by me. Were parents and children natural enemies, as some claimed?

There on that patch of ground, head on hands, I went back to our original family intent. We'd brought Barb out for *herself*, for *her* freedom. If love followed, that was a merciful bonus.

As I reminded myself of that, my anger dropped to resentment, then to disappointment. Once more I reined myself in, not letting my hopes soar.

The blue mountains I was looking at in my brown study suddenly shifted into focus. Time, they seemed to say. Things take a long time, especially forgiving. . . .

In that beneficent sun, a vast God out there, I felt love. I went to sleep on the hillside, awakened, climbed to a higher place and a huge, sun-warmed rock and observed the life around me. A miniature train coiled through Donner Pass, the chairlift was a moving toy to the right, skiers made jet-stream lines on the snow below me, there was a constant flow of people coming and going from the lodge nearby, and, forming a backdrop for all of this, beyond the great valley the gaunt Sierras soared. It had been a marvelous day and nobody had needed it more.

I climbed back, badly sunburned but restored.

I flew home to Portland by way of Reno. Ray and I fell into each other's arms and just breathed. In the days ahead, Barb was never out of our thoughts.

We survived a panicky, wild half-day on April 11 after the appeals court stayed (cancelled) our conservatorships and we didn't know where Barb had been taken.

Barb called next morning after flying down with Leslie, Jackie, and Jan to the rehab center in Arizona. She told us that the judges, before even reading the hearing transcript, had walked into the courtroom with their minds made up. After that call, we heard from her every few days.

On April 12, she phoned to ask if it'd be all right for her to go to New York City to be on the "Good Morning America" show. "Do you want to?" Ray asked. "Yes, I'm doing fine," Barb answered.

While in New York, Barb and Gary Scharff had gone to see Robert Jay Lifton, the China brainwashing expert and Yale psychiatrist. The interview consisted of three hours of Lifton's questioning Barb about her cult years, the "deprogramming," and her dreams since leaving the powerful group. He advised her to get lots of "mental fresh air." Barb told Lifton before leaving, "I can't express the amount of relief I feel about being rescued by my parents. I know I could never have left on my own. It's hard for anybody outside of the experience to understand the depth of that, but maybe you understand."

On Friday, April 15, we watched the TV program in Portland. Hovard, the only one of the Faithful Five who hadn't come out, was Barb's adversary; they'd spent an hour in a room waiting together, as a matter of fact. On the air, John vividly described the "terrors" of deprogramming, and the moderator was about to move on when Barb, composed and lovely, broke in and asked if she could comment. "My deprogramming," she said, "was one hundred and eighty degrees different from what John described. It was a compassionate experience with loving and well-informed people." Barb said she'd gone into the Church because of the ideals of the New Education Development, learned of Moon's role later, but stayed in because she felt her own relationship to God deepening and because of the incredibly fine personal relationships in the cult. "Unfortunately," she said, "I wasn't able to keep on examining my faith."

Her last sentence, and the last sentence of the program was, "I still have my faith in God, but now I have my integrity too."

Weariness, worry, guilt, anger washed away and left peace.

Twenty-five years before there had been a birth. We felt, as we watched, that we were now witnessing a rebirth.

Barb: Free of Captivity

"The earth is the Lord's, and the fullness thereof, the world and they that dwell therein."
   —Psalm XXIV

APRIL 11, 1977.
   Unadorned, the Freedom of Thought Center was a Tucson hacienda-style home on the alluvial of the saguaro cactus desert. It provided warm, understanding support for people who had just come out of religious cults. Co-director Esther Alexander, simple-spirited and intuitive, put in hours of care and counseling with the young people. Joe, Sr., her noted "deprogrammer" husband, provided the fatherly touch. Gary Scharff shared the responsibilities of running the center with Esther, helping the ex-cultists struggle to readjust to the demands of a new life.

   For me, the center seemed overly "anticult" in its emphasis, but it

did provide a much-needed and very beautiful communal family atmosphere. From April to May, I was there with seven former ex-Unification members, who became my friends. As we joined in swimming, playing guitar and piano, photography, reading, writing, and trips to Mexico, the Grand Canyon, and Phoenix, we began to rediscover lost values of equality, intimacy, and individuality. We found ourselves involved in an intense community in the aftermath of a shared and intense cult experience.

Usually, if I weren't swimming or dancing, I was pacing. It was weeks before I settled down.

"Barb," Jeff ordered, "Sit!"

"I can't," I demurred, suddenly doing a cartwheel, ending up standing on my head staring at him upside down.

Jeff was still very commanding; he upended me and pushed me into a chair. "I swear, I'm going to tie you there. Read a book. Read anything. Read Zane Gray."

I sat there laughing up at him, thinking where else in this whole earth but at the rehab center would I not have to explain to anyone what was the matter with me. It was wonderful to be surrounded by understanding people.

In the cult, of course, you're trained to think that sitting down is sinful; God requires you to keep moving, hustling. You feel guilty about sleeping. Habits of perpetual motion were only beginning to wind down in me.

"How many miles do you suppose I ran selling flowers?" I mused. Suddenly everyone was doing noisy calculations: maximum estimate, 15,000 miles; minimum, 10,000!

"I know I wore out a lot of shoes," I remarked.

"And had to pray for new ones," Evey said, dryly.

I left the Freedom of Thought Foundation on May 15, 1977, and took a Hughes Air West plane from Tucson to Portland. My parents met me with total embrace; my parents, who had shown me the meaning of true family, who had shown me that family life isn't bankrupt.

Being away from the Church community, being separated for the first time from the community of ex-members, I faced a time of great solitude. Without an intense community, I knew I'd have to look into myself, alone with God. Would I come out whole?

In this wrestle of the spirit, it was the mystery, the invisibility, the uncertainty of God's will which proved frightening; a God embodied in Moon had been so much easier. Sometimes only the wordless communion of genuine love, as Thomas Merton says, pulled me through.

I found such love during days spent in Portland with my parents, with pre-Church friends, and with my brothers. I visited briefly with Evan, a healing, time-honored friend.

I was regaining wholeness by finally taking responsibility for my inner life. And I was discovering that to know I was capable of loving and doing, and finding that I was loved beyond just what I did, enriched my faith.

During the summer of 1977 I was asked to work as a counselor for the Freedom of Thought Foundation. I had to confront several questions within myself. My reservations about going to work for the Freedom of Thought Foundation were ethical questions about "deprogramming" methods. I'd no doubt, based on my own "deprogramming" in March and April, that the process could and should be compassionate, sensitive, enlightening. But was my experience unique? I'd had a court hearing. If I were "deprogramming" others, I anticipated encounters less free than my own.

Should people who are in the Unification Church (and who, like myself, had been cut off by severe guilt and fear tactics from contact with family, friends, former cult members, and other frames of reference) be forcibly removed from the Church because their parents wanted them to reconsider their commitment? I approached this question knowing that the "will" of a Church member was a "programmed" will designed to view "deprogramming" as an annihilation of spirit. Even though the Church might be judged deceptive and antisocial and unfree, did that justify forcing a person to reexamine his or her commitment in a setting of constraint?

In addition to the potential dangers the Church represented to society because of its antidemocratic political and material goals and its totalitarian theology, what of the dangers posed to the individual? Did members of the Church stand to lose more or gain more from the experience? I had felt increased power, exhilaration, purpose, release from depression, community and comradery, and security in the Church. But I had had to be willing to subsume my common sense and my free will to dictates of "higher consciousness." Revolting against rationalism and secularism, I had had to discard the values of Judeo-Christian Biblical tradition, critical questioning, pluralism, self-reliance, individuality, my family, the "letter" of secular law, and simple honesty.

What if no one had stepped in to deprogram me? I thought of "deprogrammer" Joey Alexander's favorite phrase: "Until you are humble enough to admit the *possibility* that you might have been deceived, then you shall be deceived perpetually." I knew I was grateful that this deception had been demonstrated to me. And if I was grateful, did I have the luxury to withhold the insights I'd been allowed from others who were captive in the Church?

How did a "deprogrammer" avoid biasing a recent ex-cultist by taking an overly critical attitude toward the Church? What could a "deprogrammer" provide in security for the ex-cultist once his Church identity had peeled away?

I finally decided for "deprogramming," trusting my own delicate concern for the individual to guide me in difficult moments. From June to September I helped in seven deprogrammings. Some involved conservatorships by *ex parte* court order, some by full court hearings and others as a result of volunteer discussions. I was temperamentally most comfortable with voluntary counseling sessions where a cult member responded to his parent's pleas to talk to ex-cultists. I finally concluded that "deprogramming" can't be judged as unilaterally right, nor dismissed as absolutely wrong. Individual factors weigh heavily: love between parent and child, legal sanction, the cult member's personality and degree of involvement, and the conduct of the "deprogrammers."

One of the most painful things to face after being "deprogrammed" is the absolute separation from former loved brothers and sisters in the cult. They believe that every word you speak as an ex-believer is a lie. You present the ultimate threat to ongoing believers. For the ex-member, cult friends are glimpsed as though on the other side of a pane of glass: the member can be seen but not touched. For the member who has never left, the ex-member seems like a ghost from the netherworld, divorced from life, to be pitied or condemned.

My first encounter with an Oakland staff member, six months after the first court hearing, confirmed my most tragic apprehensions. One evening Jerry and Judy, two ex-cultists, and I, were eating dinner along the S.F. wharf, talking about our lives outside the Church. Suddenly

Jerry whispered, "Martha just walked in, but then walked out. She saw us."

I can't describe the unearthly, dark, primitive fear which crept through my body. I could hardly move my lips to talk.

"Do you think she'll come back?" I asked the others.

"Don't worry," assured Judy. "If she does, we can always leave. You can handle it, Barb." I wished I hadn't noticed that Judy herself looked shaken.

Twenty minutes later Martha marched into the restaurant with an older brother, Bill, for protection. She stalked up to our table and sat down, commanding total authority. Jerry, Judy, and I braced ourselves for a frontal attack.

"What are you doing here? What are you planning?" Martha rapped her words out.

"Well, we're eating dinner. By the way, hello, Martha. Hello, Bill. Good to see you both. It's a surprise." I offered my hand, but they conspicuously rejected the offer. Bill glared at me, solid as a flying buttress.

Martha was obviously center person for this inquisition. "Lael, what are you doing with your life? Do you pray?"

"Yes, I pray."

"Who do you pray to? And what do you pray for?"

"I pray to be more honest and good, for a better world."

Judy interspersed, "We pray for what's in our conscience; we spend our time trying to live by conscience."

"Judy, you shut up! You're not worth living. I don't care about you. I'm interested in Lael. At least Lael's still sincere," Martha said.

"Look, Martha, who are you to judge whether someone should be alive or not? Judy's my friend. I care for her and I believe it's un-Godly to talk to her that way," I flared.

"Lael, you gave your life for Heavenly Father, your brothers and sisters. You were a success in God's eyes. Then suddenly you just switched around as though you had no backbone. Why, you've thrown away everything of value and meaning."

"I'm doing what I think's worthwhile. I'm counseling people, writing; I don't exactly know about success," I tried to explain, feeling once more childlike, unable to express myself.

"Success, bah! You're a failure." Martha jeered. "You inspire only bitterness in the staff—Onni, Abba, Amos, Irene, Teresa, Micah! Why don't you stop killing people, kidnapping them? You're stealing God from their lives. Stop it now!" she demanded, enmity flaming.

"Martha, I don't want anymore to be successful or valuable in the way the Church demands. Success there means obedience, submission. I tried sincerely to obey for four years, and then at the end had to discover that the beliefs and practices weren't what they were proclaimed. Isn't that the *Church's* failure? Why am I to blame? Why does the burden of failure *always* rest on the *individual* in the Church, the glory *always* on Moon? Maybe there's something wrong with the Church system." I desperately wanted her to think.

"Yeah, if you'd take a couple of days with us, we'd be happy to share some of our new insights." Judy couldn't resist inviting Martha to a "deprogramming." "I don't feel I'm taking God out of anyone's life, least of all my own," she added.

"I agree," Jerry agreed with quiet dignity.

Martha simply ignored him. "I'm not talking to you," she snapped. "Anyway, Lael, why don't you just do your own thing away from people? Go away! Stop spreading confusion! Leave our Family alone. Why do you persecute us?"

I stared at her in quiet despair, so unable to communicate.

"Don't you believe Reverend Moon's the Messiah?" Martha persisted.

"I've been mistaken before in my life," I spoke slowly, "and I could be mistaken now. But after months of thought and research and prayer, no, I don't believe he's the messiah." My whole insides convulsed, saying that to Martha.

"But He could be!" Martha pounced. "Then where will you be?"

"I'll just be as good as I know how to be," I answered, more to myself and to God than to Martha.

"Jerry, Judy, Lael, you've no right to be alive and do this! I know God's will. He knows you're doing evil. Stop before it's too late!"

"Maybe you *don't* know God's will, Martha. Maybe Reverend Moon doesn't know God's will, either. If you only *knew* how much I'd wanted him to know God's will; for four years of my life I wanted only that. But maybe God's bigger than any of us. Maybe He's too big to know in this way," I offered.

Judy poked me. "Barb, let's go. This isn't getting any place."

"The Church," I said, moving toward the restaurant door, "will never listen to anyone who leaves it. I'm sorry it won't, because it could learn something about itself. I don't feel animosity for the people in the Church. Good-bye, take care."

We parted, Martha and Bill to go back to their witnessing, the three of us to blow off steam.

"Let's walk around the block," Judy suggested.

"They make you believe you're such a sinner, it almost tempts me to go out and *sin!*" I raged.

Jerry patted my back, and said, "You wouldn't know where to start."

"It's just hard to be hated," I confided.

Jerry put his arms through Judy's and mine. "We've got each other and ourselves," he reminded.

Ourselves. Each other. And God. The encounter just finished began to assume its right place in me.

God I knew was vaster than anything perceived in the restaurant back there. Bigger than anything in the Unification Church. Look for the God beyond the God, Tillich had begged. *The church beyond the Church and the family beyond the Family,* I thought.

When I came out of my thoughts, Judy was saying, "We've got God, because we *chose* Him." Her voice sounded final and certain, like the click of an Instamatic camera.

But I'd given up for all time believing I could capture God's image, as I'd been captured, in something stopped and framed.

Betty: Barb Is Out

"The daylight of this world which she returned to after her sojourn in the messianic abyss is not always clear or warm, but we rejoice in it because we know that whatever course she takes in the future, she will not make her conscience the prisoner or possession of another man."
—ADAPTED FROM A STATEMENT BY EX-CULTIST ALLEN TATE WOOD,
    December 1975, "My Four and a Half Years with the Lord of
    the Flies"

"He raises up the needy out of affliction,
and makes their families like flocks. . . ."
—PSALMS

MAY 15, 1977.
    With love and apprehension, we met Barb's plane when she flew into Portland from the southwest on a cloudy Monday afternoon. Joe Alexander hadn't even let her fly by way of the Bay Area

(cults fund-raise at the airports) so we were prepared for harassment, if not from cultists, by those who disagreed with our by now far too publicized action.

Besieged by curiosity callers, anxious parents of cultists, and media explorers, we welcomed Barb to a room decorated for homecoming and began to feel out where she was, where the strengths and weaknesses were in our relationship. How can I describe what it's like to respond to a much-loved adult daughter on one level, to a young stranger whose experiences have been so inimical to our family life on another? It was natural, it was old times; it was bleak, strange moments of guilt and tension born of unknowing. It was love longing to, but not quite daring to, let itself fly.

It was joyously close times and sudden shocking estrangements.

The worst of the latter happened at the end of the first week when I walked through the living room, found Barb pensively looking out the window, heard her say softly, "Maybe I shouldn't have left the Church." And instead of asking, "What makes you feel that way right now?"—how lonely and defeated she must have been feeling—in panic I trotted out the old arguments, continued at a heated dinner with the three of us. Suddenly there we were, back to four years ago, back to base one, the air thick with misunderstandings, disappointments, and bitterness.

Next day I risked putting Barb on the train to Seattle to see her brother Jeff and his friend Diane, and to visit Leslie Brown and her dear precult friend, Evan. When she returned, she was less defensive and tense. By then we had picked ourselves up and were in better shape, too.

From what she told me of her realizations during the talks shared with Evan, I learned to accept one simple and singular fact. However immoral to us some of the cult doctrine, however manipulative and unsavory some of the leadership; however unethical some of the cult practice, to Barb the four years had not been just one grand loss but had meant a deep and ecstatic religious experience and commitment, had made of her a religious person, had given her a closeness with peers never before experienced.

And so love once more taught me humility, warned me to learn from my mistakes, to stretch my perceptions and sensitivities, to reconcile anger and impatience, to sublimate personal wounds and wonders to strength, care, affirmation, and hope.

There were messages and letters, some hostile, some supportive. Our friend Mark Hatfield wrote: "I heard with great pleasure the news of Barbara's disassociation from the Unification Church. This ends a very trying and painful ordeal for you, her family, and the many others who care so deeply for her well-being. . . . Your actions will undoubtedly set an important example to the many families who suffer similar losses of their children to organizations which, under the guise of 'religion,' and through coercion, promote family hatred and fear to further their own self-serving goals."

Especially touching was a personal letter to Barb from an ex-cult friend. She wrote: "For many months I went through an incredible suffering, so much so that I truly thought my heart was breaking. I couldn't think of anything else but the Family, if I was betraying and turning away God's will. I feel very much at peace about leaving the Family now. I love them but I see bad failings, discrepancies. . . . I missed most about the Family that ideal of freely giving our love to each other. . . . But somehow even that ideal got submerged in duty and mission and finally there wasn't time to truly love. . . . No matter how strongly the Family thinks you and I have deserted God, love isn't alone in their minds, it's in God's and isn't rationed."

Then there were the letters that, in stern ignorance, reminded us that didn't we know that, in deprogramming, our daughter had been beaten and drugged?

In mid-June, Barb flew back to the rehab center to take part in working with other young cultists being "brought out." She returned the first part of September, perceptibly more secure in herself, more comfortable with us and we with her. At last we began to make positive emotional contact, began to rebuild the trust that had been so disastrously broken. At last Ray and I felt we could "relinquish" her to authentic maturing. All our children gathered, we had our first family reunion in five years. Through black nights, there had been long stretches of time when I'd thought I'd never live to see it happen.

In early October a special friend and counselor came to spend two weeks with Barb. Of her he later wrote us: "You have a wonderful daughter. She has such an intense desire for goodness. My heart is continually renewed by her presence. She is one shakily coherent, continual explosion, fueled by God, primed by trust, triggered by contact. Sometimes her vulnerability still makes me frightened for her. I have come to love her in a special, enduring way that is deeper, more freeing, and more invigorating than anything I have ever experienced with another person."

And then Gary Scharff shared with us a poem he had written to Barb:

Walk

The grip is firm,
The hand is young,
Love
  is pressed into my arm by tender otherfingers
  whose grace I know:
You are near and we walk together.

A quiet plumb at lakebottom,
This peace whose rich silence pervades this
  laughing that skims
    exuberant
      across colored
      flashing autumn,
      feelings punctuated
      in footsteps.

God per-
colates
in our newly human eyes.
Drinking the sun's smile,
Celebrating all we see:
Tying, untying delicate knots with strands of our spirits,
Building, observing, caressing in intricate intimacy,
Finding other kisses than kisses
Walking, clasping in step on a
  path
  through an
  unknown
  forest where leaves block the sun.

The California appeals court's final decision was rendered October 6, 1977. After reading our lengthy court transcript, the appeals judges declared that the provisions of the Probate Code on which our conservatorships had been granted (our claim that the danger to our children's physical, psychological, and emotional health warranted emergency intervention) were "too vague to justify" our appointment; that if the picture painted by expert testimony were a factual one, then the conclusion of the trial court that the conservatees had been subjected to coercive persuasion was valid, but that in fact the trial court had failed to establish that the Faithful Five had been "gravely disabled." The appeals court decision went up to the California Supreme Court, which denied hearing, two of the Supreme Court's justices dissenting from the high court's majority decision.

In the best of all worlds, there ought to be an America court brave enough to tackle head-on the fact of coercive persuasion applied not physically but psychologically. There ought to be a court willing to weigh, in considering rescue, the necessity recognized by the Model Penal Code—a necessity to act under a belief that intervention avoids an evil greater than the likely result of inaction.

Parents shouldn't have to do to their young people what we did to Barb. The legitimate activities of Unification should not be attacked. But laws already in existence should be used to discover if Unification systematically violates U.S. immigration laws and regulations, and/or U.S. currency and foreign exchange laws; whether Unification in its many arms engages in political, business, or other activities inconsistent with its tax-exempt status as a church; whether there have been systematic violations of the Foreign Agents Registration Act and the Arms Exports Control Act. Consumer protection laws in the individual states should be used where it is discovered that fund-raisers are deceitful. Legal methods similar to consumer protection rulings should be devised to require high-intensity cult proselytizers to identify themselves at an early stage and outline to the candidate what his or her life will be like on joining; inhibitions should somehow be placed on proselytizing by coercive persuasion such as mandatory licensing of those who practice high-powered behavior modification techniques, or requiring mandatory cooling-off periods for initiates. The chilling effect on free speech that cult lawsuits against written criticism now create should be recognized and examined. Public education about cults should continuously go forward.

With our institutions worldwide under attack and democracy, that highest development of citizenship, beleaguered, not to raise questions about the domestic use of methods so antithetical to our beliefs seems shortsighted, to say the least. Moreover, there are devoted civil libertarians who would like to see an in-depth judicial or congressional examination of the process certain cults use that robs a person of his inmost self, bends it to social conformity, and makes him feel guilty if he doesn't comply.

It comes down to what Ray said right after the "deprogramming." "It's not so much the deceit, the dictatorship, the exploitive hard work, or where the money goes, it's the rape of the self. I think that when Barb was given a chance to step back, she sensed that. The question becomes not what to do about God being 'ripped' from her, but how to find a freely chosen and magnanimous God."

Carrying memories of mixed pain and joy, Barb, like other ex-cultists, will, we hope, move on to a world that is neither cult nor anti-cult. That world of reality is often one of confusions and discontinuities, but in it choices are *made*, not mindlessly accepted—choices that can clarify, not impede, understanding, reconciliation and growth.

Barb: Conclusion

"If God had locked up all truth in his right hand, and in his left the unique, ever-alive striving for truth, albeit with the addition that I should always and eternally err, and he said to me, 'Choose!'—I should humbly clasp his left hand, saying,
'Father, give! Pure truth is after all for thee alone.'"
—GOTTHOLD LESSING

When first pursuing an ad about a Berkeley room for rent in December 1977, I appeared at the door of a brown-shingled house on Regent Street. It must have been the identical twin of the house I'd moved into five years before, when I joined the Unification Church! I was greeted by a young man who claimed he recognized me. He remembered fleeing over the Boonville fence one weekend he'd been in my group in 1975! He nearly shut the door on me, afraid I had come to infiltrate the household. After reassuring him that I came as an individual seeking only a single room, I moved in.

I lived there from January to June 1978 as a full-time student taking sociology, religion, and literature classes at Berkeley. Also in Berkeley were many of my irreplacable ex-cult friends, who comprised a close but informal "community." A communication network of mutual support and respect spread among other former members who had dispersed from Ann Arbor to Albuquerque, New York to North Carolina, and San Francisco to Seattle.

I went to New York City for the summer of '78 to work freelance for a publishing house. I lived in a Puerto Rican and Ukranian neighborhood in the East Village and survived a stringent budget, cockroach invasions, and a rickety fire escape where I read and wrote in 100-degree heat.

I also developed a warm relationship with a former PR leader of the Unification Church who left the group to pursue a professional career.

I returned to Berkeley in September 1978 after surviving my "ultimate urban challenge." I looked forward to my four housemates, a piano, my philodendrons, and no cockroaches. I continued my studies until I graduated in sociology in March 1979.

At age twenty-seven, I am no longer an adolescent. Yet I feel the full force of contradictions and complexity so characteristic of adolescence. Six years ago, I joined the Church, tempted by the possibility of leaping over the dilemmas of adolescence into what I thought of as the certainties of adulthood. Now I have to wrestle with meaning-making in a relative world (Berkeley being more relative than all the rest of the world—except the East Village!).

With the near and long-distance support of my family, I have struggled to piece together my past, to regain the positive aspects of my surging idealism. It's not easy to go from being a "world saver" to being just one person among billions. Especially as a lone student matriculating at a crowded undergraduate university, I often felt crippled by the littleness of my everyday actions. My thoughts and prayers no longer "determined" the fate of mankind. I stormed through feelings of marginality, anonymity, and purposelessness.

Often I was depressed by the harshness of real life, as it is paraded so endlessly before us in the books and newspapers we read. Confronted with conflict, violence, injustice, corruption, and gore, I experienced fleeting impulses to return to the cosmic cocoon of Church life.

I have found no community of worship nearly as energizing as the Unification Church. But perhaps the level of exhilaration I miss isn't possible without an accompanying loss of freedom and family, without courting the dangers of dogma, illusion, and totalitarianism—baggage I've chosen to leave behind me. So while continuing to seek transcendence, I float cautiously outside the bounds of institutional religion.

As I gradually and painfully learned to accept appropriate limits, I said good-bye to many of my dreams. I can no longer expect perfect love in my relations with men or women, or perfection in this life.

Nor can I expect perfection of myself, and with this realization, I am trying to work through a lot of Church-taught personal guilt. As my guilt has lessened, I have begun to experience a growing appreciation of my womanhood, an affirmation of my own sexuality as one of many ways of expressing love and care. As I gradually take on moral responsibility for my actions, even the most personal, I begin to feel the sober stirrings of maturity.

As a woman in today's world, the hardest task before me is self-acceptance, then self-actualization. The Church promises women "greatness" for submission and servitude, but I have now before me the responsibility to *accomplish* in whatever social, artistic, or family task I take up. I've learned the value of uncertainty, and the courage to risk failure. I've regained my humanity, my self.

For me, commitment to faith must find its expression in the passion and loyalty I devote to my work, be it counseling, writing, publishing, or all three, and to my relationships.

I have learned that the desire to choose goodness in God is the rock-center of my being. Spirituality has continued to be the lodestone of my life since leaving the Church. When I left the Church I made the great discovery that God exists outside of it. And as I live outside, I keep finding God's footprints, His traces everywhere.

Appendix:
Mind Control, Cults,
and Unification

"To hold power over others means that the powerful is permitted a kind of short-cut through the complexity of human personality. He does not have to enter intuitively into the souls of the powerless, or to hear what they are saying in their many languages, including silence.

The powerful person would seem to have a good deal at stake in suppressing or denying his awareness of the personal reality of others; power seems to engender a kind of willed ignorance, a moral stupidity about the inwardness of others, hence of self."
—ADRIENNE RICH, *Of Woman Born: Motherhood as Experience and Institution*

Mind Control

There are perhaps eighteen hundred cults in the United States with an estimated membership of between one and two million people, predominantly young. Best known are the Children of God, Hare Krishna (International Society for Krishna Consciousness), Divine Light Mission, Scientology, and the Unification Church. In addition to these major groups there are hundreds of smaller American sects ranging from benign "Bible" cults to Charles Manson's group, which continues to thrive in southern California despite its leader's incarceration. Many of the smaller groups, in which charismatic, often messianic leaders gather a following through claims of moral superiority or prophetic insight, are not "mind control" groups.

The larger groups named above, however, have been described as "high intensity" cults because of their widespread use of severe, intellectually and emotionally disarming pressures on members and prospective converts. Observing a deterioration of personality in their children, many members' parents have become convinced that extensive deception and techniques of coercive persuasion, or "mind control," have been used by cults to solicit, convert, and hold on to members.

The concept of "mind control" became an ugly fact of public knowledge in the early 1950s, when United States prisoners of war were released from North Korea. It was discovered that not only had virtually no American prisoners attempted escape, but also many of these men—men who had defended the U.S. and seen friends die beside them in combat—now displayed a violent, ideologically shaped hatred for America and American values which they expressed in typical Communist jargon. Many had no desire to return home to family and friends. As psychiatrists and psychologists such as Robert J. Lifton and Margaret Singer were brought in to assist the POWs to readjust to American life, it became clear that specific, consistent techniques of emotional, physical, and mental pressure had been applied with the result of effectively breaking down, or burying, the prisoners' previous personalities.

The Korean captors shrewdly orchestrated the use of violence and threats of violence, social, and emotional isolation, inadequate food and sleep, and frequent shifts of living quarters to new, unfamiliar environments in order to disorient prisoners, reduce their alertness and capacity to resist, and sever associations with memories and companions of preprison life. Individual attention was monopolized by enforced participation in a rigid, exhausting schedule. There was no time or energy to reflect upon the barrage of Communist ideas or to recall and dwell upon alternative viewpoints. Friends were separated. Opposing ideas were ridiculed; guilt was induced over past beliefs and associations, dividing the individual against himself. The normal uncertainties, misgivings and tensions the individual had had in his previous conception of the world and himself were identified and then intensified, building in the prisoners an increasing distrust of past life and environment.

Emotionally uprooted and unable to rely on their previous lives for the strength to resist their captors, the prisoners required some new framework of secure beliefs to fill this carefully created vacuum in their identities. The prisoners came to *need* their captors—for *emotional support,* for the *clarity* they required to organize the new turmoil of past memories and present confusion, and for the *approval* essential to rebuilding a positive image of themselves. Many of these techniques were effected through the use of apparently sincere affection, which broke down emotional barriers, induced emotional and intellectual confusion, and made the prisoners want to belong to the community of Communist captors as a means of acquiring a new and comfortable identity.

The phenomenon of American POWs in Korea evoked some protest and commentary, then was forgotten by the public. In 1961, Robert J. Lifton, a Yale psychiatrist who had been involved in the debriefing and counseling of Korean War POWs, wrote a book describing the methods used by Maoist Chinese in the early 1950s to achieve virtually complete mental, emotional, and physical domination over imprisoned Westerners and large groups of elite Chinese intellectuals. Lifton's classic study, *Thought Reform and the Psychology of Totalism,* contributed many insights into the process of mind control, particularly the more subtle emotional techniques used to subdue and reform Chinese intellectuals, *whose transformation occurred not in prisons,* but in "revolutionary universities." Many of the physically coercive aspects of traditional prisoner experience were absent, since the more subtle emotional pressures of mind control proved equally effective.

Lifton emphasized the importance of combining "external force or coercion" with "an appeal to inner enthusiasm through evangelistic exhortation" in Chinese thought reform. He also emphasized the power of the *sincerity* of Chinese thought reformers: "what we see as a set of coercive maneuvers, the Chinese Communists view as a morally uplifting, harmonizing and scientifically therapeutic experience." Contrary to the popular image of the brain-washer as unscrupulous and diabolical, Lifton depicted idealistic, sincere, and thoroughly indoctrinated Chinese Communists eager to save their countrymen from the immorality of their pre-Communist lives. Motivated by a messianic fervor to build the "new China," Chinese thought reformers were able to capture, through deception and a web of pressures similar to those described above, the idealism of their victims in a way which obviated physical imprisonment. The process involved thoroughly discrediting and breaking down previous identity, rendering the victim emotionally empty and vulnerable, then guiding him through a careful sequence of emotional/intellectual "rebirth" experiences in which he developed a totalistic, ideologically defined image of the evil of his previous life and of the potential for salvation in a life shaped by Communist ideology.

Though written years before the current proliferation of cults, Lifton's study of Chinese mind control is now coming to be recognized as an acute description of the emotionally coercive and manipulative techniques employed by today's high-intensity cults. Lifton described a number of interlocked processes, or "psychological themes," characteristic of Chinese Communist mind control. These patterns of group pressure, supported by a *totalistic explanation of reality* and severe *emotional polarization*—between community and outside world, the new totalist self and one's previous identity, and rigid ideological definitions of good and of evil—dissolve the previous personality by manipulating subconscious tensions and vulnerabilities.

The first of these themes of psychological pressure is "milieu control," or the control of inter- and intrapersonal communication. Relying upon social cues to orient himself to his new environment, the individual quickly perceives that certain ideas and feelings are acceptable and constantly emphasized, while others are discouraged. Isolated from other perspectives and opinions, the individual finds no support for any objections he might have. In cults like the Unification Church he may be told that he is spiritually immature or controlled by sin, so that his opinion, unless it conforms to the group viewpoint, has no validity and can even be a source of Satanic invasion into his life and, through him, into the community. Members of the community, concerned for one another's ideological correctness, become informers upon one another, relaying back to the authorities deviations in expression and feeling by fellow members. Trapped by his idealistic desire for "truth" and by the pressures of his peers, the individual comes to monitor his own words and feelings so that they conform to group sanctions. With imagination and creativity supplanted by total conformity, communication with the community and within oneself becomes an expression of obedience. Both the public and private parts of the mind become images of the group ideology.

As totalist authorities acquire control of the milieu of ideas and feelings, Lifton notes, they enforce a series of pressures for breaking down the old identity and rigidly imposing a new personality.

The first of these pressures he terms "mystical manipulation." A mystique of total goodness, value, and authority is built up around the leadership figures and their ideas, so that the individual comes to accept, in blind faith and with a childlike trust and naïveté, the obligation to obey completely. In the Unification Church, members are trained to become "part of the body of Sun Myung Moon," whose every whim is considered gospel because of the mystique of his "messiahship."

Another pressure described by Lifton is the "demand for purity." The individual's sense of integrity becomes defined by ideologically determined sanctions identifying any support of the totalist ideology and movement as absolutely good and any contradictory idea, feeling, or proclivity as absolutely evil. Any reliance upon previous ideas, opinions, or moral values that might mitigate total allegiance to the group results in intense feelings of guilt, followed by energetic efforts to expel such elements from his conscience and life.

Reinforcing the individual's inner demand for "purity" is the external pressure to confess to a leader or to the group all elements of impurity from the past so that one's previous life can be ideologically redefined and objectified as an enemy of the new totalist identity. The individual is thus denied any positive memories of his previous life as a resource through which he might privately set himself apart from the group and evaluate it from his own personal perspective.

While the above pressures are used to alienate a person from his identity and his past and to elicit total obedience to totalist authorities, other pressures are used to sharply redefine his new totalist identity. The ideology is presented, Lifton says, as a "sacred science" combining the mystical and the rational in such a way as to justify both detailed "scientific" reasoning according to ideological tenets and sweeping generalizations that accord with the cosmic significance of the ideology. The individual, intellectually and emotionally enthralled by the totality of explanations provided, worhsips the ideas themselves as his means of personal salvation. This results in a "loading of the language" of the ideology, in which particular ideological jargon is weighted with significance, regardless of its tendency to reduce complex human emotions and situations into tight "thought-terminating clichés." As the language of the totalist becomes restricted to ideological jargon, his ability to experience the world and his group becomes constricted and his perception severely oversimplified. The world exists not as he sees it, but as the ideology defines it, and gradually he comes to see the world only in ideologically defined black and white. Lifton terms this "doctrine over person," whereby the ideology's doctrinal explanation of experience comes to be more real than personal experience itself.

Lifton describes a final pressure toward "dispensing of existence." In a totally and rigidly structured world view, only those individuals supportive of the totalist group and its ideas have a right to exist. Opponents of the group are regarded as enemies of history and of the ideals of mankind; they do not deserve to exist unless they can be drawn into the totalist group. Sun Myung Moon, in a speech to members, once remarked that if opponents of his movement continued to "persecute God's will" God would "invite them to the spirit world."

The Sociology of Cults

Some people appear more susceptible than others to cultic influences. Most vulnerable are young people in transition without clear career goals or ambitions or not involved in nourishing intimate relationships. A study by Harvard psychiatrist John Clark found the majority of people who join cults to be competent, searching, highly idealistic young people caught up in the struggles of late adolescence. A minority have insecure personalities or are poorly adjusted, seeking a release from life pressures. Another minority are delinquents and criminals who crave power and control.

Isn't one man's religion another man's cult? Two main characteristics appear to distinguish cults from genuine religions. First, high-intensity cults use techniques of coercive persuasion described above, including a set of "double ethics" justifying pervasive deception of the public and of new recruits. Secondly, cults appear to have self-gain as their primary goal. Although professing traditional religious values, in practice the cults sacrifice those values for the sake of expansion. Affirmation of God's inclusive and unconditional love, individual growth through reflection and psychological integration, sacrificial service toward *all* fellowmen, emphasis on spirituality over materialism—these values are circumvented in the rush for world control. Traditional faiths do not enlist and hold clergy and laity with the same severe emotional pressures characteristic of the high-intensity cults, and traditional faiths do not sacrifice means to ends.

Cultists spend their days recruiting converts and raising funds. (The millions of dollars they raise have earned the cults the distinction of being called new growth industries.) Living communally in rigid obedience to leaders, members work seven days a week and are constantly fatigued. Health is neglected; no attention is given to education outside the cult. Caught up as they are in a momentum of control and submission, they find it nearly impossible to leave the cult.

/ 289

Why are cults so popular in the seventies? Certainly the ineffectiveness of the political activism of the sixties is one factor. Tough, unsettled times—old rules and values changing—have always seen a proliferation of cultic panaceas. Today's cult is a refuge from, as well as a criticism and exploitation of, a world without clear guidelines for personal and political morality. The confusions brought on by drug excesses and sexual experimentation, the apparent futility of individual idealism, and the impersonality, alienation, and anomie which characterize mass society—all stimulate in a young idealist desires for clarity, romantic personal importance, and totalistic commitment.

To join a cult is to turn inward, psychologically and spiritually, to seek reassuring answers to questions about self-worth. Self-purification consumes the cultist's time, energy, and thoughts. Trapped by the demands of the cult leader, whose approval is required for self-respect, he is prevented from genuinely contributing to social needs, although altruistic and idealistic goals may have been important motivations to join the cult in the first place.

The cult represents a spiritual protest against a secular milieu. It also represents a protest against the failure of the traditional church to fill spiritual voids, to provide answers, to instill fervor. And, of primary importance to many members, the cult also represents a quest for the intimacy of true community. With changing family attitudes and the breakdown of family unity, the need for genuine intimacy has increased. The Unification Church, like other cults, offers an artificial intimacy based on a shared ideological identity. For the natural family the Unification Church substitutes an "idealized" family and set of "perfect parents" that promise eternal relief from loneliness.

Despite (or perhaps because of) pressures to achieve scholastically, today's young individualistic generation exhibits a stubborn anti-intellectualism. To join a cult is to leap into a mythological world which denies reality in exchange for the apparent transcendence of illusion. Few young people have the sophistication or skepticism to see beyond the attractive illusions or to understand how intense emotional involvement can cloud and distort their perceptions.

But most importantly, to bright, idealistic young people suffering from the guilt and boredom of their privileged upbringings, the cult world (with its tentacles of deception and control hidden behind the sincerity of its adherents) presents the opportunity to engage in heroic missions in the context of what appears to be a life-and-death struggle for meaning. Whatever suffering occurs within the cult in the accomplishment of these missions is given the highest theological value.

Unification History

The Holy Spirit Association for the Unification of World Christianity probably numbers fewer than seven thousand "Moonies" in this country, an estimated three thousand of them full-time members. Depending upon the spokesman, Unification claims a world membership in over a hundred countries, of from a half-million to two million. The largest group is located in South Korea. A tightly disciplined organization exists in Japan and there has been growing strength in the United States.

Information about Sun Myung Moon is scanty and often speculative. He was born in northern Korea in 1920 of Christian parents, and sent south to Seoul to high school. At sixteen he had a vision on a mountaintop; he claims the heavenly voice of Jesus Christ told him he was designated to complete man's salvation and fulfill God's providence. It is reported that Moon studied engineering in Tokyo, then returned to Pyungyang in North Korea in 1944 to develop a religious following among a group of revivalists. Though his life record is cloudy from 1946 to 1950, it's clear he was arrested and spent several years in Hung-nam labor camp in North Korea.

Released in 1950 by U.N. troops, Moon and several of his disciples traveled south as refugees. Moon settled in Pusan and taught his principles. The Unification Church (Holy Spirit Association for the Unification of World Christianity) was formed in Korea in 1954. In 1957 Moon's theological ideas were published in *Divine Principle*, the Unification Church's "completed testament." In 1971 Moon came to live in the United States. Discipline was intensified in the Church. Most outside jobs were dropped as membership in the movement became a full-time occupation whose sole material reward was room and board. Recruiting was stepped up under the guise of a Christian youth crusade.

Unification Politics
and Finances

How can Moon's religious teachings, entangled with political and economic concerns and activities, be evaluated? In "Master Speaks," an internal publication of the Unification Church containing translations of numerous speeches by Moon, Moon says that separation of religion and government is a system preferred by Satan. The investigation of Korean–American relations made by the U.S. Congressional Fraser Subcommittee on International Organizations (October 31, 1978) came to the following conclusions:

"The Unification Church and its numerous other religious and secular organizations ... constitute essentially one international Moon organization" ... one which "depends heavily on interchangeability of its components and ability to move personal and financial assets freely across international boundaries and between businesses and nonprofit organizations."

• Sun Myung Moon has "substantial control over the economic, political and spiritual activities undertaken by the organization"; despite a church officer's protestations that Moon is simply a spiritual figurehead.

• Among the goals of the Moon organization is the establishment of a worldwide government in which the separation of church and state would be abolished and all would be governed by Moon and his followers."

• "In pursuit of these goals, the Moon organization has attempted, with varying degrees of success, to gain control over or establish business and other secular institutions in the United States, and elsewhere, and has engaged in political activities in the United States. Some of these activities were undertaken to benefit the South Korean government or otherwise to influence United States foreign policy."

• "While pursuing its own goals, the Moon organization promoted the interests of the South Korean government and at times did so in cooperation with, or at the direction of, South Korean agencies and officials."

• "A Moon organization business is an important defense contractor in South Korea." It appears to manufacture "air rifles, lathes, milling machines, boilers and parts for the M-79 grenade launcher and vulcan gun"; Tong Il Industry has denied that it assists in the manufacture of M-16 rifles, the basic weapon of the South Korean infantry.

• The Moon organization (though found to be competing for control of bank stock, not collaborating with Tongsun Park) "attempted to obtain a controlling interest in the [Washington, D.C.] Diplomat National Bank by disguising the source of funds used to purchase stock in the names of Unification Church members."

• "The Moon organization used church and other tax-exempt components in support of its political and economic activities."

• "Although many of the goals and activities of the Moon organization were legitimate and lawful, there was evidence it had systematically violated U.S. tax, immigration, banking, currency, and Foreign Agents Registration laws, as well as state and local laws relating to charity fraud and that these violations were related to the organization's overall goals of gaining temporal power."

The cult has printed a denial of many of these findings.

The cult is estimated to be worth internationally hundreds of millions of dollars. Often the estimate of an annual $60 million American income is given. In the United States the cult owns three New York estates worth millions of dollars. Moon lives in one of these estates in Irvington, N.Y. Another in Barrytown is a training center. The cult owns the multimillion-dollar New Yorker Hotel, former Columbia University property, and a newspaper, *The News World*. It has recently bought land and assets in Alabama, Massachusetts, Virginia, and California as centers to launch a major fishing industry where Moon members will work without pay. Moon is said to have bid on the Empire State Building.

In August of 1977, an ex-cultist who had worked out of the Texas mobile fund-raising center testified that cult fund-raisers nationwide for that month had brought in $5 million—an amount considered so low that a Japanese leader at national headquarters told her he was "ashamed to tell Father."

Barbara Underwood's own earnings figures are noteworthy. In a nine-month period of 1976 her six-person Oakland mobile fund-raising team made

$450,000 selling roses seven days a week, sixteen hours a day. In early winter of 1977 Barbara's six-person team was making $1,400 a day selling flowers in the worst blizzards in Michigan history. Barbara's own daily average was $400 at that time.

It is not known how many Unification members are out fund-raising, nor how much cult money leaves the American economy to support cult efforts worldwide. The fact that money does go out is corroborated by Unification doctrine. America is the cornerstone of Moon's financial theory. He has said that from America will come the wherewithal to create a world base since he deems the real mission of America to be the supplying of manpower and money.

The Divine Principle

What are the main themes of Moon's teaching, the *Divine Principle?* Ambitiously addressing problems of spirit and moral law, the cosmos and man's place in it, *Divine Principle* is dualistic and perfectionist. It divides mind and body, internal and external, and man and woman. In the literal and theological sense, *physical* as well as *spiritual* salvation is essential.

God intended that Adam and Eve and their offspring become perfect in both realms. But Lucifer (Satan) seduced Eve before she was spiritually mature, making her impure and tainting her blood. This taint was transmitted to Adam through his union with Eve. Their children—mankind—were henceforth also impure. God, wanting to redeem mankind from *all* impurity, sent Jesus. But Jesus was crucified before he could either marry or father children. Jesus thus accomplished *spiritual* but not *physical* redemption, leaving mankind's blood still impure. So a new savior, a "Lord of the Second Advent," was needed to physically restore humanity and bring in the "New Israel," this time Korea.

This new savior, this True Parent, must achieve heaven on earth by marrying a perfect woman. Their children will be the first of a new and perfect world based on a God-centered, not a Satan-centered, family. (Possibly wed several times before, Moon married an eighteen-year-old named Hak Ja-Han in the 1950s. She became the mother of Moon's large family of nearly a dozen children. Moon's aim is twelve offspring, symbolic of the twelve tribes.) Cult couples "blessed," or married, by Moon when they are spiritually "mature" will create with their perfect children the new order.

Natural parents, because they are descendants of Adam and Eve's sin, are considered blood-tainted, and must be replaced by True Parents. It is this concept of natural parents versus True Parents which is at the center of the cult's threat to family life. A "Master Speaks" issue in 1975 cites Moon as saying that in American society families are broken and parents and children alike are unhappy because of the chaos and divisiveness prevalent in contemporary American family life. Until now, because children have lacked True Parents, God has been prevented from redeeming mankind. Moon goes on to imply that only through himself as a True Parent can God fulfill his role and the true world be built.

Does *Divine Principle* claim Moon is the new Messiah? It is emphasized that Jesus must be supplanted by a second Messiah to be born in Korea between 1917 and 1930, the time of Moon's own birth. "Master Speaks" quotes Moon as saying that without having the True Parents among us, we cannot give birth to true children, and everything starts from there. That's why, he claims, God sent the Messiah to human society. As self-designated "Father," Moon repeatedly declares himself the True Parent; the True Parent is obviously the Messiah, so the conclusion is inevitable. In the minds of most Moon cultists, no matter how much they may demur in public, Moon is the Lord of the Second Advent.

Glossary

EXPLANATION OF KEY UNIFICATION TERMS

Actualize. A favorite cult word for service and action which allows for no negativity, no self-justification, but only continuous cheerful accomplishment of the mission.

Blessing. Moon-arranged marriage of "mature" followers who will have "perfect" children. Moon paired and married 1,800 couples in a mass wedding ceremony in Korea in 1975. He claims he can do a fine job of matching people from the way they talk, the way they smile. . . . Conditions are usually set before a cultist is eligible to be married, such as at least three years' membership or the bringing in of a requisite number of "spiritual children." On May 12, 1979, in New York City, Moon "engaged" 705 couples to be married some time in the future, many of them interracial betrothals.

Blueprint of history. Moon presents a startling view of both Biblical and secular "history." The last third of *Divine Principle* reads as a political statement. If Christianity hadn't betrayed Moon, it states, Korea wouldn't have been divided. After the Korean War, South Korea became the strongest anti-Communist country in the world and an anti-Communist country is the necessary foundation for the new Messiah. The Moon blueprint of history calls for the world to be dominated by Moon's leadership after a war—ideological or actual—culminating in a triumphant trinity of the U.S., Japan, and South Korea ruling the world as God's anti-Communist empire. In this trinity of nations, Korea will lead, Japan will come next, and America will be in the "serving position."

Center man. That individual (frequently male) who takes responsibility for the important activities of the cult in the rigid authority pyramid that prevails. In "Master Speaks" Moon has been quoted as saying that he is the cultists' brain.

/ 299

Chants. Developed to cause vibrations in the spirit world, certain special requests are repeated either out loud or silently in incantatory fashion.

The Fall. The Lucifer-motivated seduction of Eve's spiritual body and her subsequent physical union with Adam before they were mature (spiritually perfected). All subsequent humans have been impure. Moon tells his followers he has overcome the physical temptation course for them and paid their indemnity. He wants them to follow the road to purity. Moon claims that 83 percent of Korean males and females are chaste before marriage, 63 percent of Japanese, but that in the United States the statistics are "in rags."

The Family. Cultists refer to their communal living group by this term. It also implies the whole of mankind once restored.

Fasts. Fasting for indemnity-sacrifice is common in the Church. Water fasts extend from one to seven days.

Heavenly deception. Since every non-Moon person and thing is of the Satanic world, there is no special reason to respect noncult rights to honest dealing. Heavenly deception ranges from use of front names in proselytizing and fund-raising to disregard of solicitation and immigration laws.

Holy days. Unification celebrates four important days in the year: God's Day, True Parents Day, Children's Day, and World Day. Little regard is paid to Christmas, Easter, or Jewish High Holy Days.

Indemnity. To redeem or pay back a debt to Satan for personal sins or Satanic ancestry, cultists pay indemnities by constant work, struggle, sacrifice, and obedience. The aim for each person is to arrive at "the perfection level above the growth stage."

Jump it. The cult requires continuous hours of exertion and immediate service. One is expected to "jump it" without thinking; such response becomes part of the control pattern. However, because of this carefully created habit of instant obedience, young cultists often grow to be confident and formidable performers.

Love-bombing. Persistent psychological effort to disarm a skeptical recruit by excessive attention in order to get him or her into the cult.

Make-oneness. Constant selfless efforts to show sacrificial care for individual cult "brothers" and "sisters." The loyalty of cult persons to each other is one of the most attractive and seductive aspects of the cult phenomenon. Its pervasive aftereffect makes it hard to detach emotionally from the cult orbit even when the cultist "comes out."

Pledge. A ritualized service on Sundays and holidays where the cultists pledge their devotion to serve God and Moon and to fight Satan.

Prayer condition. Prayer life is important to the cultist—both in the form of solitary prayers and prayers of group supplication.

Restoration. Once you have moved through set stages and paid sufficient preset indemnities, salvation—or restoration—is won. Harsh and puritanical,

Unification's restoration appears not to emphasize God's grace and forgiveness so much as God's need of the cultist's good works.

Restore the material foundation. God has chosen only the Unification Church to understand his will. All money and power ought to belong to God. The cult, therefore, is the only instrument which deserves to control everything in this Satanic world. When the cult possesses all wealth and power, God can finally control, through the cult, all he serves. The material foundation will have been restored.

Satanic. Satan has seized the world and its people in history; cultists regard the world outside their group as debased, sinful. Likewise, they look upon their precult selves as pawns of Satan whose evil spirit had captured them and their lineage.

Spirit man. Moon postulates separate spiritual and physical worlds, just as in every individual there is a spiritual and a physical body. The cult spirit man grows to perfection and at the point of physical death, spirit man continues. Moon claims the superiority of the spirit world over the physical and says he alone can take charge of these spirit people.

Spiritual child. Any convert brought in by a cultist.

Subject/object. This complex transposition finds the subject (the leader) knowing God's will, but the subject is only as good as the object (server) who responds. Men are usually in the subject position, women in the object position.

Trinity. Small subfamilies in the centers which do much of the indoctrination and disciplining.

True Parents. Reverend Moon and his wife, as "perfect" humans.

OTHER GENERAL PRECEPTS

Authority. With its emphasis on aggressive growth, submission to center man or Moon within the group, and arrogance toward those outside, is prescribed Unification practice. Only the cultist knows what is best for the noncult person; the rights of the other person are submerged. In street selling, for instance, the cultist believes the purchase of a flower is the only way the buyer can grow spiritually. But typically the cultist is undisturbed that the purchaser has neither right of consent to, nor awareness of, his "restoration." Moon cultists also appear to have been taught an underlying disregard for secular legal systems, which are seen as inferior to Church morality.

Moon and Christianity. On June 26, 1977, the multi-denominational Commission on Faith and Order of the National Council of Churches of Christ in America, after many inquiries from churches around the country and after a year of study, declared that the Unification Church of Reverend Sun Myung Moon was not a Christian church. (The Council of Churches comprises over twenty mainline Protestant, Orthodox, and Catholic denominations.) The Commission emphasized that it was not calling into question the free right of the Unification Church to exist and propagate its beliefs under the Constitution of the United States, but only its right to pose as Christian, since its doctrines of the Trinity, of Christology, of salvation and grace, and of scriptural authority deny basic elements of Christian faith. Previous evidence has suggested that Moon will repudiate Christianity when his own movement is strong enough. He has said that Christians will be the ones standing in the way of a new age and "it must be decided whether Christianity belongs to God or Satan."

Racism. Moon's principles appear racist. Jews, Moon says, bear a special collective sin for their repudiation of Jesus. According to a 1977 report of the Commission on Faith and Order of the National Council of Churches of Christ in America, *Divine Principle* blames the Jewish nation for the failure of Jesus' mission in at least twenty citations. The report concludes that the attitude expressed "amounts to a prevailing condemnation of an entire people and results in an inevitable anti-Semitism." In addition, the supposed "blood taint" of "fallen" noncult people seems similar in concept to the Hitlerian obsession with the superiority of Aryan "blood." Moon has replaced Jews, as the chosen people, with Koreans whom members worldwide are pledged to defend. Koreans are considered more chosen than other nationalities; Asians in general are exalted. In "Master Speaks" Moon declares that, seen through Oriental eyes, Western people are merciless, feelingless or emotionless. Then he asks which of the two—the Oriental or the Occidental—is closer to the way of life of God? And his young American followers shout "Oriental!"

Sexism and family life. Moon says in "Master Speaks" that the man is in the central position and declares that in Oriental countries parents would like to have the firstborn be a son, without exception. He claims that that way of thinking makes the Oriental people closer to God and buttresses that claim by citing a supposed law of creation which says that "when you die, you'd rather die with your sons protecting you than your daughters." Moon demands in traditionally sexist terms that "when you are blessed in marriage, you women must be absolutely obedient to your husbands," and he harks back to the patronizing Victorian concept that women, though subordinate in other ways, are at least for a transition time morally superior to men and have the obligation to keep their men pure. Very aware of the uses of flirtation in selling, Moon states in "Master Speaks" that in flower selling, it is the women who excel and that is why he sends out more women.

Moon flatly endorses the Asian extended family over the nuclear family and orders his women to be servants to parents and grandparents-in-law and to love nephews and nieces "more than you do your own children." Cult children are ordered to be absolutely and continuously obedient to their parents who are cult members.

Sexuality. The chief sin of Unification (other than leaving it) is unendorsed sexual contact of any kind. The most severe celibacy is required. (See *The Fall.*) Moon says in "Master Speaks" that if cultists commit the "fallen act," it cannot be forgiven. They will be doomed to hell. He calls unapproved sexual intercourse worse than murder and says that if a person is murdered only one person dies, but by an unendorsed sex act a cultist "kills" descendants and lineage as well. Moon says cultists must think of their chastity as more valuable, more important, than their lives. Even after marriage, couples may be separated for a prescribed number of years.

Of necessity, the cult's communal members live as brothers and sisters in a desexualized atmosphere. Physiological changes sometimes occur. Some male cult members need to shave less often; some female members even stop menstruating.

Social outreach. Like most cults, Unification appears to have provided few social outreach programs or community services, considering how many millions of dollars have been taken from the streets of any given community. There is evidence that current projects are under way to improve that public image. But, in general, Unification is more interested in the powerful, well-off, energetic, and assertive than in the weak and needy.

Theological antecedents. Unification derives from a long Gnostic tradition, both Christian and pagan. The most interesting tenet and device of Gnostics and Moonies alike is their belief that revelation of mystical knowledge is the key to salvation. Withholding revelations is considered to be a source of power in the cult. The staff has power because it withholds secret information which will determine all cultists' lives. The rationale given for this withholding is that Satan might invade the strategy if plans were revealed. Inside information is also carefully withheld from the visiting seeker, and the indoctrination lectures appear to be built on this useful principle.

Violence. "Master Speaks," Moon's lectures to his young enthusiasts, are sprinkled with violent imagery. He declares that in training he is going to cut from the cultist those parts that are not needed. He compares this to the Biblical injunction that if thine eye offend thee, thou shalt pluck it out. How literally this is to be taken, is not clear. In reference to homosexuality, he says that that habit can be eradicated by beating on them . . . and if that is the only remedy, it will be done.

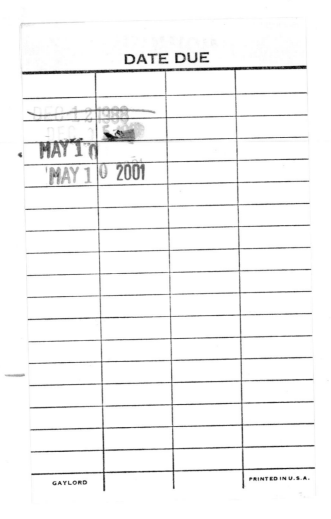

DATE DUE

DEC 12 1988			
MAY 1 0			
'MAY 1 0 2001			
GAYLORD			PRINTED IN U.S.A.